# A TIME FOR TRUTH

# A TIME FOR TRUTH

*William E. Simon*

Reader's Digest Press

McGraw-Hill Book Company

NEW YORK          CHICAGO

Book design by Ingrid Beckman.

7890FGRFGR78321098

**Library of Congress Cataloging in Publication Data**
Simon, William E., date
A time for truth.
Includes index.
1. United States—Social policy.    2. United States—Economic policy—1971–    3. Liberty.    4. Individualism.    I. Title.
HN65.S5617      309.1'73      77-25465
ISBN 0-07-057378-6

I dedicate this book to my wife, Carol, who stands by my side throughout all my battles—and to my children, so that they can never say, at some future time, "Why weren't we told?"

# ACKNOWLEDGMENTS

I wish to express my profound gratitude to Edith Efron, who assisted me with every aspect of this book, from conception to execution. The dedication to liberty which animates these pages is hers, as well as my own.

I am also deeply indebted to Managing Editor Kenneth Gilmore and Washington Editor William Schulz of the *Reader's Digest*, who spent countless hours on this project and whose guidance, criticism, and direction have been invaluable. It was they who wisely counseled me to limit the canvas of this book to domestic issues.

And finally, I wish to thank DeWitt Wallace and Hobart Lewis of the *Reader's Digest*. Without their inspiration, this project might not have been undertaken.

# CONTENTS

# PREFACE

This is a brilliant and passionate book by a brilliant and passionate man. It is a profound analysis of the suicidal course on which our beloved country is proceeding—so clearly and so simply written, with such eloquence, such obvious sincerity, such a broad base in recorded fact and personal experience, that it is hard to see how any reasonable man who wishes his fellow citizens well can fail to be persuaded by it.

Yet I know from long experience with my fellow intellectuals that many of them will fail to be. Few human acts are so difficult as to say *mea culpa*, to face facts when they conflict with long-held philosophical views. People will do so only when they suffer severe personal injury if they persist in error. That is why businessmen, who may be bankrupted if they refuse to face facts, are one of the few groups that develop the habit of doing so. That is why, as I have discovered repeatedly, the successful businessman is far more open-minded with respect to new ideas, even if he challenges positions he has repeatedly taken in public, than the academic intellectual who prides himself on his alleged independence of thought.

The socialists and interventionists, who have wrongfully appropriated in this country the noble label "liberal" and who have been the intellectual architects of our suicidal course, will suffer no severe personal injury—at least in the near future—if they fail to recognize the error of their ways. On the contrary, many of them would lose if they did so. They have found a profitable market for their views and might well be hard put to develop an equally salable new product.

The view that if there is a problem, if there is something wrong, the way to deal with it is to pass a law, set up a governmental agency (staffed, of course, by the intellectuals urging this solution), and use the police power of the state to correct it is, as Mr. Simon demonstrates so well, a superficially appealing view. It is simple, as well as simpleminded, and appeals to our natural impulse to take personal credit for the good things that happen and blame a "devil" for the bad things—an impulse that Mr. Simon documents so strikingly in his book, as he recounts the occasions on which he was the "devil."

On the other hand, the view that government is the problem, not the cure, and that the invisible hand of private cooperation through the market is far more effective than the visible hand of the bureaucrat is a sophisticated, subtle view that is far harder to get across. It requires thought, not emotion, to comprehend. It does not lend itself to ringing phrases, to high-flowered sentiment, to promises to particular people or particular groups. Moreover, the market has no press agents who will trumpet its successes and gloss over its failures; the bureaucracy does.

These forces make it in the personal self-interest of many intellectuals to adopt a statist, interventionist philosophy. Self-interest is no less powerful in the intellectual marketplace than in the narrowly economic marketplace. Self-interest has been reinforced by the herdlike instinct of so many intellectuals, by their sheltered environments, in which they tend to talk only to one another, to reinforce their prejudices, and know little of the arguments on the other side. The result has been an incredible homogeneity of views among intellectuals. There was, I suspect, no precinct in Mayor Daley's Chicago whose vote was consistently more predictable and more one-sided than the University of Chicago's Hyde Park, yet the University of Chicago is exceptional among universities in its openness, its tolerance of opposing points of view and their actual strong representation on the faculty.

Intellectuals may have a short-run interest in preaching socialism and interventionism. Their long-run interest is very different. If we continue our present trends and our free society is replaced by a collectivist society, the intellectuals who have done so much to drive us down this path will not be the ones who run the society; the prison, the insane asylum, or the graveyard would be their fate. After all, in Lenin's memorable image, the capitalists are not the only ones who sell their enemies the rope with which to hang them. The experience of Russia, Yugoslavia, and China is eloquent on this point.

Fortunately, counter tendencies have been developing, and it is to the strengthening of these that Mr. Simon's book makes so signal a contribution. The inefficiency and failures of government have become so blatant, so far-reaching that even the blindest are hard put to deny them. In the intellectual community itself the turning of bureaucratic energies to schools and universities has started to hit the intellectuals on their own home grounds—a just retribution that could be applauded if it did not have such serious implications for the preservation of our basic values. One result has been an increasing number of intellectuals who have come to recognize the threat that growing government offers to a preservation of human freedom. Another result—ultimately perhaps more far-reaching—has been the awakening of the public at large to the true situation, so socialist snake oil no longer sells so readily.

One can only hope that Mr. Simon's book will have the wide-ranging audience it deserves. It may not persuade the committed intellectual. But it will give the young intellectual whose ideas are not yet set in concrete much food for thought and strongly reinforce a change in philosophical views toward individualism that to my perhaps overoptimistic and biased eyes has already set in. And it will give the public at large—whose basic values have remained healthy—reason to renew their confidence in those values.

Mr. Simon was a splendid Secretary of the Treasury. Yet he will, I believe, contribute more to his country by this book than he has done in his often frustrating tour of duty. We have too many efficient technocrats. We have too few farsighted visionaries.

MILTON FRIEDMAN
*Ely, Vermont*
*May 2, 1977*

# FOREWORD

If, when a mutual friend had given me an opportunity to read this manuscript, I had been clearly aware that it was the work of a recent Secretary of the Treasury, I doubt whether I would have been particularly anxious to read it. Remembering only that the folder contained the work of a younger man of whom my friend expected much, I dipped into it one morning and at once got so fascinated that I could not stop until I had finished it. I still know very little about the role the author played in recent American history beyond what I learned from his own account of it. All I know is that this account of his experience and the lesson he learned from it is of the greatest importance.

How a man with his views could ever have become U.S. Secretary of the Treasury is still something of a puzzle to me. But perhaps the explanation of the opinions so unlikely to be formed in such a position is probably that he was young enough to be really shocked by what he experienced and to learn what mature politicians no longer can learn: that the compulsion under which our system of unlimited democracy places persons at the head of government to operate forces them to do things which they know to be permissive, but must do, if they are to retain the position in which they can still hope to do some good.

If this is the lesson which a first-class young brain has learned from bitter experience, we may hope to find in him a leader of opinion such as the United States and the Western world much need. But at least what he tells us in this book ought to teach many what the obstacles are to a sensible policy being followed by government. I never imagined that government could harbor a spirit opposed for good reasons to so much that was in fact done.

I can assure the reader that Mr. Simon is not unduly an alarmist. If we learn from him and the few people who think like him, we may still avert the threatening collapse of our political and economic order. Without much hope I recommend this book particularly to my fellow economists who could learn much from it never dreamed of in their philosophy.

F. A. HAYEK

# I

## *Mr. Chairman!*

... government, even in its best state, is
but a necessary evil; in its worst state, an
intolerable one.

—THOMAS PAINE

If one plans to drive from Virginia into Washington, D.C.,
April is the time to do it. The air is fragrant, the cherry trees
are massed along the Potomac, and the great white temples
that house the statues of Lincoln and of Jefferson glow
serenely in the sun. One April day I took this drive, and I
knew that this spectacle was outside my window, but I didn't
see it. I was locked inside a limousine scanning a mass of
statistics, and there was no room in my consciousness for
such pleasures. It was 1976. I was Secretary of the Treasury
of the United States, the country was emerging from a deep
recession, and I was on my way to testify before a Congressional subcommittee.

*1*

As I look back, now that I have left office, I sometimes have the impression that that is how I spent most of my four years in Washington—racing to testify before assorted groups of Senators and Representatives. I've been told that I set the all-time record for such appearances, and I'm prepared to believe it. In fact, if I ever claim any virtue for myself on Judgment Day, it will lie in my stoic patience during these incessant performances. I was unfailingly civil—as the traditions of Washington require—but as often as not, I felt like hurling a brick at some of those gentlemen whom I once described in an unguarded moment as "those coconuts on the Hill."

It is only fair to say that it was not entirely the fault of the Congressmen that I finally grew allergic to them. There is something distinctly abnormal about having to testify so frequently, on the same subjects, and often in the same words before small, competitive groups of politicians. By my last count, the number of such Capitol Hill appearances was close to 400. But given my unique situation, it was inevitable. As fate would have it, I made my political debut by landing in the very eye of the two economic cyclones that swept over the country during my years in office. I was not only Treasury Secretary during the worst inflation and recession to rock the country in forty years, but also the "energy czar" during the OPEC nations' oil embargo, which dramatized to Americans for the first time that this country had lost its energy independence. Since both our economic condition and our energy sources were of universal concern, my responsibility in these areas had given almost every committee and subcommittee in the Senate and the House the desire to question me at regular intervals for almost four years.

Most of these hearings were an abysmal waste of time. As best as I can make out, most of the Congressmen, like most of the reporters who attended the hearings, learned virtually nothing from these public investigations. It had done little or no good to answer the thousands of Congressional questions—most of which had been formulated by legislative assistants and handed to the Congressmen at the last moment—since my answers were rarely wanted or believed. Essentially, although the details of the crises changed from month to month, I was always sending the Congressmen one fundamental and disagreeable message—namely, that the government in general and Congress in particular were responsible for both the economic and energy crises and for the dangers associated with them. Nonetheless, I patiently complied with the Congressional invitations. I never neglected an opportunity to offer these gentlemen carefully documented evidence of their own historic irresponsibility.

Inevitably I was not the most popular man in Washington, and I was often unpopular within the administration itself. Republicans, like Democrats, had participated over the years in the forging of the political and legal fetters for our productive system, and like Democrats, they often demonstrated an inability to comprehend the mischief they had wrought and were still perpetuating. The frequent shortage of brotherly love in my immediate atmosphere grieved me greatly, but there was nothing I could do about it. I was entirely committed to the Dickensian view that in the economic realm "the law is a ass"—and in Washington, that was philosophical heresy.

It was also political heresy, in the narrowest sense of the word. One did not customarily achieve political success by wrangling openly with the economic decisions of the President and head of one's own political party. But I did, over and over again. I found myself compelled, in 1974, to inform President Nixon that his fiscal policies were "insane" and that a balanced budget was imperative. A year later I was engaging in a verbal wrestling match with President Ford over his proposals to "liberate" energy production in this country by intensifying and expanding state control over the energy industries.

In retrospect, I cannot imagine why both Presidents maintained me as their Secretary of the Treasury rather than send me packing. It would be nice to believe that they held onto me because they believed in private that I was right. Something like that, I suspect, is the case, for I was indubitably a public thorn in the Presidential flesh on many occasions. My years in office were punctuated with "authoritative" leaks from the White House itself to the effect that I was on the verge of being fired on the grounds that I was too troublesome, too abrasive, too controversial. My political nickname captured that view of me; it was William the Terrible. But I was not fired. And until my last day in office I kept struggling to make the government grasp that *it* was the architect of our disasters.

As I drove toward that particular Congressional hearing on that day in April 1976, I found myself reviewing my past and wondering how I had come to be in this complicated position. Certainly there was nothing in my early life, save possibly for an extremely competitive nature, that suggested that I was headed toward a Cabinet post, let alone toward the role of a "controversial" Secretary of the Treasury who was trying to weaken the death grip of government over our economy. I was born in Paterson, New Jersey, on November 27, 1927, to a family of French Catholic origins that lost its wealth during the Depression. My mother died when I was eight. While we were never in want—my father entered the insurance business, where he made a modest living as an insurance broker—the shadow of defeat hung over the head of that loving, gentle man. Early in life I was consciously determined that I would fight against life's obstacles and never capitulate. And there, I suppose, the nucleus of "William the Terrible" was born.

My battles in youth, however, were conducted on different and nonphilosophical fronts. Throughout my school years—I attended Newark Academy, and after a stint in the Army I went to Lafayette College—such ambitions as I possessed and all my capacity for grueling self-discipline were directed into sports. Surfing, physically mastering the great waves that roared onto the Jersey beaches, and competitive swimming absorbed my youthful energies—along with virtuoso performances as a cardplayer. The charm of academic study eluded me—I did not then possess the term "irrelevant"—and I harvested a crop of Cs, ornamented by a few Bs. I felt some remorse over my undistinguished academic record until, decades later, I discovered that the American intelligentsia vastly preferred impecunious Ph.D.s who destroyed the economy to successful but Ph.D.-less financiers who fought to save the economy, at which point I got some inkling of why the academic world had failed to inspire me. My remorse vanished.

It was not, in fact, until I got my own taste of life's adversities that I embarked on a serious path that challenged my intelligence and ultimately culminated in that job in Washington. In my junior year in college I married Carol Girard, a childhood sweetheart, and our children—there were to be seven in all—began to make their appearance. Responsibility and several family illnesses leaving me with a $5000 medical debt rapidly turned me into a serious citizen. In 1952 I went to work on Wall Street for $75 a week as a management trainee at Union Securities and discovered that the world of finance fascinated me. I threw myself into my work with the discipline and precision that I had once reserved for tackling giant waves, and I enjoyed it thoroughly. I instantly displayed the signs of the "workaholic" that I have been ever since, and I became quite successful. Three years after my trainee job I was named assistant vice-president and manager of the firm's Municipal Trading Department. In 1957 I joined Weeden and Company as vice-president. In 1964 I moved to Salomon Brothers, New York, where I became a senior partner and member of the firm's executive committee. By the early 1970s my share of the firm's profits was exceeding anything I had ever dreamed of as a young man. And along with this professional success came an invisible form of wealth: I had begun to acquire a much better understanding of how certain sectors of the American economy operated.

It was during the years at Salomon Brothers that I began to

participate increasingly in public affairs. Some of my interests were cultural, ranging from serving as trustee of the
Mannes Conservatory of Music to membership on the U.S.
Olympic Committee. But my path moved me closer and
closer to Washington. I met regularly with Treasury Department officials, advising them on government financing. I did
the same for "Fannie Mae" (Federal National Mortgage
Association), "Ginnie Mae" (Government National Mortgage Association), and the Department of Housing and
Urban Development. Finally, I was chairman of the Technical Debt Management Committee of New York City—a fact
that had its own ironic overtones when, in later years, New
York foundered under its burden of debt and as Secretary of
the Treasury I fought against the irresponsible bailout demanded by city leaders.

It was in the course of these activities that I acquired an
increasing knowledge of political trends in the United States.
Like many Americans in the late sixties, I was disturbed by
many developments—in particular by the economic and
military irresponsibility of the Johnson administration and
by the political violence that had broken out. I was an
enthusiastic supporter of the candidacy of Richard Nixon in
1968 and contributed my money and my vote to his landslide
election of 1972. It was both my experience and my political
acquaintanceships in these financial-governmental organizations, as well as my active support of the Republican Party,
that led the new administration to consult me in 1972 about
its appointments and ultimately to bring me to Washington.

People named to high official positions never forget the
circumstances under which they went to Washington. There
is invariably a curious story associated with such appointments, and I remember thinking about my own on that April
drive to Congress. I recalled my excitement when Penn
James, Deputy Special Assistant to the President, phoned me
in late September 1972 and asked if I would be willing to
serve in the next Nixon administration, assuming the President was reelected. I said yes and asked him, "In what

capacity?" He said, "As Secretary of Housing and Urban Development." My background in the economics of housing was good, I knew that HUD was one of the biggest snake pits in Washington, D.C., and that if ever a department urgently needed fumigation, it was that one. I expressed interest in tackling the job, and Penn James hung up the phone.

Six weeks passed, Nixon was reelected, and I had received no word. Then, at Thanksgiving time, I got a call from Fred Malek, Assistant to the President for Executive Management. He asked if I would come down the following Monday to see President Nixon at Camp David. I agreed promptly. Then a peculiar conversation took place. Malek said, "You know, this is a very important job." I said, "Yes, I know." He said, "You realize it is tantamount to running the department." I found this an odd comment since I'd always supposed that Cabinet members ran their departments. But before I could reply, he continued, "Because George Shultz is going to be given other duties." I thought, My God, are they moving George Shultz out of Treasury? I had totally ceased to understand the conversation. Then he illuminated the mystery. "Yes," he said, "the Deputy Secretary of the Treasury is going to be a more responsible post than ever before." Thus did I discover what my job was going to be.

How I was switched from HUD Secretary to Deputy Secretary of the Treasury I never did find out with any precision. One version of the story has it that I was about to be signed up as Secretary of HUD when Treasury Secretary Shultz, who happened to be in the White House mess, heard about it. He had met me while I was a financial consultant to the Treasury and, I am glad to say, thought well of me. As the story goes, Shultz had originally asked President Nixon to name me as his deputy without success. The President had asked, "Where's he from?" Shultz replied, "New York." To which Nixon is said to have responded, "[Expletive deleted]! I don't want any more of those Eastern Cadillac liberals!" Shultz had been advised to get himself "a nice Chicago or

San Francisco banker." On the day at the White House mess, however, when he heard my name was going up as Secretary of HUD, he intervened, and ultimately my name went back up as Deputy Secretary of the Treasury.

Thus, in November 1972 I came to Washington as George Shultz's deputy. And among the most rewarding periods of my life were the next sixteen months during which I worked with him. It was the greatest privilege and finest personal, as well as intellectual, experience that any man could have. His brilliance, his analytical mind, his reasoning, his patience, his thoughtfulness were incomparable. It was an enriching experience, and I emerged from it a much better man.

I did, of course, pay that visit to President Nixon at Camp David. And that, too, I recalled on that trip to Washington. I was full of anticipation; I had never met Mr. Nixon or any other President for that matter, and I was anxious to make a good impression. Needless to say, I privately rehearsed what I considered my most brilliant comments about the state of the nation. Unfortunately I never got a chance to make them. Nixon was simultaneously remote and talkative. He delivered a nonstop monologue on various affairs of state, interwoven with erudite historical references. I listened attentively and went on listening. Finally, I grasped that he was never going to invite me to express a thought or an opinion. I left, slightly bewildered by the anticlimax. To this day I do not remember a single word that he said. What I do remember is that *I* said almost nothing.

As we entered Washington on that April drive, I recalled the last meeting I had had with Nixon, as well as the first. It was that final sad Cabinet meeting at the climax of Watergate where we all sat in stunned silence, aware of the incredible calamity that had struck the nation and of the equally incredible humiliation of the President, who sat at the center of the table. None of us looked at one another. We all stared down at our laps or off into space as Nixon disclaimed any intention to resign, a step we all knew he would have to take.

I will never forget his eyes as they seemed to beseech us for support, almost begging us to say that he had done no wrong. But no one said a word. He resigned two days later.

I had been slow to realize the seriousness of the problem. I simply could not believe that a man would make and keep tape-recorded evidence of his own guilt. Furthermore, I had been artificially insulated from the Watergate uproar by another crisis. At the time I was chairman of the Oil Policy Committee, charged with bringing some order to a chaotic, counterproductive energy policy. Then, in October 1973, disaster struck in the form of the oil embargo. I was put in charge of the Federal Energy Office and was so absorbed in energy problems that everything else, even Watergate, had acquired a faint unreality for me. I do know this: that the reports that Nixon was breaking down under the strain have been greatly exaggerated. Throughout that entire period I repeatedly saw him concentrate on complex problems while under severe emotional stress. Certainly I never saw him incoherent.

He could not say as much for me. On one occasion, at the height of the oil crisis, after a succession of twenty-hour days, I staggered home exhausted to the bone and collapsed into heavy sleep. Late that night, I am informed by my wife, Nixon telephoned me to discuss certain issues. She maintains that I answered him at length but "very strangely." The next morning I remembered nothing of the phone call. I am convinced to this day that I was talking in my sleep. Whatever I said, however, it cannot have been too disastrous. On May 4, 1974, George Shultz left the Treasury, and Nixon named me Secretary in his place. I continued to hold that post under Gerald Ford after his elevation to the Presidency.

That, in essence, is how a young New Jersey surfer turned, within three decades, into a public figure—and that is how I found myself sitting in a government limousine heading toward yet another Congressional encounter. As we approached the Cannon House Office Building, my private musings over the past came to an end. My full awareness of our government-created economic crisis returned. And once again I was in contact with that deep current that ran within me: fear for the country.

That fear surfaced more vividly than usual in the testimony I gave that day. I set aside my prepared text and delivered a spontaneous speech to the listening Congressmen. It was the only time I had ever done this. I spelled out the very concerns which constitute the themes of this book. So I reproduce the relevant portion of the Congressional transcript here, edited and shortened:

House of Representatives
Subcommittee on Democratic Research Organization
Washington, D.C.
Friday, April 30, 1976
The Subcommittee met, pursuant to notice, at 9 A.M. in Room 334, Cannon Building, the Honorable Richard H. Ichord, Chairman of the Subcommittee, presiding.
MR. ICHORD:    The meeting will come to order.
We have balanced the budget only once in the last 16 years. The national debt limit was raised to about $713 billion yesterday on the floor of the House. Interest on the national debt is estimated, for fiscal year 1977, to be in the area of $41 billion a year. And for fiscal year 1976 the estimated deficits are in the area of $76 billion. . . .
We have been exploring the relationship between deficits and inflation, between deficits and jobs, between deficits and housing, between deficits and the stock market and between deficits and interest rates. And I don't think it would be possible to complete such a study without hearing from our distinguished Secretary of the Treasury. . . . May I welcome you to the committee, Mr. Secretary. . . . You are recognized to proceed as you wish.
MR. SIMON:    Thank you very much, Mr. Chairman and gentlemen.
Unfortunately, all the rhetoric about deficits and balanced

budgets obscures the real danger that confronts us: the gradual disintegration of our free society.

You know, these last 3½ years, the years that I've been in Washington—they've been like a bad dream. The kind of dream where "they" are catching up to you, and "they" overpower you, and people just walk past and don't pay any attention! But it's not a dream. It's reality. This country is in desperate danger. The danger is obscured when we talk about deficits of $40 billion or of $70 billion or about whether we should balance the budget. The real issue is the government's share of the Gross National Product—of the earnings of every productive citizen in this land. That is the issue on which we should concentrate. What does it mean for the American dream? What does it mean for our way of life? What does it mean for our free enterprise system? What *is* our free enterprise system? Isn't free enterprise related to human freedom, to political and social freedom? God Almighty, our forefathers understood that. The millions of immigrants who came to participate in the American dream understood it. When we see this monstrous growth of government, we must realize that it is not a matter of narrow economic issues. What is at stake is equity, social stability in the United States of America. What is at stake is the fundamental freedom in one of the last, and greatest, democracies in the world.

Just look at what has happened in other countries today— whether it be Italy or the United Kingdom or Argentina or Uruguay or Ceylon. Look at what has happened there when the so-called "humanitarians" try to create "great societies" by taxing and promising and spending. When the government absorbs the GNP to the levels that we have seen in all of these countries—to the levels that we are now seeing in this country—there is a tendency toward social instability, toward minority government. The very cohesion of civilized society is destroyed.

And more than that. Freedom itself must disappear. You asked, Mr. Chairman, about the consequences of deficits. But we all know what they are. We all know that neither man nor business nor government can spend more than is taken in for very long. If it continues, the result must be bankruptcy. In the case of the federal government, we can print money to pay for our folly for a time. But we will just continue to debase our currency, and then we'll have financial collapse. That is the road we are on today. That is the direction in which the "humanitarians" are leading us. But there is nothing "humanitarian" about the collapse of a great industrial civilization. There is nothing "humanitarian" about the panic, the chaos, the riots, the starvation, the deaths that will ensue. There is nothing "humanitarian" about the dictatorship that must inevitably take over as terrified people cry out for leadership. There is nothing "humanitarian" about the loss of freedom. That is why we must be concerned about the cancerous growth of government and its steady devouring of our citizens' productive energies. That is why we must be concerned about deficits and balancing the budget. The issue is not bookkeeping. It is not accounting. The issue is the liberty of the American people.

Forgive me, Mr. Chairman. I have not been addressing your specific questions. I just wanted to put the real issue in focus. I can speak to the technicalities, and I will do so. But they obscure the real issue that faces us in this country today. The problems of deficits, budget balancing, capital markets—all these are important. But it is more important, I think, to understand that these are just early warning symptoms of a disease that threatens the very life of our body politic. And if we continue to move down this same path, that disease will be irreversible, and our liberty will be lost. I speak of this so insistently because I hear no one discussing this danger. Congress does not discuss it. The press does not discuss it. Look around us—the press isn't even here! The people do not discuss it—they are unaware of it. No counterforce in America is being mobilized to fight this danger. The battle is being lost, and not a shot is being fired.

That, Mr. Chairman, is why for me the last few years in office have been like a bad dream. I am leaving Washington next January. I am going to go home to New Jersey a very frightened man.

I did not set out to make this speech. It was extemporaneous. The subject of the hearing was one of the most important in America's political life. But on this occasion most of the committee members had not shown up, the press had not shown up, and there sat Chairman Ichord solemnly reciting statistics—more of them than I have reproduced here. I, too, had come with my own carefully prepared carload of statistics. It suddenly struck me with force that this situation—an empty dais, an empty press section, and a Niagara of numbers—symbolized exactly what was occurring in the nation: an almost universal incomprehension of a glaring danger. It was that particular thought that had provoked my outburst. It expressed the essence of what I had come to understand during my years in Washington.

Those years had been intensely educational, even traumatically so. Like most American businessmen, I had concentrated, for most of my adult life, on the complexities of my own work and on surmounting the specific obstacles before me so that I might reach my goals. My years of confronting the political and economic chaos of Washington had hurled me into a wider perspective, and the responsibilities of my office were so vast that they had provided me with a vision of the state of our country that I could not possibly have acquired outside that office. What I had learned, above all, was that the country was in a precarious state, that its very cornerstone, economic and political liberty, had been seriously eroded. I knew that most Americans were still in the state that I had once been in—largely concentrated on their own special activities—and that few of them were aware of the situation. And this knowledge of an immense danger which few recognized and which was being constantly intensified by the very political direction of the country did endow my years in Washington with a nightmarish quality. I knew I carried a constant burden of fear for the country, but I had never expected to say so publicly in that intensely personal fashion.

It is my intention in this book to communicate the wider perspective that I acquired so traumatically in Washington and the reasons for my fear. I will discuss certain economic issues, in defiance of the fact that economics is said to be the "dismal science" in which few men have an interest. But, as I told the chairman of that subcommittee on that distant April day, the reason for discussing economic issues is not to inspire a national passion for bookkeeping, but to inspire a national awareness of the connection between economic and political freedom. The connection is real and unbreakable. To lose one is to lose the other. In America we are losing both in the wake of the expanding state. That was my constant thesis as Secretary of the Treasury, and that is the theme of this book. There is no surer sign of the danger we face than the fact that so cardinal a truth—that the state itself is a threat to individual liberty—should be classified today as "controversial."

# II

# *Freedom vs. Dictatorship*

> Liberty has never come from the government. . . . The history of liberty is the history of the limitation of governmental power, not the increase of it.
>
> —WOODROW WILSON

Of the many documents that have accumulated in the years during which I was Secretary of the Treasury, a particular press release has a special significance for me. Here's a brief passage from it:

*Agreed Statement for the Press, April 1975*
The joint U.S.-U.S.S.R. Commercial Commission, meeting in Moscow for its fifth annual session, has completed a wide-ranging review of trade issues and has renewed the determination of both governments to remove the barriers which prevent full development of trade between them.
During the two days in which the Commission was meeting,

*15*

the leader of the U.S. Delegation, Treasury Secretary William E. Simon and Acting Commerce Secretary John K. Tabor were received by Leonid Brezhnev, General Secretary of the Communist Party of the U.S.S.R. The leader of the Soviet Delegation, Minister N. S. Patolichev, took part in the meeting. . . .

Both delegations expressed satisfaction that despite the difficulties of the past year, bilateral trade continues at a high level. While Soviet agricultural imports declined in 1974, the overall volume of trade last year was approximately $1 billion—four times what it was in 1970. The general expectation of the Commission was that bilateral trade would reach at least $1 billion in 1975 and might well exceed that figure. Both sides agreed that in the near future they would start work on the preparation of targets for the next three- to five-year period. . . .

An understanding was reached to conduct the next (sixth) session of the Commission in 1976 in Washington.

The U.S. Delegation expressed sincere gratitude for the warm hospitality extended to it by the Soviet side during its stay in the U.S.S.R.

The joint statement indicated that the negotiations had been affable. But it did not indicate the artificial cocoon of a world in which those affable negotiations had taken place— the Moscow suburb of Lenin Hills, where the czarist aristocrats once lived, with all the luxury the dictators of the U.S.S.R. could wrap around the American negotiators to shelter them from Soviet realities. We had been in Moscow for several days—I, along with my wife, Carol; Jack Bennett, Under Secretary of the Treasury for Monetary Affairs; Gerald Parsky, Assistant Secretary; a staff group from the departments of State and Commerce; and others. I had inherited the position of détente, and I agreed with it. I knew what communism was and what the communists were trying to do, but I was convinced that, with properly structured relations, we could maintain peace. So I found those days challenging. Leonid Brezhnev is a clever, jovial man, and I found the Soviet Foreign Trade Minister, Nikolai Patolichev, as always to be friendly, intelligent, and informed. What they felt, of course, I never knew. The facades they wore masked all inner feelings. I often sensed a deep emotional difference between us, some profound way in which they were unlike me, but I couldn't give it a name. Nonetheless, we all had worked hard and in between sessions had been treated to those monumental sturgeon, caviar, and vodka orgies that the Russians offer honored guests. We had been treated splendidly in our royal cocoon.

Somewhere outside that cocoon, in some other dimension of reality, we knew that there was an oppressed populace. Somewhere outside it, we knew, citizens were ill clad, ill housed, ill fed, and unfree—some being torn from their families and homes and hurled into prisons and insane asylums for the crime of disagreeing with our jovial hosts. But none of this was visible in our opulent nest. Only the most pleasurable sights and sounds had been allowed to filter into that artificial world prepared for us by the lords of the Kremlin. Soviet society itself had little or no reality.

When our "agreed statement" was handed to the press, we prepared to depart. We exchanged our formal compliments, made our farewells and boarded Air Force Two. Still caught up in our official roles, we continued to discuss the ramifications of East-West trade. Then, abruptly, the roar of the motor broke into our conversation, and as the plane taxied down the runway, we all fell silent. After a moment or two Air Force Two lifted off. We heard the dull thump of the locking wheels. The ground fell away beneath us. We were no longer on Soviet soil! And everyone burst into applause.

I'll never forget the moment of elation that possessed us all. It needed no translation. I knew exactly what the emotion was: a sense of oppression being lifted from all of us who had never known oppression. It felt, for a crazy moment, as if we were staging a great escape. I remember that sense of "I can breathe again. I can talk again. I'm not being spied on anymore." It was a sudden vanishing of all the menacing things that characterize the Soviet Union, the shadowy intrusions that you can feel but cannot see. Throughout all the long, cooperative working hours, underlying the jovial ceremonies, lurking beneath the flash of crystal, the flow of vodka, the unspoken awareness of unseen oppression had been with each of us. We too had felt unfree. So all of us, seventy-eight dignified representatives of the United States of America, shouted and applauded like youngsters in sheer relief because we had emerged from that mammoth jail called the Soviet Union, because we were flying home, flying toward freedom. And at that moment that's all that "home" meant to every one of us—blessed, blessed freedom.

And it was then for the first time that I could put into words that sense of a deep, unnamable difference between the Soviet officials and myself. It was the difference between men who have never known freedom and men who were born free. Most of them, I suspected, didn't even know that difference between us existed. They heard about it, they read about it, but they couldn't comprehend something they had never known. I was certain that they couldn't understand that rush of joy and relief that was racing through us like a powerful tide. I realized something disturbing: Those Soviet officials are men who do not *know* that they live in a dungeon. And as I realized that, I understood down to my very roots how important my liberty was to me, that the need for it was a part of my very identity. My God, I thought, without it, I would not be *me*!

I learned afterward that this intense awareness of the value of freedom is a common response of Americans leaving the U.S.S.R., but for me it was an extraordinary moment. For I had never, until then, thought philosophically about my own feelings about freedom. It was only at that singular moment when Air Force Two soared over Moscow that I got my first real insight into what political freedom actually was and how intensely I valued it. It taught me why, until that moment, I had never experienced that intensity or even understood what it was I so deeply valued. It also taught me I was not alone in this lack of self-knowledge.

Freedom is strangely ephemeral. It is something like breathing; one only becomes acutely aware of its importance when one is choking. Similarly, it is only when one confronts political tyranny that one really grasps the meaning and importance of freedom. What I actually realized in Air Force Two is that freedom is difficult to understand because it isn't a *presence* but an *absence*—an absence of governmental constraint. People who are unfamiliar with severe political constraints—severe enough to make them aware that they have lost their freedom—often don't know what freedom is and on what it depends.

This was true of me, and it tends to be generally true of Americans, who have had the unique privilege of living in a nation that was organized, constitutionally and economically, for one purpose above all: to protect that freedom. Our Founding Fathers, for whom the knowledge of the centuries of tyranny that had preceded them was vivid and acute, were guided in the creation of our political and economic system by that knowledge; virtually every decision they made was to bind the state in chains to protect the individual's freedom of thought, choice, and action—to protect that ephemeral thing called freedom.

I have also come to realize that of all the aspects of political freedom guaranteed to us by our Constitution, freedom of action—most particularly, freedom of productive action or free enterprise—is the least understood. For years, in Washington, I have been watching the tragic spectacle of citizens' groups, businessmen, politicians, bureaucrats, and media people systematically laying waste to our free enterprise system and our freedom even as they earnestly— and often sincerely—proclaimed their devotion to both. Again, this widespread incomprehension is largely due to the fact that freedom of action, including freedom of productive action, is simply a subdivision of freedom; it, too, is an *absence* rather than a *presence*—an absence of governmental constraint. By whatever name one wishes to call this category of free human action—free enterprise, the free market, capitalism—it simply means that men are free to produce. They are free to discover, to invent, to experiment, to succeed, to fail, to create means of production, to exchange goods and services, to profit, to consume—all on a voluntary basis without significant interference by the policing powers of the state. In the most fundamental sense, the right to freedom in this entire chain of productive action adds up to the right to life—for man, by his nature, is a being who must produce in order to live.

Our Founding Fathers, in whom I grow progressively more interested as I grow older, were well aware of this. One of the British philosophers who influenced their thought most profoundly was John Locke. And when I discovered his existence fairly recently (I was no scholar in college, and he is not the usual reading material on Wall Street or, for that matter, in the Treasury Department!), I felt as if he were speaking directly for me. "A man . . . having, in the state of nature, no arbitrary power over the life, liberty or possession of another, but only so much as the law of nature gave him for the preservation of himself and the rest of mankind, this is all he doth or can give up to the commonwealth, and by it to the legislative power, so that the legislative can have no more than this."

In other words, government's power, said Locke, was logically limited to the protection of each individual's right to his life, his liberty, and his property, and any government that interfered with these rights instead of protecting them was illegitimate. It is this language that ultimately appeared in our Constitution as the rights to "Life, Liberty, and the Pursuit of Happiness." Our Founding Fathers, intellectual heirs of Locke, consciously and deliberately created the first limited government in the history of man.

A philosopher I cherish equally is Adam Smith, the Scottish theoretician of free enterprise—that political system in which the state leaves producers and consumers free to produce and consume as they choose. Smith, too, believed in the natural right of the individual to liberty, and his essential message to all government was "laissez-faire," or "leave people alone to act." In *The Wealth of Nations*, published by happy coincidence in 1776, Adam Smith denounced the "mercantilists" of his period who (precisely like our contemporary "liberals") argued that a government should control all aspects of domestic and foreign trade if it wished to enrich the nation. Smith, on the contrary, argued that if the goal were wealth, the productive individual should be free of all such state controls, in accordance with "a system of natural liberty." In total liberty, he said, wealth would necessarily be produced on a scale yet unforeseen. And this Scottish philosopher made a series of points that continually amaze me with their prophetic power.

Cooperation among men, he said, would flow naturally from self-interest alone: "It is not from the benevolence of the butcher, the brewer or the baker that we expect our dinner, but from their regard to their own self-interest."

And, he declared, the totality of interacting self-interests would find, in nature, a spontaneous form of self-regulation—namely, the law of supply and demand. This natural order, working through the self-interest of individuals without their knowledge, promotes the public interest. Smith wrote:

> As every individual, therefore, endeavors as much as he can both to employ his capital in the support of industry that its produce may be of the highest value; every individual necessarily labors to render the annual revenues of the society as great as he can. He generally indeed neither intends to promote the public interest nor knows by how much he is promoting it. . . . [H]e intends only his own gain, and he is in this, as in many other cases, led by an invisible hand to promote an end which was no part of his intention.

Our Founding Fathers must have read *The Wealth of Nations* with great satisfaction, for, as Smith himself observed, the American colonies had been practicing what he preached for more than a century. In their dedication to individual liberty, the earliest leaders of this nation were determined to leave citizens free to seek their fortunes with a minimum of state interference, and a free-market system rooted in "natural law" had been the brilliant result. From its very birth America was a natural laboratory for the liberty-loving philosophies of such men as Locke and Smith, and this country proved to be the noblest experiment ever devised by man. Not coincidentally, it also proved to be the form of society that produced a degree of wealth and a standard of living for the "common man" that had never before been seen. America was by the very definition of its founders a capitalist nation.

In sum, individual liberty *includes* the individual's economic freedom, and the Founding Fathers knew it. They had good reason to leave the productive activities of men as free as possible. Their calculations, like those of Adam Smith, were correct. When men are left free by the state to engage in productive action, guided by self-interest above all, they do create the most efficient and powerful production system that is possible to their society. And the greatest misfortune in America today is that most people do not understand this. They don't understand our traditional economic system precisely because it is not, in the ordinary sense, a system at all—meaning a conscious organization or detailed plan. Essentially, as always, what they don't understand is how, in the *absence* of conscious planning, millions of men can function efficiently together to produce wealth. But it is precisely that *absence* of conscious planning that accomplishes the miracle! To this very day—obscured by a tragic amount of governmental intervention since the thirties—it is *still* Adam Smith's "invisible hand" and "the system of natural liberty" that are producing our goods and services, creating our jobs, paying our salaries, financing our government, and generating American wealth.

The enormously complex and productive system known as a free market operates without conscious supervision and direction. It works as follows: Day in and day out, people engage in economic activities called businesses—small individual ones and gigantic ones held together by a tissue of voluntary individual contracts. They organize and allocate resources by selling and buying in markets which respond sensitively to the wishes of individuals. Each consumer "votes," in effect, with his dollar in untold thousands of market "elections," and his vote is automatically translated into shifts of resources into the desired products and services. The products for which people are willing to pay an adequate price are produced; things for which people are not willing to pay an adequate price are not produced.

The free market is nothing but the sum of these interacting individual decisions. It is the most individualistic and the most democratic economic system conceivable. It works with no conscious direction. There is no single purpose or goal. Each "voter" has his own purposes and goals; he seeks to maximize his rewards, to avoid or to cut his losses. There are literally billions of purposes, billions of decisions, billions of adjustments every day as inventors, entrepreneurs, middlemen, employers, workers, buyers, and sellers pursue their own respective self-interests.

And what is the end result of these billions of individual decisions? It is the torrential outpouring of man-made wealth that characterizes the history of American capitalism—in which 28 percent of the total production of the human race is created by only 5 percent of the world's population. American capitalism has generated the most astounding flood of imaginative goods and services ever to have appeared on the face of the globe—goods and services produced in inconceivable variety and abundance and (until the relatively recent invasion of government into the marketplace) with maximum efficiency. This is the system that has endowed the average American with the highest standard of living in the world and in history—even if the job of eliminating the last pocket of poverty is not yet completed. That is what Adam Smith said would happen if men were left free by the state to produce, and that is exactly what happened. Paul McCracken, former chairman of the Council of Economic Advisers, observes: "Great masses of the world's people do not . . . have a material level of living significantly better than did their ancestors a generation ago. . . . But we have been doubling the material levels of living for the average American roughly every 40 years."

Defenders of the free enterprise system, struggling in the face of growing antagonism and noisy heresies, often seek to defend it by reeling off statistical evidence of the productivity of the free market. For example, a memo that landed on my desk in the Treasury Department contained these figures to illustrate the "success of the free enterprise system":

—96 percent of all American homes have a telephone;
—50 percent of all Americans own at least one automobile;
—96 percent of all American homes have at least one television;
—after American farmers finish feeding the U.S., they export 60 percent of their wheat and rice; 50 percent of their soybeans; one quarter of their grain sorghum and one fifth of their corn. The U.S. provides half the world's wheat.
—American farms produce this despite the fact that since 1940 the number of U.S. farms and farm workers has decreased by two thirds. During that time, however, agricultural output has increased by 75 percent.

Now all this is very true, and indeed, it doesn't scratch the surface of what one could say about the American economy, if one wished to make such lists. The extraordinary wealth of our nation is well known throughout the world. The statistics which record the tangible results of that system nevertheless miss the invisible dimension. The single most awe-inspiring thing about our economic system lies in what is *absent*, what is *not* perceivable to the naked eye. It is the fact that the flood of wealth emerges from the lack of any direction of the economic process, from the lack of government control, from the lack of state-imposed or "national" purposes and goals. The capitalist miracle occurred in the United States, the politically freest nation in the world, precisely because this explosion of wealth is uniquely a result of *individual liberty.* That is the true defense of capitalism. That is what most people do not understand—and that is what deserves to be shouted from the rooftops.

There is nothing subjective or biased about this view that political and economic freedom are inextricably related. It is conceded as objective fact by even the most interventionist of economists. Arthur Okun, for example, a liberal economist who was chairman of Lyndon Johnson's Council of Economic Advisers, readily grants the integral relationship of a free market and political freedom. He says:

> A market economy helps to safeguard political rights against encroachment by the state. Private ownership and decision-making circumscribe the power of the government—or, more accurately, of those who run the government—and hence its ability to infringe on the domain of rights. In the polar case of a fully collectivized economy, political rights would be seriously jeopardized. If the government commanded all the productive resources of the society, it could suppress dissent, enforce conformity and snuff out democracy.[1]

Ironically, this connection between political and economic freedom is perfectly understood by totalitarians. Their "understanding," however, has a morbid cast. The communist theoretician knows precisely how to *destroy* individual freedom; he destroys economic freedom, and the job is done. More specifically, he expropriates private property, the means of production, and he forbids profits. He places the entire production-exchange-consumption chain under the direct rule of the state, which means, of course, that he places the physical life of each individual at the mercy of the state. That is the essence of tyranny.

The totalitarian, of course, never announces that his intention is to enslave people. Quite the contrary, he invariably proposes to "liberate" them. He rationalizes his tyranny righteously in the name of the collective well-being of the "proletariat," "race," or "fatherland" or in the name of the "public interest," "brotherhood," or "equality." But all these are invariably just rationalizations; the goal of tyranny is tyranny. And inexorably it destroys economic life. The ultimate result is inevitably grinding poverty, an inability to produce.

If America historically has been a test tube case of the brilliantly fruitful connection between political and economic liberty, the communist world has been a test tube case of the economic destruction that automatically accompanies the destruction of political liberty. Many of the intellectual and political leaders of this nation have never understood the overwhelming economic impotence of the Soviet Union. Until recently I did not understand it either. But I do now. And I believe that nothing can be more important for the American citizen to know today, in an era where "advanced" and "progressive" thinkers are advocating economic collectivism and increasingly centralized state control of the economy as the wave of the future. And so, in this next section, I am going to describe the polar opposite of the free-market system as it has existed in the Soviet Union.

The Soviet Union in our era is seen by many Americans and by people all over the world as a sort of communist Horatio Alger that transformed itself from primitive peasant nation into a major modern industrial power by one means alone: collectivization and centralized economic planning.

The truth is that the Soviet economic system doesn't work. It has functioned from beginning to end by relying on Western capitalism, above all, on American capitalism. By 1921, four years after their revolution, the Bolsheviks had destroyed the czarist economy and were themselves faced with revolution. But Lenin had a brilliant idea: He would abandon "pure communism" and create his New Economic Policy (NEP). Thus, in 1921, he invited the capitalists of the West to rebuild the Russian economy.

Lenin thought himself Machiavellian in devising the NEP, which he called "industrial cohabitation with the capitalists." And he declared, "As soon as we are strong enough to overthrow capitalism, we shall immediately seize it by the throat."

Western capitalists, who knew nothing about ideological venom but everything about production for profit, leaped to the Russian bait. Lenin offered them generous "concessions" in exchange for the rapid industrialization of Russia. American and European industrialists fell over their own feet in their zeal to sell to the Soviets. The International Barnsdall Corporation and Standard Oil, for example, won oil-drilling concessions; Stuart, James & Cooke, Inc., reorganized Russian coal mines. The International General Electric Company sold Moscow electrical equipment. And other major American firms—Westinghouse, du Pont, and RCA—assisted in various ways.

In the thirties our businessmen shipped and installed replicas of complex American production centers to the Soviet Union, where they were assembled like gigantic do-it-yourself kits. The Cleveland firm of Arthur G. Mackee provided the equipment for huge steel plants at Magnitogorsk; John K. Calder of Detroit equipped and installed the material for tractor plants at Chelyabinsk; Henry Ford and the Austin Company provided all the elements for a major automobile works at Gorki. Colonel Hugh Cooper, creator of the Muscle Shoals Dam, planned and built the giant hydroelectric installation of Dniepostroi. *The most grandiose "Bolshevik achievements" of the thirties, which glorified communism throughout the world and convinced two generations of American and European intellectuals of the economic potency of the U.S.S.R. and of centralized planning, were all achievements of Western capitalism.*

By 1941 the Soviet Union was desperately begging the West for aid against Hitler's armies. And the phenomenon known as lend-lease was created. Between 1941 and 1945 a vast flood of goods was flown and shipped to Russia: raw materials, machinery, tools, complete industrial plants, spare parts, textiles, clothing, canned meat, sugar, flour and fats, as well as purely military supplies—an unending stream of arms, trucks, tanks, aircraft, and gasoline. Lend-lease was equal to more than a third of the prewar level of Soviet industrial production—a gift of at least $11 billion worth of the most advanced technology in the world.

The war over, the communist dictatorship, protected by private agreements between Roosevelt and "Papa Joe" Stalin, plundered the conquered nations. Russia, writes German historian Werner Keller, collected "loot on an unprecedented scale from Europe and the Far East." The total, in 1938 dollars, was $12.27 billion. From Germany alone the Soviets took iron and steelworks, chemical plants, shipyards, motorcar factories, electric power stations, railway networks, armaments factories, and the huge underground V-2 works; 41 percent of Germany's industrial equipment, Keller reports, was dismantled, packed, and transported to Russia. Additionally, reparations to Russia totaled as much as the Marshall Plan aid given by the United States to all Western Europe.

Within little more than a decade the Soviet Union had leaped into the advanced industrial era and was producing atomic bombs, hydrogen bombs, intercontinental rockets, sputniks, luniks, and manned satellites. And a "major world power" was born. That is how contemporary Americans—and the rest of the world—suddenly "discovered" the miraculous power of the communist economy. It would indeed have been miraculous if this development had occurred independently. But it didn't. During this "advanced industrial era" the average Soviet citizen was about as poor as he had been under the Czar. Average living space, calculates economist Warren Nutter, was about as large as a gravesite.

In fact, the U.S.S.R. had not entered into an authentically advanced industrial era at all, but remained as dependent as ever on Western technology for its industrial development. Throughout the 1950s, as the Soviets ceaselessly imported technology, their exports consisted almost entirely of non-manufactured materials. In the 1960s and 1970s the trade pattern of the U.S.S.R. was still essentially the same preindustrial pattern as that which had existed in the 1920s. The Soviet Union had never stopped exchanging raw materials for Western technology. A half century under centralized planning had rendered the country virtually incapable of technological innovation. To this day, "Bolshevik achievements" are dominantly the achievements of Western capitalism.[2]

During the summer of 1976, a year after my visit to the Soviet Union to discuss trade, the American press began to discover the immensity of the communist dependency on the Western capitalist world. The astonished stories sounded exactly as if they had been written in 1921. On July 26 Arnaud de Borchgrave wrote in *Newsweek*:

> In recent years the Soviets have imported vast quantitites of Western technology, consumer goods and food. . . . The communist appetite for Western technology is staggering. The Russians have purchased nearly 1000 "turn-key" plants—ready-to-go enterprises complete with a trained technical staff. Some of the current deals are even bigger. The Russians are buying several chemical plants, a new steel mill, oil drilling equipment and a complete shipyard from Britain. France is putting up a timber complex in Siberia and chemical refineries in central Russia.

And on September 6 *Time* magazine, innocently unaware of history, reported:

> Now the Soviet bloc is following [a] heretical strategy that might be called credit-card communism. . . . Totally violating Marxist prejudices, the Soviet Union and its six economic allies in Eastern Europe are trying to modernize their antiquated economies by borrowing heavily from their supposed class enemies, the capitalists of the West.

And this is exactly where I came in when I started this story—with the birth of this "heretical strategy." What I have learned since my enlightening trip on Air Force Two is that Lenin's emergency "cohabitation with the capitalists" has actually been going on incessantly for fifty-five years. In fact, the rulers of the Soviet Union are impaled on the horns of a frightful dilemma and do not know where to turn. They are fully aware that they preside over a sick and stagnant economy, dependent on a Western capitalist crutch, and they are also aware that they cannot go on indefinitely starving their own people and depriving them of the most modest amenities of life. When I was last in the Soviet Union, the Minister of Trade told me about the "incentive" programs being instituted to give workers money for additional production. Unfortunately such limited "incentives" have been tried many times before and do not solve the fundamental problem: lack of freedom. The Soviet leaders know exactly how America generates its technological innovation and wealth. They know that only by decentralizing and individualizing the decision-making process and allowing free, competitive markets to develop across the length and breadth of the Soviet Union can they generate technology and wealth. As one observer has said, "To cure the patient would kill the doctor." To introduce true incentives and economic freedom into the Soviet Union would destroy the communist state. And so the communist rulers, in despair, turn eternally to the capitalist world for their continuous economic fix.*

These, then, are the polar systems of political-economic

---

*Clearly, the Western nations, above all the United States, have been desperately unwise in providing the U.S.S.R. with that continuous economic fix. We have supplied the Soviets with vast amounts of technology and know-how but have demanded almost nothing in return, no cutback in military spending, no end to the "wars of national liberation" that the Kremlin supports the globe around. I am a strong advocate of economic cooperation and free trade, but I have come to believe that it is imperative for Western governments to stop financing Soviet industrial expansion, by either direct loans or credits—$40 billion in recent years. Certainly there is no moral or economic justification for taxing American citizens in order to finance the industrialization of nations that seek to destroy them.

organization: at one extreme, a free, unplanned, individualist market in a free individualist society which creates a powerful and inventive economic system and produces wealth; at the other, totalitarian-collectivist planning which destroys both the political and the economic freedom of the individual and produces collective poverty and starvation. Only when one has a good grasp of these polar alternatives is it possible to understand what has been going on—and going wrong—in Western countries, and in our own country in particular, in the past few decades.

To understand it, one need merely ask one question: What would happen to a society if someone tried to *mix* these contradictory polar systems in the life of a nation? What would happen if one tried to mix the free and the totalitarian, the unplanned and the planned, the individualist and the collectivist elements in economic life? For an answer, we must examine the industrialized nations of the West— Britain, France, Italy, Norway, Denmark, Sweden, the Netherlands, Austria, West Germany. Their economic "mix," of course, is known by many names—"liberalism," "interventionism," "mixed economy," the "welfare state," "social democracy," "democratic socialism," even "socialism."

None of these terms has a precise definition, but societies with such economies share certain characteristics: Their intellectual and political leaders share the illusion that a comparative handful of individuals can substitute their judgment for the billions and trillions of decisions that go on in a free market. Generally, they believe it possible to use central planning to "correct" free market processes without destroying the market itself. They advocate planning to increase economic efficiency, to enforce competition, to eliminate the business cycle, to manipulate the money supply and rates of interest, to determine prices and profits, to redistribute property and income, to speed up or slow down the growth of the economy, to prevent discrimination, to eliminate pollution and several hundred other things. Whatever such gentlemen deem to be in need of improvement is sufficient cause for them to turn to central planning as a solution. The result of such political leadership is a system that was accurately described by *Newsweek* magazine (October 18, 1976) in an article entitled "Is Socialism in Trouble?" "By and large," the writer said, "social democracy seeks a middle ground between communism and capitalism."

The advocates of economic intervention clearly believe that their aims are worthy. But if one deflects one's attention from the meritorious motives and goals of such planners and simply looks at the nature of the system they have created—"a middle ground between communism and capitalism"—one sees that this is a regressive trend.

Few people would have any difficulty in understanding that if communist countries were to move in the direction of capitalism, that would be a decided sign of progress. If we were to hear, for example, that the Soviet Union was abandoning its centralized planning, opening up the nation to individual initiative and to free markets, most people would realize that totalitarianism was on the decline, that freedom was on the rise, that technological innovation and wealth could be expected to increase. But most of the same people cannot see that when a politically and economically free society starts to contract individual initiative, to contract the freedom of the market, political liberty is on the decline, inventiveness must decay, and wealth must decrease. Yet, if one really understands the polar systems, there is nothing particularly difficult about this calculation. A nation that decreases its economic freedom *must* be less politically free. And because freedom is a precondition for economic creativity and wealth, that nation *must* grow poorer. It follows as night follows day. *If* one understands the polar systems.

There are, of course, significant differences in the various mixes of freedom and coercive control in the Western countries. The nature, the degree, the rigidity, and the duration of the government's power over the economy; the slowness or speed with which this government takeover of economic control has occurred; the number of areas affected; the momentum of the prior free economy; the degree to which the people are accustomed to state control of their lives; the history of the society, its culture, the very temperament of its people—all these elements and doubtless many others will determine the nature, speed, and severity of the deterioration. As a result, I am in no position to account for all the various differences we see in the Western nations and for their different rates of deterioration. All I can do, like everyone else, is to observe some of these differences.

In Italy and France the trends are clear-cut: Both nations are drifting in the direction of totalitarianism. In Italy, where the dominent modern experience has been that of strong government controls, we see incessant economic disturbance, intransigent poverty, chaos, endless strikes, and the strong development of a communist movement. The New York *Times'* Graham Hovey has written that Italy has "arrived at the point where a democratic government must depend for survival on communist benevolence in Parliament." Communist "benevolence," of course, consists of educating the public to believe that all social and economic problems will vanish with total government control over the economy.

In France, where the prewar economy had been virtually calcified by government controls, the postwar "cure" once again was centralized planning. Again, such planning has resulted in economic chaos, strikes, riots, "revolutions," and in severe economic, political, and social disturbance. A large communist movement—which has worked closely with socialist François Mitterrand—is gathering greater and greater support by assuring France that the "cure" for its ills is a complete government takeover of the economy.

In both Italy and France a number of factors have both camouflaged and delayed the crisis—mainly the Marshall Plan and the enormous postwar injection of U.S. wealth into these economies, plus, of course, the surviving strength of their own increasingly hobbled markets. But it is now becoming apparent that both these nations are drifting, almost helplessly, toward communist economies. Needless to say, in both countries there is tremendous fear of this trend in certain sectors and strong resistance to it. But it seems fairly certain that communists will now be a staple element in the political leadership of those countries, that the steady destruction of the market will continue, and that political freedom itself is grossly threatened.

In West Germany the development has been strikingly different. National Socialism and war had reduced Germany to ashes. A brilliant Minister of Economic Affairs named Ludwig Erhard, who knew what he was doing, pulled West Germany out of collapse by the simple expedient of yanking out most government controls and letting a free economy rip. The result was an extraordinary laboratory demonstration of the relationship of a politically free economy and the production of wealth. Erhard launched a free enterprise Germany to the top of the list of productive nations in a few short years. On the communist side of the Berlin Wall the poverty remained deadly. One might suppose that with such a comparative experiment going on under their noses, the West Germans might have learned the value of a free, untrammeled economy. But they didn't. They turned back to government intervention and became a "social democracy." Their incredible growth has slowed considerably. And today, while Germany remains a powerful nation, few realize that its wealth and strength are a result of that massive productive momentum generated by the freedom given to the postwar market and by the resolve, even by a socialist government, to resist easy money and inflationary ruin.

In Sweden yet another variation on the theme has existed. For a variety of reasons an "advanced welfare state" has developed in Sweden and remained relatively stable for forty-four years. The stability has been due in part to the gradual development of the Swedish social system, a slow, steady move in the direction of state control over individual life without traumatic swings between free market and severe regulation as in Germany. It has been due in part to the fact that those ambitious citizens who could not tolerate the growingly oppressive bureaucracy and the economic ceilings that menaced their goals simply left. In addition, there is a culturally and psychologically homogeneous working class which places immensely high value on economic security and economic equality and is relatively indifferent to competitive individual achievement. For these and other reasons the Swedish people on the whole have willingly accepted almost suffocating bureaucratic supervision of every detail of their lives—the state dictates the color a man may paint his house; he may choose from shades of *tan*!—in exchange for cradle-to-grave protection.

For this protection—exceeded nowhere on earth—the Swedes have been willing to pay an extraordinary percentage of their income. The average industrial workers' pays $4125 in taxes on a salary of about $11,000. The most successful members of Swedish society, in business, the arts, and all the independent professions, have as much as 85 percent of their income confiscated. In one famous case, author Astrid Lingren was taxed at the rate of 102 percent. Successful professionals are now working part time to avoid such a fate—their incentive to produce severely damaged, if not destroyed. And many arts are in disarray; Sweden's Minister of Education and Cultural Affairs Bertil Zachrisson has expressed the view that it is morally objectionable that some authors earn more than others. He has suggested that all writers' royalties be pooled and divided among writers according to their need!

In a revealing "Letter from Stockholm" published in *The New Yorker* in 1976, author Steve Kelman makes it clear that a significant number of Swedes—"a phantom opposition not represented by the parties"—is deeply disturbed by this suffocation of liberty, and many are "obsessed" by taxation. "Perhaps a fifth of the Swedish electorate sees Sweden as . . . drowning in bureaucracy and stifling the individual. Others, whose alienation is not so great, nevertheless have feelings that no politicians vent: that the country has too many 'welfare chiselers' . . . that taxes should be cut drastically." Such ideological opposition to the Swedish welfare state has almost never been noted by Western journalists, and Mr. Kelman may be the first to explain why. The reason is that *no political institutions are tolerated in Sweden by means of which such opposition can be expressed.* He writes: "Leaders here consider their duty to be *educating* voters as much as *representing* them; a University of Gothenburg survey revealed that only 7½ percent of the members of Parliament feel that if their constituents held a view on an issue which differed from their own, this fact should affect the members' public stand."

Inevitably in such a system the cloven hoof of the police state has appeared. Privacy is continually invaded by the state's tax collectors, who remorselessly police the citizenry for unreported funds. Swedish law gives tax authorities the right to enter houses and businesses without court orders to inspect bankbooks and survey medical records, and tales of midnight visits from officials of the National Tax Board are common. The entire world became aware of this totalitarianism when director Ingmar Bergman was dragged off a theater stage by policemen for alleged nonpayment of taxes and suffered a nervous breakdown.

Inevitably, also, signs of economic deterioration are present in Sweden. In 1976 a study by Hudson Research, Europe, showed that Sweden had the slowest growth rate of fourteen industrialized nations—second only to that of Britain.

In the election of 1976 socialist Prime Minister Olof Palme was defeated at the polls. He had been challenged by three nonsocialist parties which campaigned on the issues of high taxation, the "arrogance" of bureaucratic power, the increasing power of labor unions, and the centralization of government. Nonetheless, the election reversal cannot be construed as a repudiation of Swedish collectivism. All the challenging politicians piously pledged to maintain all the "protective" legislation of the system—while lowering taxes, cutting the power of the bureaucracy, and limiting the power of the centralized government at the same time! Most Swedes, too, have yet to grasp that their mammoth "public sector" is slowly devouring their wealth and that they cannot allow the government to "protect"—*i.e.*, dictate—every aspect of their lives and be free of government oppression.

And finally, there is the United Kingdom, which offers yet another variation on the mixed economy theme. Economically wrecked after World War II, the U.K. did not emulate the wisdom of Germany's Ludwig Erhard, but moved in the opposite direction. Most British intellectuals and political leaders appear to have suckled Fabian socialism with their mother's milk and in consequence learned nothing from the fact that Britain—and all Europe—had been saved from Hitler's hordes by America's free market economy, which was simultaneously holding up the war effort of America, Europe, and the Soviet Union. To "cure" their society, they turned massively to socialist measures. Ralph Harris, director of the Institute of Economic Affairs in London, summarizes the results in a pungent phrase: The socialist leaders of Britain created a "progression from socialist planning to planned chaos." The Labor Party's pledges of abundance that would follow from such ingenious solutions to British poverty as the nationalization of the coal, gas, electricity, railway, and steel industries, along with their other interventions into the economy, culminated, says Harris, in "shortages, austerity and restrictions." And this occurred despite American "loans equal to about one eighth of the British national income." And the postwar "planned chaos" has simply grown worse. In 1975 Harris called British central planning a "total failure": "Cumulatively, since 1960, record levels of unemployment and inflation have come to exist with flagging growth and a sinking pound, whilst a standard of living overtaken by most European countries is now prevented from falling further only by massive foreign borrowing."[3] Since Harris wrote those words, the standard of living has crashed still further.

No one predicted this tragic outcome more accurately than Winston Churchill. Ousted from office by the socialists in 1945, this eloquent statesman, whom I consider the greatest leader of this century, wrote:

> I do not believe in the power of the state to plan and enforce. No matter how numerous are the committees they set up or the ever-growing hordes of officials they employ or the severity of the punishments they inflict or threaten, they can't approach the high level of internal economic production achieved under free enterprise.
>
> Personal initiative, competitive selection, the profit motive, corrected by failure and the infinite processes of good housekeeping and personal ingenuity, these constitute the life of a free society. It is this vital creative impulse that I deeply fear the doctrines and policies of the socialist government have destroyed.
>
> Nothing that they can plan and order and rush around enforcing will take its place. They have broken the mainspring, and until we get a new one, the watch will not go. Set the people free—get out of the way and let them make the best of themselves.
>
> I am sure that this policy of equalizing misery and organizing scarcity instead of allowing diligence, self-interest and ingenuity to produce abundance has only to be prolonged to kill this British island stone dead.

The British "planned economy" *is* "stone dead." It has survived to this day only by devouring the productivity of its citizens. The British now pay taxes that allow the government to confiscate 60 percent of the national income. A royal commission has reported that the *richest* 1 percent of the British populace earned more than $13,700—the same year that the *median* American income was $12,965. The most successful of the "rich"—those who earn more than $40,000 a year—lose an average of 83 percent of their income to the government. And profits—considered by Keynesian doctrinaires as socially noxious—are virtually confiscated; they are taxed at 98 percent! Inevitably throughout the decades there has been a leakage from Britain of the enterprising, the productive, the ambitious, and those intellectuals and artists who place a high value on their individual achievements— the same "brain drain" that has occurred in all "social democratic" countries. Physicians today are fleeing in great numbers because Labor policy seeks to eliminate what remains of private medicine and private hospital care. But above all, *capital* is leaking out of Braitain to be invested abroad, where it will not be confiscated. There is no longer the slightest incentive for a Briton to invest his capital in British industry.

The most powerful force behind the massive destruction of the British economic system is the labor movement, which continues to be obsessed with Marxist fantasies of "expropriating the expropriators." Laborite Anthony Wedgwood Benn, now Secretary of State for Energy and former Minister of both Technology and Industry, had the imaginative idea, a few years ago, of converting failing businesses into government-subsidized workers' cooperatives. The result was disastrous; it cost the British government more than $100 million. Currently the "solution" seen by many—such as Labor leader Arthur Scargill, known as "Little Lenin"—is a government takeover of the successful, not the failing, businesses! "We would not nationalize the lame ducks," he says, "but the golden geese." In 1976 the *Times* of London warned that "the present trend portends the progressive liquidation of manufacturing industry and with it most of the differences between the standard of living now and the standard of living 200 years ago when the Industrial Revolution began."

Political freedom, along with economic freedom, is being chipped away. As in Sweden, the British state may now enter people's homes without warning to search for violations of the tax codes. And a Labor commission has recommended that the entire press—radio, television, and newspapers—be nationalized to take them out of the hands of the "special interests." The proposal was repudiated by the British, but it is of immense significance that in the land of Magna Carta so explicit a bid to destroy press freedom was proposed at all.

There are other case histories of comparable developments in mixed economies or "liberal" social democracies, but these are ample to make my point. Whatever the variations on the theme, those nations that have sought a genuine mix of the polar opposites of a free and an unfree economy, of the unplanned and the planned, of the individualist and the collectivist—of communism and capitalism—are slowly deteriorating or rapidly rotting, both socially and economically, and liberty itself is being corroded. And although in every one of those nations there is acute unease and anxiety over political trends, rare are the Europeans who fully understand why their worlds are running down or collapsing. All have been taught that the political directions in which they have moved constituted "enlightenment" and "progress"; all have been taught that the free market was an archaic and reactionary concept. And all have grown decreasingly concerned with liberty and increasingly concerned with security and equality, this shift in priorities necessitating a proliferating growth of government and "the public sector." The result is the same, in principle, if not detail, for all: Economic growth is shrinking.

As I mentioned earlier, the Hudson Institute, Europe, has done a revealing study of the relationship between the growth of the public sector and real economic growth in fourteen countries. The findings show that overall growth is the lowest in countries where the government sector is largest.[4] These findings have been supported by other studies conducted in Britain by economists Robert Bacon and Walter Eltis and by David Smith, using a nineteen-nation sample during the sixties. All such studies conclude that the expansion of government in the Western industrial nations results in shrinking profits, falling investment, and plunging growth rates.

Many of these facts crossed my mind as I flew back from

the Soviet Union, 40,000 feet above those European nations whose mixed economies are stagnating and whose citizens see their liberties ever more restricted. The speed of my plane made me think of the speed with which the disease has spread to the United States, where a younger, more vibrant nation, only one year into its third century, is itself degenerating into a social democracy. But the American picture, although it is obviously similar in many ways to those I have sketched here, is also extremely different—and consequently confusing in a very special way.

As compared to the European nations mentioned, the United States is apparently in the least amount of trouble. Our industrial sector, riding on the awesome momentum of more than two centuries of freedom, is still, for all the intervention and regulation, breathtakingly inventive and rich, compared to others in the world. And in worldwide terms we can still describe ourselves as a free enterprise or free market economy. But today these terms have only a relative meaning. In the context of our own past and by the standards of our once exceptionally free market, we have ceased to be a true free enterprise economy, and we are today a mixed economy or "welfare state."

Despite our comparative wealth, our situation is unusually ominous, for cultural, as well as economic, reasons. In the United States a population accustomed to historically unprecedented liberty is now ruled, almost exclusively, by a political-social-intellectual elite that is committed to the belief that government can control our complex marketplace by fiat better than the people can by individual choice and that is ideologically committed to social democracy or democratic socialism. So blinding is this commitment that this intellectual elite can watch the social democracies slide into stagnation and chaos around them and never question the interventionist assumptions which have caused that stagnation and chaos—assumptions they share. They believe, tragically, that one can drastically mix polar political opposites, that, to quote *Newsweek* again, one can fuse the dynamics of "communism and capitalism" within one society with no evil consequences.

Since this book is dedicated to providing an overview of that irrational mixing and its consequences, I will not here go into any details save to say that America, too, is suffering acute economic and social dislocations and a capsizing of trust in our governmental institutions. We are also suffering from one other thing: an apparently permanent case of intellectual confusion, indeed incoherence, in our political leadership, an incoherence so intense that it became the object of almost universal scorn during the 1976 elections. If one understands the underlying forces that are at war in our "social democratic" society, the reasons are not too hard to discover. Our political leadership today, which is committed to the "ideals" of the mixed economy, is required to articulate a coherent advocacy of individualism *and* collectivism, of the free market *and* a planned economy, of individual liberty from government coercion *and* of government control over individual life. The American political language has become paralyzed by these conflicting assignments. It is impossible to articulate such massively contradictory "ideals." And those politicians who attempt to resolve this problem end up speaking a mediocre kind of double talk so rife with self-contradiction that they are winning the contempt of millions of Americans.

There is a reason for our special degree of incoherence and confusion. The United States, in changing with relative speed into a social democracy, has undergone an alteration that is more fundamental than any other nation's. It has actually repudiated its own *identity*. As I said earlier in this chapter, America was born a capitalist nation, was created a capitalist nation by the intent of its founders and the Constitution, and developed a culture and a civilization that were capitalist to the core. But this capitalist, or free enterprise, identity is true of no other nation. Only America was invented from scratch by libertarian philosophers! France, for example, is an ancient nation that has had many political systems, many economic systems; it has survived and remained France under monarchies, emperors, revolutionary tribunals, military governments, democratic and now heavily socialist parliaments. The "Frenchness" of France is not tied to its political and economic arrangements. And the same is true, in varying degrees, for all European nations. Consequently, France can go socialist, as can the other nations, and remain France. But this is not true in America. America *is* tied to its original political and economic arrangements because they were the *definition* of America. And an American who is hostile to individualism, to the work ethic, to free enterprise, who advocates an increasing government takeover of the economy or who advocates the coercive socialization of American life is in some profound sense advocating that America cease being America. He is advocating values that are not American and are philosophically antithetical to America itself.

Indeed, he is actually striking out against the most fundamental unifying principles of our society. Historically the "Americanization" of the immigrants to our shores has followed their voluntary acceptance of the capitalist culture, its economic modes and its ethics. An ethnic, racial, and religious "melting pot" was able to turn into a unique and new culture, precisely because that "melting" required the unification of all around the Horatio Alger ethic and the free enterprise system. The American culture offered each individual the ideal of hard work, competitive achievement, and self-fulfillment in freedom. The ideal may have been imperfectly fulfilled for some and unjustly denied to others, but it was universally recognized throughout the world as an ideal. And to repudiate that ideal is to repudiate the very philosophical glue that holds together our many different kinds of citizens. It is inevitable that, as this has happened, the culture has been fragmented into what Michael Novak now calls the "unmeltable ethnics." It is also inevitable that recent political trends have been described by such thoughtful people as Howard K. Smith and Midge Decter as "anti-American," that our present culture is described by intellectuals like Irving Kristol as an "adversary culture" and by the adversaries themselves as a "counterculture." What is happening in this country is a fundamental assault on America's culture and its historic identity. Before he died a few years ago, Arthur Krock, the retired Washington bureau chief of the New York *Times*, wrote in his memoirs: ". . . the U.S. merits the dubious distinction of having discarded its past and its meaning in one of the briefest spans of modern history."[5]

It is not surprising, in this situation, that our political leaders should become virtually incoherent and unable to articulate the ideals of this nation and that our public should become confused and suffer from a crisis of distrust in its leadership. Nothing else could really have been expected once the ideals themselves were repudiated by the "enlightened" with contempt and with hatred. It is widely sensed that a "mysterious" malady is eating away at the core of our society, but we are drowning in shallow and nonessential explanations. Yet the reason is plain. The "mysterious" malady is that the freest land in the world is becoming unfree, that America's unique historical attributes—the brilliant interlocking of political liberty and economic liberty—are slowly being destroyed.

# III

---

# Dictatorship in Microcosm

We've always had a finite amount of
energy. . . . We had finite supplies of wood
in the early pioneer days. How did we make
the transition from using wood to using
coal, from using coal to using oil, from
using oil to using natural gas? How in God's
name did we make that transition without a
Federal Energy Agency?

—MILTON FRIEDMAN

In December 1973 I myself became an illustration of a
free-market principle—the very one that allowed Winston
Churchill and such economists as F. A. Hayek and Milton
Friedman to predict the disastrous outcome of the British
welfare state decades in advance. That principle states
that government planning and regulation of the economy will ultimately lead to shortages, crises, and, if not

reversed in time, some form of economic dictatorship. That is precisely what happened in the realm of energy production in the United States. Years of incoherent government intervention strangled energy production, domestic supplies diminished, artificial shortages emerged, a foreign embargo on oil precipitated a crisis, there was a violent public outcry for an instant solution, an energy "dictatorship" was established to allocate the rare commodity—and I, incredibly, became the "dictator."

The American energy crisis is a classic case out of a free-market textbook, and for that reason I shall describe it in detail because unless one sees the planning and regulatory system close up, it is difficult to resist the entrancing notion that conscious planning by the state is a reasonable process. Even so, there is no guarantee that the lesson will be understood, and to this day, in the energy realm, it has not been understood by most people.

To be fair about it, in the beginning I barely understood it myself. On December 4, 1973, with the nation reeling under the Arab oil embargo, President Nixon named me energy czar, the American euphemism for a mini-dictator over a portion of the economy. Throughout the crisis I constantly found myself fighting with one hand to ease the government death grip on energy production and with the other to unify and centralize government control. But my own confusion did not last. I had the kind of education on the subject that focuses the mind. There is nothing like becoming an economic planner oneself to learn what is desperately, stupidly wrong with such a system.

Needless to say, I did not acquire that strange role overnight. I passed through an apprenticeship of sorts. It began immediately after I was named Deputy Secretary of the Treasury under George Shultz. I arrived at the Treasury in November 1972, and I was boning up on financial matters, law enforcement, and the various international issues in which Treasury is involved when I was summoned one evening by Shultz. He told me that he and the President had decided to make me chairman of the Oil Policy Committee. I was astonished and replied, "But I don't know a thing about oil." Shultz said, "That's all right. You'll learn. We both feel that what's needed is a man without any built-in prejudices or vested interests."

It took no time to learn why a neutral personality had been chosen for the job. No sooner did the rumor get out that I was to chair the Oil Policy Committee than I was deluged by advice, demands, and warnings from an incredible number of interested parties, ranging from the fifty-five federal agencies which had been regulating the oil industry to the industry itself—the major companies and the independents, marketers, producers, refiners, and jobbers. The assult was dizzying.

My first two-hour meeting with the Oil Policy Committee appalled me. I was new to government, and I had had no experience with the bureaucratic moles and bag carriers. They all seemed half asleep to me. That committee, I thought, badly needed an activist from the business world who was accustomed to the idea of solving problems, not just ruminating over them.

To learn everything I could about energy, I set up the equivalent of a school for myself. I chose as my "professors" the men who had impressed me most strongly as knowing what they were talking about: James Akins of the State Department, who was soon to become the ambassador to Saudi Arabia; Peter Flanigan of the White House; Stephen Wakefield of the Department of the Interior; and Duke Ligon and William Johnson, energy advisers in the Treasury Department. And for three months—for up to five hours a day, almost every evening and solidly through weekends—they educated me on energy in general, oil in particular, the mandatory import quota policy, and the international implications of all the issues involved. Often we'd work until one o'clock in the morning; we'd eat pizzas or greasy hamburgers for dinner at 10 P.M. in my office, while my "professors" crammed information into my head, using a blackboard and giving me specific assignments for study. I worked hard, and so did they. By the end of the three-month period, in the spring of 1973, I had received from these gentlemen the equivalent of a master's degree on the subject of energy.

I had worked with such fervor because I was determined to assist the Nixon administration to achieve its goal: energy independence. In both 1971 and 1973 President Nixon had sent energy messages to Congress to that effect. He wanted the deregulation of natural gas and the simplification of various regulatory procedures that were greatly delaying energy development. The more I learned about the energy problems of the nation, the more certain I became that there were few more important things on the agenda. I was shocked to learn the degree to which our energy industries were stagnating and struggling futilely against regulatory shackles. In the oil realm, demand was rising constantly; but domestic exploration and production were declining sharply, and from year to year we were growing more dependent on imports. All the elements of an impending energy catastrophe were visible. Those fifty-five federal agencies and the hundreds of state and local committees and commissions that had been regulating bits and pieces of the oil industry had been strangling energy production in the country.

Congress had been warned of an emerging energy shortage for more than two decades but had done nothing. The idea that this incessant government intervention was actually damaging production was hopelessly unreal to these gentlemen. I got a remarkable taste of the uncomprehending animosity unleashed in many Congressmen when they were forced to face the fact that an oil shortage existed. Clearly, they felt, it was somebody's fault—but whose? During one of my first appearances before a Congressional committee I found myself under attack by then Congressman John Culver, now a Senator from Iowa. He screamed and yelled and frothed at the mouth, blaming *me* for the energy crisis. I thought he'd gone insane. I remember leaning over to Gerald Parsky and Bill Johnson of Treasury, who had accompanied me, and whispering, "I've only been in government for sixty days, for God's sake! Even I can't do that much damage in sixty days!" The Congressman's staff later apologized to me, and I learned he was fabled for his ill temper. I remember it to this day because it symbolizes the difficulties I was to face.

For some months I concentrated on the import problem. We were by then importing 30 percent of our oil, and the national security implications were disturbing. What would happen if war broke out and America were caught without an assured and adequate oil supply? I had an unexpected chance to present my views on this problem to the President and to stress the necessity to liberate production. On one occasion, when Shultz was on a trip, I attended a Cabinet meeting as Acting Treasury Secretary. I had been asked to report on the economy, but I decided instead to speak on the energy situation. I made a strong plea that major action be taken. Customarily, President Nixon was bored by discussions of abstract economics, but this interested him—if for no other reason than that the Democrats, led by Senator Henry Jackson, were making energy a major political issue. He reacted the way he always did when he was interested; he pulled the top of his fountain pen off with his teeth and began to scribble. I noticed Vice President Agnew, who was sitting next to me, scribbling, too, and then passing a little note to the President. The next day I discovered what the Vice President had scribbled. He called me up, told me he had been impressed with the urgency of the situation and would like to work with me in the energy field. And then he asked a question which stunned me: Would I be kind enough to intervene with President Nixon and ask him to assign Agnew to that job? I was a lowly Deputy Secretary of the Treasury, and I thought it inconceivable that I lobby the President. So I didn't. But the memory of that Vice Presidential plea stayed with me. I had, like all other Americans, heard that the Vice Presidency was a miserable job. How miserable I had never dreamed until that moment.

My political education was being advanced rapidly, and I had become a walking repository of energy lore; but I was very much in the position of being all dressed up with no place to go. Nothing happened except the appointment of Colorado Governor John Love as head of a newly created Energy Policy Office.

Then, without warning, the unthinkable happened. In October 1973, in the wake of the Yom Kippur War, the Arab countries unanimously decided to place an embargo on their oil sales. Suddenly America had no access to imported Arab oil. The long-dreaded energy crisis had arrived.

No reader of this book who lived through that period needs any description of the collective hysteria that ensued. The political heat was on both Congress and the executive to solve the problem overnight.

As far as the executive branch was concerned, it soon became obvious that Love was not cut out for the job. One Friday at the end of October he turned to Rogers Morton and asked, as if it were the end of a normal workweek, "What are you doing this weekend?" Morton drawled, "John, I'm going to go out and get me some quail." And Love drawled back, "Fine idea! That's what I will do too. I'm going quail hunting." And both of them disappeared. I stared at them in stupefaction. Quail hunting—when the United States was in the middle of a catastrophic oil embargo? I knew then that Love never fully grasped the magnitude of the emergency, and I was not alone in this judgment. Shortly thereafter President Nixon decided to replace Governor Love as energy czar. I was the replacement.

Strangely the President and I did not actually discuss the job itself, only the means of executing it. Nixon told me I would have to leave the Treasury and that he would advise each head of the relevant agencies to send me thirty-five or forty of his best men to staff my organization. I repressed my desire to laugh. By then I had been in Washington long enough to realize that without a bureaucratic base of my own, I would be cooked. Those helpful agency heads would simply dump on me all the Civil Service deadwood they had been longing to get rid of for years. I refused to run the energy program unless I could remain at the Treasury as Deputy Secretary with my own bureaucracy to support my efforts. Nixon understood and agreed. And that is all we talked about. I still did not know exactly what he had in mind.

It was only at the Cabinet meeting two days later that I learned, along with the Cabinet, just how much of a czar Nixon intended me to be. I was to have "absolute authority," he said. I was to decide everything and to decide it rapidly. He equated our energy crisis to the kind of problem one has in wartime, and he likened the job he was giving me to that of Albert Speer in the Third Reich when he was put in charge of German armaments. Nixon told the Cabinet that if not for the power that Hitler had given Speer to override the German bureaucracy, Germany would have been defeated far earlier. And I, William Simon, he said, was to be given that same kind of power. I was less aware, then, of the value of this comment to psychohistorians than I was of the immensity of the responsibility he was placing on my shoulders.

And so, by executive order, Nixon named me the nation's second energy czar. I immediately learned that my plans to operate in an efficient, businesslike manner had been an illusion and that efficient business management had nothing on earth to do with the centralized allocation of resources by a government agency. Compared to what went on at the Federal Energy Office, production for the marketplace was breathtakingly simple. In the market essentially all that happens is that a man or a company creates a product or a service and sells it to anyone who wants it at a price deemed advantageous by both. The pricing system automatically allocates resources, and that's that. There are no other considerations. When a government—or a czar—allocates resources, a thousand other considerations enter into the picture, none of which are relevant to the production or distribution process.

The first problem I faced, for example, was an explosion of political mythology which denied the very reality of the oil shortage. Thanks to a press which emphasizes the minutiae of the day and supplies few, if any, of the connective links, the American public had never learned adequately about the dangerous decline in oil and gas exploration—all caused by shortsighted policies—and the consequent rise in our dependence on foreign oil imports. I had testified repeatedly about it before Congress, usually in the presence of the press. But those sections of my testimonies were apparently not considered sensational enough—or were viewed merely as unimportant background—and were rarely covered. What made the headlines was what I was going to do today or tomorrow. Few people realized that before the embargo we had been importing one-third of our oil—6.5 million barrels a day out of a total of more than 17 million barrels used. Of these 6.5 million, about 2.7 million came directly or indirectly from the Middle East. Thus, the embargo left a shocking hole in our economy.

This reality could not be contested save by the ignorant, and the voice of ignorance was heard in the land, churning out accusations that the shortage had been contrived by the oil companies to get higher prices, that thousands of tankers were lingering offshore until the prices rose. These charges surged through the network news mechanisms and flooded the country with paranoid suspicions, after which the newsmen dashed around, collecting the feedback from citizens who repeated the suspicions as fact, and retransmitted them over the air waves. Vastly more coverage was given to the false rumors than to the actual facts of the shortage. I spent a ludicrous amount of time simply struggling to convince people that the crisis was real.

Even many of those who acknowledge the reality of the crisis were gripped by the equally mythical belief that a rigid program of gasoline rationing could solve the problem. It was an idea I opposed with every ounce of strength. So, to his great credit, did President Nixon, who knew that rationing would wreak havoc with the market and would be a bureaucratic nightmare. But as the clamor for rationing increased, Nixon ordered the stamps printed and held in reserve. "Maybe that will shut them up," he said to me. It didn't, and many continued, unsuccessfully, to demand implementation of rationing.

As for the centralized allocation process itself, the kindest thing I can say about it is that it was a disaster. Even with a stack of sensible-sounding plans for even-handed allocation all over the country, the system kept falling apart, and chunks of the populace suddenly found themselves without gas. There was no logic to the pattern of failures. In Palm Beach suddenly there was no gas, while 10 miles away gas was plentiful. Parts of New Jersey suddenly went dry, while other parts of New Jersey were well supplied. Every day, in different parts of the country, people waited in line for gasoline for two, three, and four hours. The normal market distribution system is so complex, yet so smooth that no government mechanism could simulate it. All we were actually doing with our so-called bureaucratic efficiency was damaging the existent distribution system. As the shortages grew more erratic and unpredictable, people began to "top off" their tanks. Instead of waiting, as is customary, to refill the tank when it is about one-quarter full, all over the country people started buying 50 cents' worth of gas, a dollar's worth of gas, using every opportunity to keep their tanks full at all times. And that fiercely compounded the shortages and expanded the queues. The psychology of hysteria took over.

Essentially the allocation plan had failed because there had been a ludicrous reliance on a little legion of government lawyers, who drafted their regulations in indecipherable language, and bureaucratic technocrats, who imagined that they could simulate the complex free-market processes by pushing computer buttons. In fact, they couldn't.

Throughout this period I was working sixteen-, seventeen- and eighteen-hour days. I don't believe I slept more than four hours in any single night, including weekends, from the end of November until the embargo was lifted. My life was further enriched by being continually threatened, and over my objections George Shultz ordered Secret Service men to accompany me on my rounds. After one particularly trying day I arrived home at midnight. I had had a couple of apples to eat for dinner at eight o'clock. I wasn't so much hungry as I was bone tired. All I wanted to do was to flatten myself with a strong scotch and go to bed. I opened the front door to find my wife, Carol, in a most uncharacteristic mood. That normally loving and cheerful woman sprang at me like a termagant. She had stopped going to our customary gas station because, in view of my widespread unpopularity, she did not want to be recognized. She had stopped using charge accounts that carried the name William E. Simon. She had been skulking around in a shawl and dark glasses. "Do you know how long I waited in line?" she shouted. "You have to do something." I groaned, "*Et tu, Brute?*" The hysteria had hit my own home. I knew then that I didn't have much time left to crack the gas lines.

Toward the end of January I told my bureaucracy in the Allocation Center that I wanted additional allocations from our reserves sent to all the pockets of shortages in the country to break the gas lines and stop the hysteria. The bureaucracy was appalled. "You can't do that," I was told. "Why not?" I demanded. "Because six or more months from now, when midsummer comes and the demand is at its greatest, we will have no reserves." I understood the risk, but I also understood *when* to take a risk. The hysterical buying and hoarding had to be stopped. Frenzy was spreading around the country, and I could envision the gas lines growing deeper and deeper with plenty of gas available. The bureaucracy was stonewalling me, so I summoned Gerald Parsky and Frank Zarb, and said, "This is ridiculous. We must do it ourselves." We worked for thirty-six hours straight. We called every governor of every state where there were problems. We called every oil company distribution line. We worked out the allocations, sent the forms over to the FEO, and I ordered that they sign them. By the end of the thirty-six-hour period the gas lines were cracked. The embargo lasted another six weeks, but the fever had been taken out of the public response. As far as I was concerned and as far as the American gas buyer was concerned, the emergency had been handled successfully.

That was by no means the assessment of the Washington bureaucracy, however, which poured its protests into the press. On March 22 the Federal Trade Commission staff, after a study of the FEO, wrote: "By most tests of administrative effectiveness, FEO has been found wanting and increasingly so as the problems to be dealt with grow in severity." At about the same time the FEO's Congressional liaison man resigned and in a memo to me charged there was organizational chaos: "One is left with the feeling that there is a total lack of internal cooperation and cohesion . . . among the various offices and branches of the organization." In sum, I was charged with being a rotten bureaucrat, and by their standards, I *was* a rotten bureaucrat. In fact, I was worse than that. I was an *anti*bureaucrat. I flouted the pre-set plan, relying on my own judgment and that of my kitchen cabinet. I ignored most of my bureaucracy and worked with only a handful of brilliant, mostly non-Civil Service staffers. I could discover no other way to accomplish anything. In the crunch I had used the decisive methods that had served me well in the marketplace. They were not the methods admired or desired in Washington.

That is how I ultimately realized the profundity of the difference between the businessman and the government bureaucrat. The businessman's standard of efficacy is a solution to the problem, and the more responsive he is to external reality, the better. The bureaucrat's standard of efficacy is obedience to the rules and respect for the vested interests of the hierarchy, however unyielding of a solution; response to external reality is often irrelevant. That is why bureaucracies so often produce nothing but wastepaper and destroy the productive institutions they supervise. Bureaucrats are actually the first victims of their own regulations, the primary effect of which is to inhibit individual thought and the courage to take responsibility. To believe that a bureaucracy is *ever* the solution to a complex problem is to believe that a system which outlaws those qualities can be efficacious. It is a flat contradiction in terms. To believe further that imposing an efficient business manager on the bureaucracy will solve the problem is nonsense. The businessman will either go limp and become a good bureaucrat—*i.e.*, he will passively let the Civil Service hierarchy perform its sterile ballet—or, as I did, he will impatiently bypass the bureaucracy, violate its procedures, and outrage the Civil Service mentality. I have never so profoundly appreciated the swift and goal-oriented operations of the marketplace as during the days in which I functioned as a direct economic "dictator."

While I was playing the philosophically preposterous role of William E. Simon, Invisible Hand, I got my first insight into the extraordinary irresponsibility of that collection of economic planners known as Congress. My most vivid experiences, of course, came from participating in Congressional hearings, which are merely one of Congress' many functions. But they are immensely revealing of the psychology of these planners, of their occasional ineffable silliness, their frequent stony ignorance, and their paralyzing interventionist ideology. I cite here illustrations of all three.

Sometimes the hearings were almost surrealistically funny. One such was a session before the House Agriculture Committee, headed by W. R. "Bob" Poage. Because I had to testify two more times that day, I agreed to testify at night. The committee was concerned about the allocation of fuel to farmers, and in my opening statement I assured the committee that food was my number one priority and pledged on my sacred honor that American citizens would not starve to death during the crisis.

On the face of it that doesn't sound unreasonable, but the

hearing room was, in fact, a madhouse. For one thing, Chairman Poage had a startling high, shrill voice, like a mouse's scream. Secondly, throughout my testimony, the Congressmen were talking to one another with all their microphones open, so they were in effect jamming my voice. They never heard me. In addition, before every Congressman was a cellophane bag of Planter's peanuts. Peanuts are a heavily subsidized product, and Congressmen eat them all the time at agricultural hearings. While I was testifying and they were talking, they were also ripping open their cellophane bags before the open mikes, and ferocious cracklings and chompings were compounding the furor. Running like a crazy counterpoint through the entire racket was the incessant squeaking of Congressman Poage. I never did hear a single question that they asked me. I merely replied to what I guessed they were asking. It was all preposterous nonsense, but you would never know it from the published transcript.

Then there is the demagoguery that is often unleashed at these hearings and is a gross caricature of the process of seeking information. A hearing before the House Small Business Committee six months before the embargo perfectly captures this phenomenon. The committee had been holding a series of hearings on all aspects of energy and was extensively informed about not only the growing fuel shortage but the allocation methods to deal with it. Yet Representative Joseph McDade of Pennsylvania tried eight times in a row to force me to guarantee that every city, town, and hamlet in the United States would have enough gas. I quote some of the exchange from the transcript. It runs a little long, but it's an instructive example of the bullying pseudoresearch in which many Congressmen engage:

> MR. MCDADE. Your statement indicates that you intend to give priority to municipalities, even so under the regulations you have written, are you unable to assure the committee that a city will not have to stop its sanitation collection or police patrolling or use of fire equipment because of a lack of gasoline? Can't you make that assurance?

MR. SIMON.   I can tell you that all of our efforts are going to be directed to make sure that that does not occur. But I cannot stand here and say yes, sir, everybody is going to have enough gasoline because we are going to make sure of it—I just don't have that confidence.

MR. McDADE.   Is that because of any deficiency in the legislation Congress has granted you to date?

MR. SIMON.   No, sir. As I said, I think a mandatory program would do more to tie our hands than help us. Right now we are asking the majors and others to supply those people whom they supplied in the base period. Now, this base period goes back prior to many contracts. They say, "We have contracts which we cannot break legally. The voluntary allocation program does not give us the legal authority to break our contracts." What I hope that they will do is to say to their contract customers, "Look, we are going to do our best with this bad shortage that we have, and we are going to supply you with as much as we can, but it is going to be a little less."

If we go to a mandatory program, I can envision this sanctity of contract problem will be even greater because we will end up in the courtrooms.

MR. McDADE.   Yet, I find it inconceivable that you cannot assure the committee that every municipality will have sufficient gasoline to provide essential services.

MR. SIMON.   That and the farmers are our number one priority, and we are going to break our backs to give them what they need.

MR. McDADE.   But you won't give me the assurances that the municipalities will be taken care of. That is what I am looking for. I am seeking a statement from you, indeed, an absolute assurance, that every municipality will be able to provide its citizens with essential government services.

MR. SIMON.   Congressman, that is exactly what we are striving for. I feel confident—

MR. McDADE.   I do not want to be engaged in a game of semantics with you. Can't you give me the assurance that every municipality will have the gasoline to provide those services?

At this point Darrell Trent, Acting Director of the Office of

Emergency Preparedness, seeing that the Congressman had turned into a broken record, intervened with a long explanation of the "number of variables involved," and he explained to Representative McDade that these variables meant "that we just don't have the power to predict." He recited a whole list of those variables as they would affect the supply problem for the entire nation for the next year and ended: "As far as assurances, that would be difficult." The dialogue continued:

> MR. McDADE. I haven't asked you for all areas, I have asked you for one. I have asked for the municipalities in the United States, and I cannot understand why you cannot give that. We are not in that great a deficit with respect to gasoline.
>
> MR. SIMON. Well, a ten percent shortage is desperate in some areas where we have a faulty distribution system.
>
> MR. McDADE. I understand that, but I thought we were talking to the people in the U.S. government that had the authority to institute an allocation program. I have asked you for one assurance involving municipalities which have to provide very basic services to their citizens. I ask you for assurances, and I cannot get it. I don't understand that.
>
> MR. SIMON. As Darrell explained, in predicting of weather and the uncertain supplies from the Mid East and the instability of the supplies, Congressman, if I sat here and said, yes, sir, we are going to provide all of these priorities with everything they need, I would be going out on a terrible limb. . . .
>
> MR. McDADE. Suppose you have no supply for five municipalities in the United States of America. Let's say 100,000 population per city. Are you at that point going to institute rationing?
>
> MR. SIMON. That would be quite a serious situation, and I would have to take a look at the overall cause. I cannot foresee we would not be able to supply the needed gasoline to cities under the present circumstances.
>
> MR. McDADE. Do you believe you can run an allocation program that would not supply the essential needs of the cities of America?
>
> MR. SIMON. No, I don't. I envision this program working and being able to identify, as we have, these priority areas.[1]

This entire exchange could have been boiled down to one question and one answer. *Question*: "Can you guarantee needed gas to all cities?" *Answer*: "No, but we will do our best." But the Congressman could not, or would not, grasp that a guarantee was impossible. Although his committee had been holding a string of hearings on the growing fuel shortages, he did not appear to know what a shortage was. I knew I was faced with an economic illiterate or with a political hypocrisy so great that it stunned me. I was to experience this broken-record "cerebration" over and over again from Congressmen—from the very gentlemen who have given themselves the right to rule over our economy. I would respectfully argue that if production were dependent on this kind of mind, the human race would still be crawling on its belly in the primeval slime.

And then there was the quasi-religious liberalism—with its capacity to ignite into moral outrage and to go on antibusiness witch-hunts at the drop of a rumor. One striking example of this took place in January 1974, when the Shah of Iran suddenly announced to the world that the United States was importing more oil than ever before. We were at the height of the Arab embargo, and this was an absolute falsehood. I had examined personally the Customs Bureau receipts which showed a dramatic fall-off in oil imports, but it was easy enough to know what our "friend" the Shah was up to. He, after all, was mainly responsible for quadrupling the price of oil, and he was now trying to deny the damage he had inflicted on the American economy. He offered no evidence for his charge, and there were no rational grounds for believing him. Indeed, he was a notoriously unreliable source. The gentleman had continual hallucinatory chats with God, an eccentricity that was later discussed on CBS' *60 Minutes*. At one point I myself was quoted as saying, "The Shah is a nut." The remark had been made in an off-the-record conversation, and my denials were diplomatic. Nevertheless, despite the absurd nature of the source, the press blew up the Shah's latest hallucination into a major story—and Congress rushed to "investigate."

At 5:30 A.M., reading the headlines about the Shah's charge, I said to myself, "Oh, my God, it's going to be a busy day." I gave the actual import figures to the press office so that it might reply to questions. I then went off to a meeting with the lieutenant governors of the states, who had been put in charge of energy problems in their areas. While we were in conference, I got a message that Representative Al Ullman, chairman of the House Ways and Means Committee, wanted me. At the end of the conference I rushed out to my car, from which I intended to phone him. Actually I rushed backward, since I was followed by two lieutenant governors who were talking to me. As I backed into my compact car—I had already "grounded" all government limousines—I cracked my head, splitting the back of my scalp wide open. Blood started to pour from my head. I held a handkerchief to it and phoned Al Ullman. He said, "We want you up here immediately to answer the Shah of Iran's charges." I replied, "I've just split my head open. I'll have to see a nurse first." I visited the Treasury nurse, who told me that my scalp required a half dozen stitches. I relayed the information to Congressman Ullman, and that kindly fellow said, "Absolutely not. Get down here right away. We'll keep you for only a half hour." In fact, I was there for about five hours, bleeding incessantly, in considerable pain and facing Congressmen who were screaming and yelling. The exchanges were brilliantly informative; to wit:

> CONGRESSMAN VANIK: Are you telling me the Shah of Iran, the world's most renowned oil expert, doesn't know what he's talking about?
> MR. SIMON: That's what I'm telling you.

The sheer brutality of keeping me there for hours while blood was dripping from my head and while I was obviously suffering is in itself notable. It inspired Representative Omar

Burleson, Democrat from Texas, to ask me why I, a man of independent means, put up with such treatment. And Irving R. Levine, NBC newsman, was moved to express his personal sympathy to me—a kindness I shall not forget. But the brutality was merely a symptom of something far deeper: the compulsion in a dominantly liberal Congress to believe any rumor, however baseless, from any source, however absurd, which suggested that the shortage was "unreal," a product of a vicious oil company plot, and the compulsion to "demagogue" whenever the red light of the television camera lit up.

Those compulsions were themselves Congress' most damaging contribution to the energy crisis simply because they kept most legislators from understanding the actual causes of the crisis, which in turn rendered them incapable of projecting rational solutions. To get a perspective on the immensity of this self-blinding, one must have a more detailed understanding of the causes which had been incessantly explained to Congress over a period of two decades. I have broken them down here in simple form so that they can be readily grasped.

1. Congress had been repeatedly told that there was no shortage of fuel as such. The known sources of fossil fuels are abundant, and we have barely begun to explore vast areas of the United States, including Alaska, the offshore resources or the sea. Only in terms of what we have *already* discovered, not of the vast unknown potentials, the facts are these:

## COAL.

We have half of all the coal reserves in the noncommunist world, of which at least 425 billion tons are immediately recoverable. At 1973 levels of consumption we have enough coal for 800 years.

## NATURAL GAS.

We have potential natural gas reserves of 920 trillion cubic feet, according to the U.S. Geological Survey—enough for forty to fifty years at 1972 rates of consumption.

## OIL.

There are an estimated 50 to 127 billion barrels of oil still untapped in continental America, according to the U.S. Geological Survey. In addition, we have proved resources of 40.6 billion barrels, despite the fact that we have explored by drilling only 4 percent of the Outer Contintental Shelf.

## NUCLEAR.

We are the world's technological pioneers in nuclear energy production, which, in its various forms, can yield limitless energy.

2. Congress had been repeatedly told that despite those great potential fuel reserves, not to mention the vast unexplored areas, production had been severely inhibited.

## COAL.

Our coal production today is barely more than it was thirty years ago. In 1960 coal represented 23 percent of our energy consumption. By 1974 it had dropped to 18 percent.

## NATURAL GAS.

Since 1968 our gas production has been steadily shrinking. By 1973 new reserve additions were less than one-third of consumption, and the nation's total natural gas reserves dropped from a fifteen-year supply in 1967 to a less-than-ten-year reserve. Since that date there have been serious gas shortages.

## OIL.

There has been a steady decline in the number of oil wells drilled in the United States. Between 1955 and 1972 the number dropped from 31,567 to 11,306 a year. Additionally, construction of new refineries in this country has come to a standstill. Federal energy policy actually encouraged the exportation of our refinery capacity, despite the obvious risks to national security.

## NUCLEAR.

After thirty years of development, nuclear energy in 1975 was supplying only 2 percent of our energy needs, with Germany, France, and Japan systematically outpacing us in construction of nuclear plants.

3. Congress had been repeatedly told that various laws and regulations were primarily responsible for this inhibition of exploration and production in all energy realms.

## COAL.

In 1969 and 1970 the Coal Mining Health and Safety Act and the Clean Air Act were passed. The latter forbids the burning of high-sulfur coal, the most readily accessible, unless it is first cleaned in scrubbers, which are exceedingly costly and in many cases technologically infeasible. The immediate result of both laws: Coal production crashed 30 percent. The problem was compounded by the Congressional attempt to pass legislation restricting surface strip mining of coal. The likelihood that such legislation would be signed into law effectively prevented the development of massive quantities of our low-sulfur Western coal.*

## NATURAL GAS.

In 1954 the Supreme Court clamped a complex system of price controls on all natural gas sold for transmission in interstate commerce. Incentives for industry to spend billions of dollars developing new supplies and technologies and exploring the methane-rich waters along the Gulf Coast were all but destroyed by the artificially low prices that followed. By the late 1960s shortages had developed throughout the nation except in the non-price-controlled intrastate gas-producing areas. Industries located in areas with local supplies of natural gas have been able to pay a higher, market-determined price to acquire a significant competitive advantage over competitors forced to rely on other forms of energy. Plants in huge numbers, which could have used coal and oil, were it not for the exaggerated costs of ill-conceived environmental and pollution regulations, have simply relocated to gas-producing states. Today four gas-producing states consume 34 percent of the natural gas used in the nation, 91 percent of which is used industrially. Thus, government has created major shortages in supply for those homes, schools, and hospitals which have been unable to move to the producing states.

## OIL.

A system of quotas instituted in 1959 restricted the importation of crude oil but encouraged the importation of refined products. Thus, construction of refineries in this country slowed to a standstill, and when President Nixon announced his goals of Project Independence, there was

*Such legislation was signed into law by President Carter on August 3, 1977.

insufficient capacity to make possible the shift to domestic crude oil sources. In 1973 Nixon was able to scrap the mandatory quota system—as I had urged—but the damage had been done over the previous fourteen years.

In addition, environmental restrictions blocked exploration and drilling, prompted further stagnation in the building of refineries, and led inevitably to soaring costs. In 1969 Congress passed the National Environmental Policy Act, which requires that "environmental impact" studies be prepared by the Department of the Interior and reviewed by Congress before any drilling or construction can be done. The act allowed environmental groups to block every stage of the proceedings. Since that law was passed, it takes three to five years to obtain site approval alone and a similar period for construction, not to mention the time spent meeting the incessant lawsuits by environmental groups. Oil companies started to leave the country; it had become simpler and cheaper to set up refineries in the Caribbean and in Canada.

On top of this, oil exploration on both the West and the East coasts, as well as in Alaska, was strangled by environmentalists. More than 7 million acres of the Outer Continental Shelf, primarily in the Gulf of Mexico, were leased to oil companies for exploration between 1954 and 1970. But in 1969 a blowout at a platform in the Santa Barbara Channel generated so much hostility by environmentalists that in 1971 and 1972 politicians halted virtually all new leasing of offshore acreage.

In Alaska, where the already known reserves total nearly 10 billion barrels of oil, environmentalists blocked the building of the pipeline for five years. Construction was again halted by a court suit. It was only when the energy crisis exploded full force that the importance of the Alaska pipeline was acknowledged.

In addition to all this, the Arabs began to confiscate the oil companies' properties abroad. "Partnerships" were imposed on the oil companies by Saudi Arabia, Qatar, Abu Dhabi, and Iran, with the object being the total confiscation of these companies. Libya nationalized 51 percent of the major companies outright. The American oil companies were not properly remunerated for this confiscation, and the State Department did little to protect the valuable investments of its citizens, just as the government never adequately responded to the confiscatory actions of assorted Latin American dictators.

To cap the climax, the record of deliberate strangulation of the thousands of companies that make up our oil industry can be matched in idiocy only by the simultaneous record of financial indulgence to the oil companies. With the left hand the U.S. government paralyzed their operations, and with the right hand it granted them absurd tax exemptions and a variety of subsidies "to stimulate incentive"—an incentive which the government itself had done its utmost to destroy.

The result of all this, in a magnificently energy-rich and technologically superior nation, is that the United States paid the OPEC oil cartel more than $40 billion in 1977 versus $2.7 billion in 1970. And each year our dependency on imported oil grows, our dollars continue to flow to the OPEC nations rather than to our own domestic companies and workers— and the national security is further threatened.


## NUCLEAR.

A crazy quilt of environmental regulations has so inhibited the creation of nuclear power plants that it now takes as much as eleven years to build such a plant, almost three times as long as it takes in Europe and Japan. The costs of such prolongation of the building process are such that they are destroying economic incentive and driving the price of nuclear energy to noncompetitive levels. Already major and experienced firms are leaving the nuclear energy industry. In Europe, by contrast, the building period is only from four to four and a half years, with the consequence that the nuclear industry is growing steadily—and safely—despite the opposition of European environmentalists.

For years Congress has been told that we are on a collision

course with reality, that shortsighted, politically expedient policies are denying us the energy we need to survive and jeopardizing our very future. But Congress has proved incapable of grasping these simple facts or of seeing its own ludicrous culpability in the matter. The reason for the Congressional blindness is clear. The very regulatory philosophy that has chopped prices, jacked up costs, and outlawed fuel production represents the highest liberal "good." Men cannot perceive their "good" as the source of evil, and the liberals are no exception.

Thus, the liberal hue and cry in the course of the energy crisis were precisely what one would expect. Liberals on the whole perceived no fault in government and tried to interpret events in terms of the few facts that were left when one omitted the government's destructive role. Many perceived the shortages as the end of energy sources and began to emit apocalyptic shrieks. Modern man had greedily plundered the earth, they cried, warning that Americans must immediately return to a life of simplicity. Primitivism became a fad in the trendy upper middle class; the well-to-do took to eating alfalfa sprouts and growing organic tomatoes on high-rise terraces. Leftist ideologues eagerly recited their cherished myth that "capitalism was in its final crisis." Finally, the Establishment liberals, committed to having their free enterprise cake while eating it too, perceived only the role of the oil companies; they denounced them as conspiratorial monopolists who had invented the shortages out of whole cloth to increase their "obscene profits."

Captives of their special distortions, liberal politicians opened their mouths in an orchestrated squall. Senator Lee Metcalf of Montana warned the nation of an oil company conspiracy but didn't bother to back up his warning with any facts. Indeed, by his own say-so, he had no facts: "We now have an energy apparatus dominated and controlled by the major oil and gas-energy companies. . . . [They] influence federal energy policy in secret through advisory committees and voluntary agencies—*perhaps for their own special benefit*." (Italics mine.) Senator Metcalf did not explain why, if the oil companies "dominated and controlled" federal policy, they had subjected themselves to incessant price controls and to the blocking on environmental grounds of their own profitable projects.

On June 8, 1972, at a meeting of the Anti-trust Subcommittee of the Judiciary Committee of the Senate, Edward Kennedy strongly suggested the existence of a conspiracy between the Justice Department and the oil companies—and then angrily demanded that someone supply him with proof of his charges. He called for "the convening of a grand jury for an inquiry into the antitrust implications of the recent activities of the major oil companies. *This may be the only way we can obtain the information to determine whether antitrust violations actually have occurred,* and to discover to what degree the current oil shortage in this country had been manipulated to the advantage of the oil companies." (Italics mine.)

On June 12, 1973, Senator Hubert Humphrey, before the Agriculture and Forestry Subcommittee on Research and Legislation, warned against the "vertical integration" of the oil companies: "I think the major oil companies have been tightening control over the distribution system on what we call vertical integration from the domestic crude to the refinery to the broker right out to the filling stations." He did not explain why he was not distressed by the equivalent vertical integration of those major newspapers which own lumber companies, pulp plants, newsprint, printing presses, and delivery trucks.

And so on, and so on, and so on. It should be said that some individuals, even when they jumped on the conspiracy-monopoly-obscene profits bandwagon, displayed greater awareness of the real causes than others. Senator Humphrey was one of them. He at least was keenly aware of the severe clash between environmental regulation and oil production and knew that regulation had been irresponsible: "We have never had any coordination between the environmental part of our legislation and the industry . . . we assumed there was plenty of electricity and fuel to go around the world. We saw there was smog, pollution, solid wastes, and we proceeded with environmental controls without any regard to what was going to happen in terms of availability of fuel supplies."

By 1975 such men as Senator Edward Brooke of Massachusetts and Senator John Tunney of California had finally grasped the fact that price controls were choking the production of natural gas. They jointly launched a recommendation that "new" onshore natural gas be deregulated. "I strongly believe that such deregulation will protect the Massachusetts consumer from exorbitant gas price increases in the long run," Brooke told his constituents.[2] Congress in general, however, had not achieved even this minimal insight and deregulated nothing.

Such limited perceptions as these were equally rare in the whole liberal world. For the most part, the verbal barrage about the oil "monopolies" and their "obscene profits" continued nonstop for several years with the enthusiastic cooperation of the networks and the print press until "oil company" became for the average American citizen a synonym of "evil."

By 1976 the terrain for hatcheting the oil companies to bits had been prepared. In June the Senate Judiciary Committee approved by an eight-to-seven vote a bill sponsored by Senator Birch Bayh, later modified by Senator Philip Hart, called the Petroleum Industry Competition Act. It proposed the breakup of eighteen of the nation's largest oil companies into separate production, refining, transportation, and marketing entities on the grounds that they constituted a monopoly. But the charge had no rational base. As of 1976, there were 8,000 different oil and gas producers, 130 refiners and 16,000 wholesale marketers—to say nothing of 186,000 service stations, the vast majority of which were run by independent businessmen. And this was a monopoly? One of the most thorough examinations of the industry on record—a collection of analyses called "Vertical Integration in the Oil Industry," edited by Professor Edward J. Mitchell of the University of Michigan—demonstrates that none of the characteristics of monopolies are present in that industry. In 1969, reports one contributor, Professor Richard Mancke, the largest single producer of crude oil, Exxon, accounted for less than 10 percent of production and less than 10 percent of gas refining. The four largest firms together accounted for only 25 to 30 percent of production and the eight largest for between 40 to 50 percent. In 1974 more than 85 percent of all onshore oil exploration was conducted by the independent oil producers. In 1974 the top marketing firm, Texaco, had less than 8 percent of all sales, etc., etc.

In sum, it was ludicrous to charge that a monopoly existed. The oil industry fought bitterly against the proposed divestiture legislation, and its widely circulated arguments won considerable acceptance. More than 250 newspapers, including the Washington *Post*, took strong antidivestiture stands. *Post* publisher Katharine Graham doubtless had an additional reason; by that same bizarre definition of "monopoly" Congressmen could demand the dismemberment of her $370 million communications empire, which includes the Washington *Post*, the Trenton *Times*, *Newsweek*, a major news service, five broadcast stations, and 49 percent of a paper mill—despite nationwide competition from less wealthy and influential media. Many Congressmen, too, were affected by simple facts. The anti-oil Congressmen discovered that they would lose, so rather than let the oil companies win a victory, they quietly put the bill on ice.

Essentially the same blindness to fact has been present in the uproar over the oil companies' "obscene profits." That charge, too, is baseless and equally easy to disprove.

It is true that after the OPEC embargo hit, oil profits did reach a historic—and onetime—high. The sudden shortage, followed immediately by OPEC's 300 percent price increase, drove domestic prices up. The result: a recorded leap of 81.5 percent over the profits registered at the same period the year before, which, incidentally, was the worst profit year in nearly two decades. But there is something bizarre about people who see in this statistic a cause for battle but remain indifferent to far greater profit leaps in other industries. During the same quarter, compared to the year before, metalworking machinery and equipment profits rose by 700 percent, almost nine times the oil leap; primary nonferrous metals profits rose by 237.3 percent, almost four times the oil leap; and other fabricated metal products showed a profit rise of 152.8 percent, almost twice the oil leap. Oil, in fact, ranked seventh in a group of industries whose profits surged ahead in that period, but the liberals in Congress screamed only about oil.

And even that does not adequately reveal the magnitude of their selective perception. In 1974 the Treasury Department did a study of the profits of the nineteen biggest oil companies, based on data collected by the FTC, as compared to other industries. Between 1958 and 1973 the petroleum industry ranked in the middle range of the twenty-nine industries studied. At the highest end of the scale were the instruments and metal products; the printing, publishing, and television industries; and big lumber, with respective profit growth rates of 17.3, 15.3, and 14.7 respectively. At the lowest end of the scale, ranking twenty-ninth, was iron and steel, which had a profit growth rate of 1.4 percent over a fifteen-year period. A later profit study, done in 1977 by Warren Brookes of the Boston *Herald-American*, updated the FTC-Treasury figures. Brookes compared the profits of communications conglomerates with those of other industries. He discovered that between 1973 and 1975, pretax profits for food retailers were 1.3 percent of sales; for the oil industries, 8.2 percent; and for the television industry, 19.1 percent. Again, oil profits were in the middle range.

In both the Brookes and the Treasury Department studies, newspaper, magazine, and television profits towered above oil profits. This is particularly ironic since, for years, the worst barrage of oil company demagoguery has come over the network air. Reporters transmitted the liberal Congressmen's canards about oil company profits without even bothering to check on the profits of their own industry, which are more than twice as great.

Because the big lie has been repeated over and over, the notion that there is an evil oil "monopoly" making "obscene profits" has now congealed into the conventional wisdom, and the call for the breakup of the big oil companies is incessant. Economist John Kenneth Galbraith, who came out of the closet in 1973 to confess he was a "new socialist," describes the demand for divestiture as "the sophisticated liberal position." Like many other "sophisticated liberal positions," this one is not worth the paper required to summarize it.

My education in the energy realm was not complete until I truly understood the nature of the oil hysteria of the liberal Democrats. It is a symbolic mania sheltered by a profound refusal to look at the facts. Such writers and journalists as Theodore White, Irving Kristol, Howard K. Smith, and the late Stewart Alsop have observed that their liberal brethren were out of contact with reality, trapped in a maze of preconceived notions. That maze, I realized, is the liberal ideology itself—a hash of statism, collectivism, egalitarianism, and anticapitalism, mixed with the desire for the *results* of capitalism. This murky conceptual mess renders even the most innately brilliant of men stupid.

And I would stress sharply that by stupidity I really mean stupidity. Too many Americans, particularly pro-free enterprise conservatives, have assumed immense intelligence in the liberal world and have concluded that when liberals destroyed U.S. production, they knew what they were doing—*i.e.*, that they were guilty of a conspiracy. They are not conspirators; they are intellectual basket cases in the realm of basic economics. It takes an immense resistance to logic and fact not to know that one cannot simultaneously control prices, inflate costs, ban production, increase taxes, grant counterproductive subsidies—and expect healthy, vigorous production to result. Amy Carter could understand perfectly well what was wrong with such a system if her father "regulated" her lemonade stand the way the liberals in Congress have regulated the energy industry. Unfortunately her father, who made his money in a regulated, subsidized industry, does not understand it. And clearly most Democrats in Congress do not understand it. They appear to be compelled by their own distorted thought processes to keep rushing down the route to the destruction of our productive system, emitting shrill cries of moral outrage all the way and staring with astonishment at the economic disasters that spring up, unaccountably, about them.

Strangely enough it was not until I understood the liberals, who dominate our political life, that I was finally able to understand my own fellow Republicans, with whom I have been on a restless four-year journey. All sorts of people have been writing essays in recent years trying to answer the question "What is a Republican?" It's a legitimate question because the answer is not at all obvious. A friend of mine once wisecracked, "A Republican is a Democrat who knows he's crazy." And there is truth to his claim. Too often, the Republican tends to buck but ultimately follows Democratic trends. Unlike the Democrat, however, he commits his economic misdeeds in a state of moral depression and is not in the slightest astonished when the disasters occur because he always knew they would. That is the only way I know to capture the inner sense of being a Republican and to account for the way that Republicans talk to each other when Democrats aren't listening. It is also the only way I can find to explain Republican conduct during the energy crisis.

If Republicans know anything at all, they know what is involved in the production of wealth. Thus, the intelligent Republican free enterpriser knows exactly how to solve the energy crisis. He knows he should deregulate the tortured productive system; drop price controls, destructive bans, and crippling subsidies; and let exploration and production rip with the profit motive as guide, allowing prices to find their true market level. And then, when the United States is roaring with oil production, gas production, coal production, and nuclear energy production and vice-presidents in charge of research and development are poring over innovative technologies to release yet other forms of energy, he should go off to play a healthy round of golf. That is the Republican at his best and at his most useful to the nation.

But for forty years those free enterprise values that made America a lusty, inventive giant have been discredited. And after decades of functioning as a minority in a philosophically inimical atmosphere, the Republican—with notable exceptions—has lost his moorings. To survive politically, he has often felt obligated to modify, compromise, abandon, and betray many of his own standards. Most of the time he has no hope of being able to do what he thinks is right. So he frequently does what he thinks is half right or wrong or even god-awful. He floats trial balloons to see if he can sneak through something economically sane, but if they fail, he scuttles quickly to safety, which means an imitation Democratic position. Since this is, in fact, a shameful way of life, he has devised certain standard rationalizations for it. I heard all of them, over and over again, throughout the energy crisis, when two Republican Presidents were in the White House but facing a Democratic majority in Congress.

One of the most frequent is: "If *we* don't propose or accept some bad legislation, the Democrats will propose worse." And this is usually followed by the corollary: "So long as that legislation is in *our* hands, *we* won't damage the country or the free enterprise system the way *they* would."

I witnessed the precise enactment of this little drama one day when I was no longer in charge of energy policy and, as Secretary of the Treasury, was attending to the related chores that accompany that post. I got a phone call from a reporter for the *Wall Street Journal,* who asked, "What do you think about extending the life of the Federal Energy Administration?" The FEA was supposed to go out of business after the emergency but had lingered on to proliferate, malignantly. The thought that it was being further extended horrified me. I exclaimed, "Extend its life! That place is a menace. It's strangling the energy industry at the very time when we need production. It should be wiped out of existence." My views appeared in the next day's *Journal.* But that same day I learned that President Ford had already decided to extend the life of this bureaucratic abortion.

I went charging over to the 8 A.M. White House meeting

with blood in my eye, and there I heard the classical Republican rationalization from my very close friend Frank Zarb, the FEA director. "At least we're keeping all the garbage in one place so *we* can control it rather than distribute it all over government." I answered, "You've forgotten one thing. One day *you're* not going to be here, and *I'm* not going to be here; but *that horrible thing* is still going to be here. You know damned well it is!" And the chief economic counselors to President Ford—Alan Greenspan, Paul MacAvoy, and Paul O'Neill—all spoke almost simultaneously and said, "Yes, get *rid* of the damned thing." But it was too late.

It was only after I had left the White House that I remembered the day that George Shultz had said to me, "I'm so glad it's *you* who's heading up the energy bureaucracy. That way it *will* go out of business, and you'll be able to keep the damage in check."

Well, I didn't keep the damage in check—it outlasted me. And Zarb didn't keep the damage in check—it outlasted him. "We" are all out now, "they" are all in now, and "our" detestable bureaucratic creations, devised by "their" standards, are in place, waiting to be used for purposes "we" privately deplore. It is obvious to me that one does not acquire virtue by becoming a "better type" of prostitute. Nor, obviously, does one win votes.

Yet another Republican rationalization for violating free enterprise principles is this one: "If liberals can use state coercion and public taxes to push through their goals, why can't we? Let's use their bag of statist tricks to build up our productive system before those fools destroy it altogether." The result of this kind of thinking was President Ford's espousal of Nelson Rockefeller's grandiose plan for a $100 billion energy corporation to lend funds to private industry to develop new fuel technologies. The President—whose attitudes were fiscally conservative but who sometimes deviated—justified the scheme in a public statement as a "catalyst and stimulant" to inspire energy independence. But it was, in fact, an economic outrage—a gargantuan welfare boondoggle for the energy industries, lifted right out of the taxpayer's wallet, an inflationary scheme that would additionally put serious strains on the capital markets.

Even with taxation and inflation set aside, however, there is no conceivable justification for the government to subsidize a massive construction program for an industry that the same government has actively prevented from functioning! If the energy industries are simply freed from their regulatory bondage and are allowed to function sanely, they will pay for their own expansion out of their own profits. *That* is free enterprise, and in the entire history of mankind nothing has ever served better as a "catalyst and stimulant" to invention and innovation than the profit system. That system will quickly bring about the increased production necessary for self-sufficiency. There is time, using fossil fuels alone, the resources yet to be discovered (oil in Alaska and the North Sea were unheard of just a few years ago), and nuclear energy for the energy industries to devise synthetic fuels and new technologies like solar, geothermal, and tidal energy. Nuclear energy alone could, if need be, sustain us forever. There were no grounds whatever for the Rockefeller boondoggle.

I am aware, incidentally, that my reliance on the insurance policy of nuclear energy flies in the face of the revealed wisdom of the environmentalist, consumerist, and public interest factions led by Ralph Nader, which have ceaselessly sought to ban nuclear energy production as "unsafe" and have mischievously tried to equate it with nuclear bombs. Reactors are not bombs. They do entail risks as, for that matter, do all forms of energy production. One of the most important functions of technological development is to diminish those risks. But the various Naderite factions seem incapable of differentiating between the type of risk that may affect a tiny fraction of the population and the certain destruction of an entire civilization that would result from paralyzing energy production. They have, in fact, sought to block all forms of energy production in this country as unsafe either for people or the environment. While I, too, am concerned for health, safety, and the well-being of our environment, I cannot take such a position as evidence of serious thought.

I am vastly more impressed with the wisdom of Hans Bethe, that giant of theoretical physics who helped discover nuclear fission by using the sun as his "laboratory," one of the greatest intellectual feats in the history of man. Bethe and several hundred other physicists of great national and international repute, including many Nobel Prize winners,[3] are fighting to save nuclear energy production in this country from the Naderites and the major media, which serve as their press agents. These scientists are well aware of the risks entailed in nuclear production, and they consider it remarkably safe—safer, in fact, than all other types of energy production. What's more, the national and international safety record of the past twenty years of nuclear energy production bears them out.

I am also more impressed by the Committee for Economic Development, which, after extensive study, urges that we move ahead full speed with nuclear energy production. Finally, I am more impressed by the common sense of the American people, who have repeatedly rejected Naderite measures to restrict or kill off nuclear plants—in California, Arizona, Colorado, Montana, Ohio, Oregon, and Washington.

Given all this, I aired my strong objections to Rockefeller's $100 billion scheme at the top of my lungs, as did Alan Greenspan, chief economic counselor to President Ford. But to no avail. Incredibly, the President endorsed Rockefeller's proposed raid on the Treasury. Fortunately, Congress never acted on it.

The last Republican rationalization for betraying free enterprise is a time-honored one: "It's necessary to stay in power. We can accomplish nothing if we're out of office. So we have to throw the voters the kinds of bones to which the Democrats have accustomed them." A man who uses this rationalization so frequently that he believes it is known as a progressive Republican. President Ford, a conservative, didn't believe it. He just used it on occasion. And the fearful result was his acceptance of the Energy Policy and Conservation Act of 1975. One of the provisions—the one emphasized by the press—was the promise to give voters cheaper energy. After long years of battling for a sensible energy policy, Ford caved in. Anxious for a quick political fix just before the New Hampshire and Florida primaries, he signed the bill. It may have got him a few votes in New Hampshire, but it lost him a great deal of moral support in his own party and was in part responsible for the conservative rebellion against him.

The EPCA was, in my judgment, the worst error of the Ford administration, which, on the whole, sought to be economically responsible. The administration started out bravely enough. The President vetoed shortsighted strip mining legislation that would have cut back on desperately needed coal production. He pressed for expanded oil production in the frontier areas of Alaska and the Outer Continental Shelf. He sought to remove the regulatory roadblocks that were crippling the nuclear industry and to guarantee that by 1986, 300 nuclear plants would be supplying 20 percent of the nation's electricity. Finally, the President recommended the immediate lifting of all price controls from oil and natural gas since it is impossible to have increased exploration, production, and innovative technology when the government holds the price artificially below the market price. But the Democrats resisted. And with each round of resistance Ford cut down his own proposal, prolonged the price control period, until by about the third round of compromises, he was accepting a forty-month extension of price controls and other provisions virtually identical to those in a bill he had vetoed a year earlier. "We'd better sign this or we'll lose the New Hampshire primary," argued the political "realists" at the White House. So principled were these advisers that I am convinced, if Texas had been the nation's first primary, these men would have been urging a veto. As it was, the President finally ended up agreeing to *more complex* price controls on *more* oil than had ever existed before. His subsequent pleas that Congress deregulate natural gas were simply ignored, and the nation was saddled with a disastrous energy law.

There is no way, briefly, to describe the rest of that statute. It is a nightmarish botch of specifics. But the most important aspects of it are these:

1. The law contained no serious attempt to remove the throttles on energy production. On a piecemeal basis certain timid modifications were made in the franctically excessive environmental and pollution regulations—permitting increased use of coal in particular—but this major energy bill sought no true solution to the problem.

2. The law tacitly assumed that our energy production would be strangled forever, and it concentrated heavily on conservation measures. Conservation, by definition, is a short-range emergency measure. If you are in a lifeboat with seven people and only one jar of water, you conserve it, meaning you dole it out by drops so that the group may stay alive *until all are rescued.* But to demand of a giant industrial nation that it "conserve" energy without simultaneously offering an ultimate rescue plan is insanity. The unstated implication of that energy law was simply that we had become helplessly dependent on the extortionist OPEC nations for our very survival and that, should our relations with them go awry, we would die.

3. The law established a series of new controls for both the oil industry and for all energy-using industries—*which is to say, for virtually all industry in the United States.* It contained a variety of emergency powers to permit the executive and congress to supervise energy production, to alter its nature and methods, to coerce industries into switching from one fuel to another, to allocate and ration. In effect, the law turned energy production, without saying so, into a national utility, and it gave the state the right to rule

arbitrarily over our *total* industrial system and to allocate crucial resources on a grand scale. Because of the absolutely vital role that energy must play in the nation, that law was a major leap in the direction of a centralized, controlled economy.

That Republicans who claim to be dedicated to free enterprise and to the welfare of this nation should have cooperated in the framing of this bill and that a Republican President should have signed it are tragic. Gerald Ford and Frank Zarb, who participated in the formulation of this conference legislation, both said that it was the best that could possibly be accomplished given the Democrats' attitudes. That is true only on the assumption that Republicans were required to compromise on an energy bill no matter what it contained. But I challenged that assumption then, and I challenge it now. In this life there are issues on which men may reasonably compromise, and there are issues over which one must fight, even if one goes down in flames. As far as I am concerned, energy production, the vital life-force of the United States, is an issue over which one must fight. I did—and lost.

Thus, the Energy Policy and Conservation Act became law. It did not, of course, assure Gerald Ford's election the following November. With the inauguration of Jimmy Carter we all went back to our various homes, and I proceeded to work on this book. It is with inexpressible indignation that I report here that while this book was being written, we had our next energy crisis—a frightening shortage of natural gas in the coldest winter in 100 years. Natural gas was concentrated, of course, in those states where the free market price existed and ran short in those states where federal price controls had reduced the supply. According to the press, about 10,000 factories, deprived of energy, closed. More than 1.5 million people were hurled into the deadly winter to stand on unemployment lines. And this time Americans actually died of the cold. The ultimate result of an energy shortage in an industrial nation—death—had made its appearance.

Had anything been learned at all? For a moment, yes. Some politicians understood this time that the solution was to run as fast as their legs would carry them to rip the price controls off the interstate transmission of natural gas—at least temporarily. Even some of the press grasped this. The New York *Times* and CBS, for example, explained the effect of those price controls on the natural gas supply clearly and accurately.

But many in the liberal world learned nothing at all. I watched, disbelievingly, the idiotic replay of all the events I have described in this chapter. Once again liberal voices exploded hysterically that the shortage was "unreal," contrived by natural gas companies to rip off the public. Congressmen bayed righteously at the scandalous refusal of American industrialists to produce at prices lower than their costs. And on February 7 the *Village Voice,* New York City's ultraliberal weekly newspaper, carried a huge front-page headline: KILL CON ED—A CALL FOR PUBLIC POWER. The "KILL" was four inches high, each letter was one inch thick, and it took up almost a quarter of the page.

In April 1977 the Carter administration committed itself formally to the idea that only centralized planning by the state could solve the nation's energy problems. The legal base had been prepared by the Energy Policy and Conservation Act of 1975 and by another horrendous piece of legislation—the Energy Conservation and Production Act—which was authored by Senator Edward Kennedy and signed into law by President Ford during the 1976 campaign. All the new administration had to do was to elaborate on the provisions of the two statutes, and Carter did just that. Focusing almost entirely on conservation, Carter proposed to restrict the use of energy by a complex design of taxes which, if enacted, would paralyze incentives in the energy industries. Specifically, they would make it impossible for our energy producers to earn the profits needed (1) to explore the vast areas of the earth and ocean that have not yet been investigated; (2) to extract what may be a 1000-year supply of gas in the Gulf of Mexico; (3) to extract an estimated 50 to 100 billion barrels of oil in Alaska; (4) to devise the new technology needed to recover 105 billion barrels in existing oil fields and to recover possibly two trillion barrels in U.S. oil shale deposits.

In addition, Carter sought to ban America's single most reliable long-range energy insurance policy, the liquid metal fast-breeder reactor. By that action the administration was actually refusing to use 200,000 tons of uranium 238 that are now being stored in steel boxes at Oak Ridge, Tennessee, and elsewhere—the depleted uranium that remains after its fissionable isotope U-235 has been extracted. Petr Beckmann, professor of electrical engineering at the University of Colorado and editor of *Access to Energy*, clearly explained the meaning of that refusal:

> The stuff in those steel boxes, if bred into fuel, contains a staggering 8000 quads, or a century's worth, of energy at the present rate of consumption.
>
> Mind you, this is merely the fuel asset that has already been mined and is stored around the country as "waste."
>
> It does not include the as yet unmined uranium reserves of this country, estimated by ERDA at about 3.5 million tons. They could be bred into fuel while producing energy in the process of breeding it. Only 0.7 percent of it is fissionable in current reactors.
>
> The total amount of energy available from these reserves represents a staggering 140,000 quads, or about 1750 years of energy at the present rate of U.S. consumption.

What, instead, did Carter offer the nation? He proposed a giant bureaucracy which would control every aspect of pricing, production, and consumption, not only in the energy-producing industries themselves, but also in all industries that use energy or produce machines that use energy—automobiles, refrigerators, stoves, air conditioners, washing machines, electric typewriters, office equipment, etc. The tentacles of the proposed bureaucracy would reach into every home, office, and factory in the land. In effect, with that program Carter was advocating the effective nationalization of American industry.

Equally significant was the philosophical message that accompanied these proposals. Calling for sacrifices for a great national purpose, Carter asked American citizens to view his project as the "moral equivalent of war." This is a collective state of mind always longed for by men who dislike the "inefficiency" and "chaos" of free societies in which individuals determine their own purposes and do not submit to great national purposes imposed by the state save to defend the nation itself. In fact, war always creates an economic dictatorship, and the "moral equivalent of war" is merely a call for a peacetime economic dictatorship.

Inevitably, those who valued the free market and understood its role in generating innovative technology and wealth were stunned by the Carter proposals. Milton Friedman denounced them as a "monstrosity," as did other free-market economists like Murray Weidenbaum and Alan Greenspan. And so did I. It was all too clear that the proposals could result only in a decline in present production, and waste of capital in the rise in costs of an incalculable number of commodities, a paralysis of technological innovation, a decline in economic growth, an intensification of shortages, an increase in inflation, a general depression of the economy, and loss of jobs. What's more, there was not an economist in the country, including Carter's own Secretary of the Treasury, Michael Blumenthal, and his chief economic counselor, Charles Schultze, not to mention Carter sympathizers Walter Heller, Arthur Okun, and Otto Eckstein, who was not aware of these potentialities. All they could do was to debate, not if, but how much, the proposals would damage the economy.

What all this added up to was this: The Carter administration had the power to safeguard freedom, to allow profit incentives for further oil and natural gas exploration, and to make full use of current nuclear technology, all of which would guarantee constant economic growth and expanding employment. Instead, Carter proposed a strangling economic dictatorship. I described it publicly as a call for an "energy police state," and that is exactly what it was.

The President's "moral equivalent of war," consisting mainly of shackles on industry, ignored the ingenuity of Americans and their problem-solving dynamism. If there is any single trait that has characterized our culture, it has been an aggressive eagerness to overcome practical problems, and the technological and economic history of this country bears witness to it. Individual initiative and private enterprise are the forces which made us an energy-rich nation, which moved us from wood and whale oil a century ago to breakthroughs in electricity and petroleum and to our astounding developments in atomic technology. In a crisis the productive forces of this nation will instinctively strain to solve the problem.

The Carter program was opposed by both industry and labor for its failure to focus on production. But we cannot eternally rely on the subconsciously held values of our producers to fight an essentially philosophical battle. It is only a minority that has challenged Carter on the grounds of principle. He is still being described by the press as an "idealist," and the opposition to his program as resistance by selfish "special interests." And *that* is the deepest danger we face, for it is the principle that the Carter program embodies which must be understood if this destructive "idealism" is to be defeated permanently. The Carter program, like the energy legislation that preceded it, is a dramatic illustration of the principle with which I began this chapter: Government control of production results in artificial shortages which produce crises, and if not corrected, it will culminate in a drive to economic dictatorship. The principle is inviolate. Our capacity for innovation must decay, our standard of living must drop, and our wealth and freedom—and the wealth and freedom of those nations which depend on us—must deteriorate until the principle is finally understood.

# IV

## Disaster: Visible and Invisible

The problem of the managed economy is like the problem of the waves of the sea. We have identified the forces that cause them, we apprehend the conditions which must be met for a solution of the problem, and we can even reduce it to an equation—but its solution is hopelessly beyond our capacities.

—JACQUES RUEFF

In April 1974 President Nixon named me Secretary of the Treasury. The press of the period described the appointment as "noncontroversial." That didn't last. I was very shortly to become an extremely "controversial" Secretary of the

Treasury, and primarily for one reason: I had resolved to fight for the free enterprise system. And shout, "Stop!" to bigger and bigger government.

As my intentions and determination became apparent, I was warned by friends and associates that I could expect substantial animosity from the liberal press, which was given to a primitive cartooning of politicians as "good" and "evil"—with free enterprisers being cast in the "evil" role. They were right. I was soon the object of systematic attack by certain "prestigious" elements of the press.

The first target was my mind. The New York *Times* pronounced me "nonconceptual." Washington columnist Joseph Kraft described me as the mental "prisoner of a theology which sees market forces as totally benign and government as evil."

A second target was my motive for being a free enterpriser, which was pronounced either neurotic or opportunistic or both. Edward Cowan in the New York *Times* quoted an "economic planner" who described me as getting ego kicks out of "rear guard action": "Simon likes to see himself in that role. It turns him on to be the guy out there on the limb all by himself." And a Washington staff writer on the *Wall Street Journal* quoted a "well-placed source" as explaining that my fight for my principles "may only be Simon's way of polishing up his conservative credentials before returning to private life."

A third target was my free-enterprise psychology— variously described as frenetic, inhuman, and either devoid of moral feeling or, conversely, harshly moralistic. Kraft described me as "hysterical" and admonished me to stop screaming about the budget. Washington *Post* columnist Hobart Rowen, with thicker nerve endings, merely found me "near-hysterical," with the moral sensibilities of an "Archie Bunker." The *National Observer* published a fellow who ascertained in me the psychology of a mass murderer; he claimed that I "longed for a Genghis Khan who would decimate the unemployed." The *New Republic*'s TRB, however, perceived me as revealing a streak of "conscious rectitude" and compared me to "the professor of moral philosophy at a Calvinist divinity school." And of course, I was endlessly described as a political "Neanderthal" and as an "18th-century economist"—the New York *Times* being especially fond of that line.

But while reporters were busily denouncing me in the name of the "social democratic" mythology, I was making the most important discoveries of my life, discoveries I knew to be of long-range importance to the country.

As Secretary of the Treasury I could see the entire picture of what was going on in the economy at every level, from macrocosmic to microcosmic, in vertical slices and horizontal slices, in graphs, charts, and tables. The experience was shattering. It was very much like being a physician staring at a wall full of X–rays and a stack of sophisticated test results and realizing that the patient was not just sick but that every vital organ was threatened. Add one fact—that the physician loved the patient—and you have my state of mind in viewing the American economic condition.

Many of these facts and trends, of course, appeared in print—in bits and pieces and splinters scattered throughout many publications, usually business magazines and financial sections of the major press. But in this nonintegrated and incoherent form the information was virtually useless. Certainly the average citizen who received his briefings about the economy from the general press, particularly from the networks, scarcely knew what was happening. Above all, he did not know what he could have known had he been shown a systematic picture of the major economic trends: that the very life of the American economic system was in danger.

In the next few pages I will present some of those trends—the "X–rays" and "test results" and "symptoms" that I was contemplating. I have selected only those that a layman with no education in economics should be able to understand. I have broken these "symptoms" down into categories which give you an initial, if rough, sense of causal relationships.

## TAXES.

Washington was taking about one-quarter of the national income. That meant in effect that we all would be working from January 1 to the end of March only to turn our total income over to the federal government; in addition, we would be working through April into early May only to turn our total income over to the state and local governments. On an average, more than four months out of every citizen's year of labor were being confiscated by the government.

\* \* \*

The share of the Gross National Product eaten up by government had been inflating feverishly. In 1930 spending by federal, state, and local governments accounted for 12 percent of the GNP. By 1976 it was 36 percent. If the trend continued, it would hit 60 percent by the year 2000.

\* \* \*

The tax bill—federal, state, and local—was rising more rapidly than the cost of living. While the cost of living had climbed about 40 percent from 1969 to 1973, the tax bill had increased 65 percent.

\* \* \*

Taxes on business levied by federal, state, and local governments had climbed 320 percent between 1960 and 1975, while industrial sales had risen only 180 percent.

## GOVERNMENT SPENDING.

Federal spending had flown out of control. It had increased 232 percent from 1961 to 1975. The federal government was spending more than $1 billion a day.

\* \* \*

Federal spending had grown faster by far in the past twenty years than the private economy that supported it, rising nearly 400 percent. State and local spending had mushroomed 520 percent.

\* \* \*

Government at all levels had become the nation's biggest employer, bigger than the auto, steel, and all other durable-goods manufacturers combined. One out of every six working people was employed by a federal, state, or local government.

\* \* \*

The redistribution of wealth from the productive citizen to the nonproductive citizen had become the principal government activity. This process—carried out through a vast array of "social programs"—had roared out of control in the sixties and had continued to proliferate. In 1960 federal, state, and local governments spent a total of $52 billion on assorted social welfare programs. After Congress passed the Economic Opportunity Act in 1965, expenditures soared, rising over the next decade from $77.2 billion to a staggering total of $286 billion in 1975.

\* \* \*

The actual number of federal programs for transferring producer's income to nonproducer's pockets had proliferated. In 1960, at the end of the Eisenhower years, there were approximately 100 federal programs. By 1963 there were 160 such programs. By 1976 there were more than 1000.

\* \* \*

Only one category of federal spending was shrinking: Defense spending had a negative real growth rate. It had declined by half—from 43.5 percent of the federal budget in 1969 to 24.8 percent in 1976.

## GOVERNMENT DEBT.

The U.S. government was in hock up to its ears. This catastrophe had taken decades to develop. Before the New Deal the American government had kept its federal budget in surplus for four years out of almost every five. Since the New Deal the federal budget had been in the red in nearly four years out of every five. In sixteen of the past seventeen years we had rolled up deficits. From 1965 to 1975 the national debt had soared from $313 billion to $533 billion.

\* \* \*

The governmental statement of the federal debt was grossly deceptive. Enormous liabilities were not listed on the budget at all but were described as off budget items. Consequently, the citizens rarely realized the magnitude of the government debt.

\* \* \*

The missing off budget items themselves were staggering. By 1975 $11 billion was owed by "independent" agencies like the TVA and the Export-Import Bank. Government-sponsored enterprises, such as the Farm Credit Administration and the Federal Home Loan Board, owed $88 billion. Loans totaling $237 billion were guaranteed by the Federal Housing Administration, the Veterans Administration, the Farmers Home Administration, and others. But the biggest and still growing obligation was Social Security, estimated at more than $4 trillion—a figure which did not include Civil Service and other pensions.

\* \* \*

The interest on the federal debt alone in 1975 was $38

billion. Interest on the debt had nearly tripled in a decade and become the third largest item in the federal budget after transfer payments—redistribution of wealth programs—and defense.

## REGULATORY AGENCIES.

Although the President's Council of Economic Advisers estimated in 1975 that regulation cost the citizens $130 billion a year, no one knew how to calculate precisely either the inhibitory or inflationary effects of these agencies. They exercised control over every aspect of the operations not only of interstate transportation, power generation, the securities market, electronic communications, and the maritime, automobile, drug, food, agriculture and defense industries, but of small business as well.

\* \* \*

Regulatory agencies were clearly strangling economic activities. For instance:

—Government regulations had slowed the construction period of a nuclear plant to eleven years in the United States as compared to four to four and a half years in Europe and Japan.

—The 1973 automobile was subjected to forty-four different government standards and regulations involving about 780 different tests of equipment. In 1974 General Motors reported that it cost them $1.3 billion to comply with government regulations—costs that were, of course, passed on to the consumer.

—The Interstate Commerce Commission had on its books about 400,000 tariff schedules and 40 trillion rates telling the transportation industry what it might charge customers.

\* \* \*

An estimated 130 million man-hours were being spent filling out bureaucratic forms at a cost of at least $25 billion, that sum being added to the basic price of America's goods and services. And government processing of that paperwork cost taxpayers a minimum of $15 billion more.

## INFLATION.

To pay for both budget and off budget items, as well as interest on the debt, the government was printing more money every year. From 1955 through 1965 the money supply had grown at an annual rate of 2½ percent. Since 1965 the money growth rate had averaged nearly 6 percent.

\* \* \*

Prices had been soaring since the mid-1960s. From 1960 to 1964 inflation had averaged 1.2 percent a year. Then, from 1965 through 1968, the inflation rate doubled to 2.5 percent a year. In the next three years it doubled again, to more than 5 percent a year. The politically inspired imposition of wage and price controls artificially blocked inflation for the next two years. But when the controls were removed in 1973–74, inflation soared more than 12 percent—the highest figure in our peacetime history.

## HOUSING SHORTAGES.

The explosion of high prices had virtually destroyed the housing market. The median price of a new house was close to $45,000, nearly double the 1970 price. In six years the price of new houses had risen almost twice as fast as the average level of consumer prices and was still rising. By 1980, if the trend continued, a typical new house would cost $78,000.

\* \* \*

Apartment house construction had been hit even more severely. Inflation had greatly increased the risk of long-term investment. High interest rates on construction and mortgage loans had cut deeply into profits. Rent increases had lagged far behind rising costs. Since 1973 rents had increased about 15 percent, while costs of operating apartment houses had increased over 25 percent.

\* \* \*

The price explosion, compounded by rent controls in effect in 200 communities containing 15 percent of our urban population, had bankrupted many landlords. There was a massive abandonment of buildings by owners who could no longer maintain them or pay their taxes, resulting in the creation of huge housing "cemeteries" in big cities.

## PROFITS.

Since the mid-1960s, under the impact of rising taxes, inflation, redistribution of wealth programs, and proliferating regulation, profits after taxes had been plummeting throughout the business world by every standard measurement used by economists. In ten years the actual profits made on every dollar of sales had plunged by 50 percent—from 10 cents to less than 5 cents.\* Retained earnings—what is left over after corporate taxes and dividends are paid—had suffered an even worse drop: 85 percent between 1965 and 1973.

\* \* \*

By 1974 retained earnings fell to a record level of minus $16 billion as companies devoured their own seed corn.

---

\*Ironically, public opinion polls showed that the average American believed profits represented 35 cents on the dollar.

## CAPITAL INVESTMENT.

The government was usurping funds needed for private investment. Approximately 70 percent of the long-term capital funds available in private money markets was being borrowed by the federal government and 80 percent by government at all levels.

*   *   *

Capital investment was falling far short of that required for long-overdue plant expansion and technological innovation. From 1960 through the early 1970s private investment in the United States averaged less than 18 percent a year of our GNP. By comparison, investments averaged 35 percent a year of the GNP in Japan, 26 percent in Germany, 25 percent in France. Capital investment in the United States was the lowest among all industrialized nations, including the United Kingdom.

## PRODUCTIVITY.

Productivity growth—heavily influenced by investment in new plants, equipment, and technology—was declining rapidly. Between 1948 and 1954 output per man-hour had increased by 4 percent annually. Between 1956 and 1974 the increase had dropped to 2.1 percent. And between 1970 and 1974 the increase was only 1.6 percent. Since 1960, of eight major industrialized nations, the United States has ranked last in productivity growth.

## UNEMPLOYMENT.

In 1974-75 all these destructive trends came together, and the situation was worsened by several onetime factors, like the quadrupling of oil prices by the OPEC nations. The result was the worst inflation and recession in this country's history save for the Great Depression of 1929. Production declined drastically in many industries. Millions of people lost their jobs, and the unemployment rate hit 9 percent.

Those are the "symptoms" I was looking at as Secretary of the Treasury. I have left out hundreds of others of a more technical nature, but all of them added up to a frightening diagnosis.

On the *visible* level—the result of years of increasingly irrational government manipulation of the economy—the diagnosis was inflation, recession, and unemployment. This diagnosis was easily made and communicated to the public because everyone could *see* the higher prices on merchandise and could *see* the lengthening unemployment lines. Network cameras could take pictures of the tangible symptoms and of demoralized people. The political dialogue and press coverage centered almost exclusively on what was visible to the average citizen.

On the *invisible* level—which is to say, the long-range causal level—the diagnosis was more extensive and even more disturbing, but it was rarely talked about at all. Its elements could be summed up as: (1) a tax system that was stripping citizens of ever-increasing proportions of their wages and profits; (2) deceptive budget practices which kept citizens from grasping the full magnitude of massive federal deficits; (3) an ever-increasing national debt that was devouring the funds needed for capital investment in our productive system; (4) a federal printing press that was pouring increasingly valueless dollars into the economy, fueling both inflation and inflationary expectations; (5) a runaway "transfer" system which was compulsively redistributing the wealth from the productive citizens to the nonproductive; (6) an ever-expanding regulatory system which was wrapping increasingly tight coils around our productive institutions; (7) an entrenched profits depression; and (8) inadequate capital investment and a collapsing productivity rate that had fallen below those of the impoverished United Kingdom.

That collection of long-range invisible symptoms added up to only one thing: a government-engendered dynamics which was set *against* productive citizens, set *against* productivity, and set *against* the productive system. To all intents and purposes, a "stop growth" pattern had been built into the economic structure by the state itself.

This was not a minor problem. No economy can survive a structural war conducted against it by the state. The pattern was all the more horrifying in that it was identical in concept, if not in detail, to the economic pattern of the U.K. It embodied the insensate promise to the electorate of an eternal something for nothing. And since that is impossible, since wealth must be produced and cannot be conjured up out of thin air, the promise took the only practical form it could take: the pillaging of the productive for the sake of the nonproductive, both in the present and in the form of a mortgage on the future. That was precisely the cannibalistic pattern that the British had set into motion after World War II and tolerated blindly until even the London *Times* was able to grasp that if it continued, Britain faced economic extinction.

What had brought the United States to such an impasse? There are a great many ways to explain it, but the simplest, by far, is to give you two kinds of explanations—one dominantly economic, the other dominantly philosophical and political. In effect, I will first explain the visible crisis and next the invisible.

The symptoms and trends I have set forth in this chapter all culminated in an inflationary crisis and recession. They can best be understood by reviewing them in the context of the four major government policies that caused them. Those policies were deficit spending, inflation of the money supply, regulatory policy, and wage and price controls. I will discuss them briefly, one by one.

## DEFICIT SPENDING.

The inflationary cycle began, as all such cycles begin, with the extensive stimulus of government fiscal policies. For years American political leaders had been buying their way into power by promising to pay for and solve every problem, real or imaginary, domestic or foreign, that was declared by any sufficiently vocal and influential group to exist. Partisan versions of history notwithstanding, the malady was of both Democratic and Republican parentage.

By the time Lyndon Johnson's Great Society was in full swing in fiscal year 1966 federal outlays had reached $135 billion. Eight years later, under Nixon, expenditures had doubled to $269 billion. Even when the Vietnam War was over, during the next two fiscal years 1974–76, federal spending had increased again by 35 percent to $366 billion. Another large increase was to occur in fiscal year 1977 with President Ford proposing a budget of $396 billion and the concurrent resolution of Congress calling for an outlay of $413 billion.

In part, this dizzying acceleration of spending was due to the recession itself, which had triggered the "automatic stabilizers" such as unemployment compensation benefits. But most of the spiraling spending was simply a function of the permanent social redistribution programs that were already in place and which had become "uncontrollable."

Why were they "uncontrollable"? One reason was that many of the social programs are endowed with an "entitlement authority" which makes the actual outlay open-ended, depending on the eligibility, rules, and benefit levels established. Various income maintenance programs have been liberalized so that they rise automatically as inflation occurs. Yet other outlays are required by specific laws and contractual agreements. Today approximately three-fourths of the federal budget is considered "uncontrollable" because of such incessantly expanding obligations.

In theory no such thing as an "uncontrollable" budget

commitment exists, since Congress controls the nation's purse strings and has the power to determine what the nation shall spend each year. But in political reality men running for Congressional reelection do not choose to eliminate or reduce existing programs. Typically they keep making promises in exchange for votes and keep piling new programs on top of old ones. What is actually "uncontrollable" are the promises of politicians, who perceive votes as absolute and the budget as infinitely flexible. These "uncontrollable" political promises and government programs must be financed, and they are heavily financed by borrowing from the citizens themselves. Since 1929 deficits have become a cardinal feature of our economic life. There have been deficits in thirty-nine of the last forty-seven years, and since 1959, those deficits have become huge and virtually permanent. During the single decade 1968–77 the cumulative federal deficits totaled more than $265 billion.

Such federal deficits distorted allocation of resources, damaged the stability of financial markets, and, because the money was borrowed from the capital market, inhibited the formation of capital. Since capital investment is necessary for productive growth and high levels of employment, the "uncontrollable" deficits constituted a direct assault on the productive system and a direct cause of unemployment.

Further to complicate matters, the federal budget has itself been touted by government economists as a "tool for economic stabilization." Rationalizers of deficit spending have argued that increased federal spending and the resultant deficits were a creative act, that they were actually required to replace private demand during periods of slow economic activity. Thus, at every dip of the economy, the proposed cure was always deficit spending. Unfortunately the deficits never disappeared. They continued during both "stop" and "go" periods, during periods of both weak and strong economic activity. There were two destructive results of this alleged "stabilization" by deficits: The momentum of government spending was incessantly upward and inflationary, and the capital markets were further drained of investment capital.

Deficit spending, furthermore, generated its own pathological form of "bookkeeping." Politicians discovered that they could launch federal programs and win the enthusiastic support of grateful voters without taking a penny out of the Treasury. As every obligation fell due, all the government had to do was to sell new bonds to replace the old ones. As government borrowing became astronomical, a new "convention" in record keeping gradually emerged, and this also occurred on state and local levels of government; it consisted simply of hiding the true amount of the debt.

Thus, in addition to the recorded debt, there developed massive forms of debt which went unrecorded in the official budget numbers: price support programs and a variety of public assistance and social welfare programs to all classes of society. These and many other governmental obligations showed up in the budget, if at all, as footnotes; they were casually described as off budget items, and the citizens were not aware of them.

Their ignorance has been contrived by politicians, who have chosen to keep this information from the public's attention, and the choice is often conscious. In 1976, in testimony before the House Appropriations Committee, I condemned the practice of describing legislated spending for future programs as "future liabilities." That, I said, was a deceptive formulation; they are *present* liabilities, payable in the future, and the budget should make this clear by using the accrual accounting method. Before I testified, bureaucrats in the Office of Management and Budget read my statement and warned me excitedly, "Remove that section!" I ignored their advice and made the criticism. Congress knew what it was doing. There was only one possible dupe: the American people.

We have continued to proliferate both the recorded and unavowed debt at rates substantially greater than the growth of our ability to pay. The visible or acknowledged debt alone has grown at an annual rate of 14 percent in the past decade, while the GNP has grown at a far lower rate. Clearly this system cannot go on indefinitely.

## MONETARY POLICY.

Meanwhile, in the Federal Reserve System our monetary policies were being rendered unstable by our fiscal policies. Indeed, "monetarists" like Milton Friedman would argue that our monetary policies themselves had permitted politicians to get away with irresponsible fiscal policies. Whichever causal relationship you choose, it is certain that the government was printing money hand over fist to help finance its expenditures. The rate of growth in the money supply had risen dangerously. From 1956 to 1965 the money supply expanded at an average annual rate of 2.3 percent. But between 1966 and 1975, as the government engaged in runaway spending and was piling up increasingly huge deficits, the average annual money growth rate rose to 5.8 percent. And in 1976 the announced target for expansion of the money supply was within a range extending from $4\frac{1}{2}$ percent to 7 percent. The excessive growth of the money supply further aggravated inflation as more and more dollars chased virtually the same supply of goods and services.

In addition, both inflation of the money supply and deficit spending by the government had a direct impact on the economic attitudes and actions of citizens. It became approved public policy to live beyond one's means. By pumping fiat dollars into the economy, the government sought to keep interest rates artificially low. In fact, the government itself went into the lending business with veterans loans, educational loans, housing loans, and business loans. On all levels of society, citizens borrowed—in imitation of their government.

The banking system, encouraged by government policies, was caught up in the go-go craze, both at home and abroad.

The once hardhearted banker, who traditionally had demanded too much collateral, suddenly became "our friend," grinning at us from the TV set, encouraging us all to drop in at lunchtime for a quick low-interest loan—and please do call me Irving!

The resultant figures on individual debt tell the tale. In 1945 nonfarm families owed $5.7 billion, consisting primarily of installment debt. By 1974 those debts had risen to $190.1 billion—a leap of 3235 percent.

Corporate balance sheets similarly eroded. Many businessmen and financiers came to believe what the politicians were telling them: that the business cycle was dead, that the government could now keep the economy expanding indefinitely. Disciplines and responsible management procedures that had been developed through years of hard experience were condemned as old-fashioned and were abandoned or forgotten. Younger businessmen, also gripped by speculatory fever, never learned them at all. The statistics tell the sorry tale. At the end of World War II, corporate liquidity—a measure of cash, cash equivalents, and assets that could readily be converted into cash—stood at just under 50 percent of total liabilities. By 1960 the ratio was down to almost 30 percent. And at the end of 1970 it was on the order of 19 percent. In sum, it was not just the federal government that was on an inflationary spending binge. That binge had extended to the populace at large.

## REGULATION.

Simultaneously government regulation of industry was proliferating, and its effects, too, were simultaneously inflationary and restrictive of productivity. As I have already mentioned and will discuss in detail later, hundreds of government policies were launched which inhibited the efficiency and effectiveness of our economic system. The result was a mass of regulatory and administrative restrictions on industrial and agricultural production—and a prop to inefficient industries. Where dynamic new industries might have emerged in a free competitive market, regulation was actually maintaining archaic and noncompetitive production systems. This in turn extravagantly wasted resources and shriveled the production of goods and services, thus generating further inflationary pressures.

## WAGE AND PRICE CONTROLS.

Yet another inflationary explosion was caused by the government's attempt in 1971 and 1972 to pen up the inflation that its own policies had caused. Under the Nixon administration there were three years of wage and price controls. Controls are politically cosmetic and allow the government to be perceived as fighting inflation. In fact, they distorted the economy by rendering impossible the flexible price and wage adjustments needed to allocate resources, and they disrupted competitive relations, diverted capital investment, created shortages, and generated artificial motives for exports. As the record of World War II, the Korean War, and this last peacetime plunge into price controls reveals, federal intervention only suppresses but cannot stop the underlying wage and price pressures. The moment the controls are eliminated, the accumulated distortions that have been building up during the control period burst forth—and a surge of further inflation follows.

These four government policies brought inflation upon us in inexorable fashion. To compound the problem, the American economy was afflicted by several unusual factors. In 1972 and again in 1974 many nations suffered severe drought. The abnormal vulnerability of the world to drought was the direct consequence of the decline in food production caused by centralized planning or collectivized farming in the U.S.S.R., India, Argentina, and China—nations which had once been able to feed themselves and, in the case of U.S.S.R. and Argentina, to export food to other countries. With such giant land–masses rendered dependent on U.S. and Canadian wheat and with the demand for food rising in the Western nations, an accident of nature had overwhelming economic consequences.

Add to this a simultaneous "boom" in the industrialized West, which drove up the prices of internationally traded raw materials, and two devaluations of the dollar, and inflation spiraled still more rapidly.

Yet another inflationary trend was set off by the actions of foreign governments: The Arab oil cartel quadrupled the prices of crude petroleum. This obviously raised the prices of gasoline and home heating fuel. Less obvious were the pervasive inflationary effects on the costs of chemicals, plastics, transportation, man-made rubbers. There was no way on earth that after such compounding of inflationary trends we could have avoided the inevitable consequence of severe recession and unemployment.

This is the purely economic explanation of the crisis. Whether its genesis lay in fallacious policies of the past two decades or in onetime factors, every element in the crisis save one was the product of interventionist government—at home or abroad. The only factor in the crisis for which politicians were not responsible was the weather.

Congress, particularly the Democratic majority, has never wanted to understand the governmental causes of inflation—above all, the policy of deficit spending—because to understand them would require the most disciplined restriction of their interventions into the economy. They perceive that, tragically, as a threat to their "liberal" aspirations for the poor. The incredible irony, of course, is that inflation is, above all, an attack on the poor because it means their few dollars can buy less and less. During the budget discussions that took place during the Ford administration, several of us went before Congress and argued desperately against this frightening shortsightedness. We tried to show them the implications of their indifference to inflation. The Congressmen listened attentively and courteously, but they didn't have the slightest intention, ever, of adhering to our budget ceilings. And they didn't. That is why veto after veto came from the White House. There was actually no way to communicate with them. The English language had no effect in the face of this quasi-religious commitment to spending.

I don't want to suggest here that wisdom on this issue was distributed in a partisan fashion. It wasn't. Nothing illustrates that more clearly than the ludicrous "Whip Inflation Now" crusade launched by the White House, with the assistance of "WIN" buttons. It was conceived of by Bob Hartmann, an ex-newspaperman who served as assistant to President Ford and who argued that buttons and a snappy PR slogan could "whip" inflation. Every time the "WIN" issue came up we at the Economic Policy Board would hide our heads in embarrassment. I still have a box of old "WIN" buttons at home which I look at any time I develop partisan delusions. Nonetheless, it must be said that Mr. Ford's counselors understood the issue, and with few exceptions, he followed their advice. He fought Congress as Congress should have been fought.

As the administration's chief economic spokesman I was the most visible and vocal fighter against inflation and its major cause, deficit spending. I was fighting, in fact, for a certain constituency that went virtually unrepresented in our allegedly representative government—those millions of Americans who may not have understood the complexities of our economic problems but who knew full well that their taxes were oppressive, that the government was growing steadily more authoritarian, and that their voice was virtually unheard in Washington. I had actually been fighting for that constituency from the moment I took my oath of office under President Nixon as Secretary of the Treasury, and I spoke on behalf of the American taxpayer in every possible forum— from the town halls of the nation to the White House itself. Much of the history of my tenure consisted of this nonstop

battle against the very economic policies I have just analyzed. And it is relevant here to summarize that battle briefly
because it illuminates not only my role in fighting to restore
the American economy, but also the nature of the political
forces mobilized against such restoration. They were present, in strength, within the Republican Party itself and
accounted for a difficult relationship with some members of
my own party.

In 1974 I urged President Nixon to start a systematic
campaign against the pathologically inflated budget. I urged
him to cut taxes by $20 billion, to be accompanied by a $20
billion reduction in federal spending. There was no difficulty
in finding aspects of the budget to slash. I aimed directly at
those which had proved to be the centers of the most
obvious waste. "At present," I argued, "we are subsidizing
higher education far too much. Manpower programs have
been far more noted for their scandals and failures than for
their economic success. Housing programs are notoriously
wasteful." I had named a group of liberal sacred cows, and
reaction was swift. Roy Ash, head of the Office of Management and Budget, argued strenuously that nowhere in the
budget could sizable cuts be made. White House aides who
understood little about economics, and cared less, rushed to
party leaders, arguing frantically that the program was
politically suicidal. A distorted version of my plan was
leaked to columnist Joseph Kraft, who proclaimed that it
was "morally, administratively and politically disastrous."
The President retreated to San Clemente to decide between
Ash and me on the question of budget cuts. But the decision
was never made. The tide of Watergate grew ever stronger,
and consideration was given to only one concern: beating
back impeachment.

After President Nixon resigned, I continued to speak out
strongly in the Oval Office. The Congressional elections were
nearing, and as the campaign heated up, many Republican
politicians were urging President Ford to battle the recession
in the typical liberal manner: to loosen up the money supply

and cut taxes while boosting federal spending to create make-work jobs for a token number of unemployed. It was, of course, a certain formula for greater inflation and, ultimately, for even greater unemployment.

As debate raged within the administration, I implored President Ford, as did Alan Greenspan, chairman of the Council of Economic Advisers, James Lynn, head of the Office of Management and Budget, and Arthur Burns, not to follow this destructive formula. "Don't try to cure the economy with the very methods that have wrecked it," I told him. "If we can't finally control inflation, we won't have an economy left to argue about." To his everlasting credit, the President accepted the advice of his counselors and rejected election-eve political compromises.

But no sudden cures were possible for an economic crisis which had been building for decades. When the election results were in, the Republicans had suffered heavy losses—forty-three seats in the House, three seats in the Senate, four governorships. And since I had been the most vociferous public spokesman for the Ford policies, I became the target of those Republicans who actually believed that if President Ford had pretended, at the last moment, to be a convert to liberal economics, the party could have prevented its losses.

A Republican campaign to drive me from government began. I had actually predicted it. I had told columnist Tom Braden before the election, "If I were the President, I'd get rid of Bill Simon about next May because by that time he'll be so bloody that Gerald Ford will get credit for letting him go." And I had told my wife, Carol, one day after a particularly bitter confrontation with White House "pragmatists," that "If they get me, they get me. But at least I'll know I was right." My clash with a certain type of Republican partisan was inevitable. The blunt truth was that I had been far less interested in salvaging a few Congressional seats for the Republican Party than in the economic health of the nation.

My intransigent position turned into a party "crisis" when, after the election, I continued with equal intensity to make public denunciations of runaway spending and when I publicly characterized the proposed deficit in the new Ford budget—$51.9 billion—as "horrendous." Quivering with an indignation based on everything but concern for principle certain White House aides—most notably chief of staff Donald Rumsfeld—argued that I was "betraying" the President. News was leaked to the influential *Commercial and Financial Chronicle* that my resignation had been accepted and that I would leave "before or just after the end of 1974." When I declined to take the hint, the leakers used UPI's Helen Thomas to report that my resignation was imminent. And columnist Joseph Kraft eagerly passed along to his readers the "good economic news" that "Simon is on his way out."

Finally, President Ford, who had an admirably high tolerance for diversity of views within his administration, became aware that the White House infighting was excessive and moved to terminate it. He did not, in fact, feel "betrayed" by my judgment that the deficit was "horrendous"—he knew quite well that it was. He announced flatly, "Bill Simon is my Secretary of the Treasury, and he will stay in that job." Even then the anti-Simon campaign continued, with the assistance of liberal journalists, who were only too delighted to cooperate with Republicans in ridding the country of a Secretary of the Treasury who was crusading against deficit spending. *Newsweek* quoted administration sources as saying that I "would be let go after a decent interval and that the search for a successor is already under way." The Washington *Post* reported again that I was about to resign. *New York* magazine disclosed that "the word is that despite the President's considerable admiration for him, Simon will be out of office this winter or spring."

But winter came, and so did spring, and I was still in office—still fighting those economic trends which, if not arrested, would inexorably destroy the country. I did not confine my battle to government circles. I was equally intent on awakening the public to the dangers of continuing the economically suicidal policies of the past. I accepted every interview I could—from the Asbury Park *Press* to *Iron Age* to *Playboy* to the TODAY show. I logged tens of thousands of miles speaking from Miami to Portland, spelling out the danger. "It took us a hundred and seventy-one years to get a federal budget of a hundred billion dollars a year," I said time and again. "That was 1960. Within nine years we had reached two hundred billion dollars and four years later gone over three hundred billion dollars. And two years from now, if present trends are not reversed, we will reach four hundred billion dollars. The very existence of our free economy depends on getting government spending under control."

I did my best to communicate to the public the most urgent symptoms of economic disaster I have just analyzed in this chapter. Over and over again, to audience after audience, I explained the basic government policies which had led our country to the crisis of inflation, recession, and unemployment in which we were still trapped.

On the surface, I was behaving quixotically. A Democratic majority controlled Congress and had no interest in such views. Indeed, as I was traveling across the country talking in every forum I could find, the Democrats elected in the fall of 1974 were racing to adopt their historical cure-all: spending nonexistent money to "stimulate" the economy. The Ford budget had called for a deficit of "only" $51.9 billion. Now Chairman George Mahon of the House Appropriations Committee suggested that the vast new programs moving through Congress could push the deficit to $150 billion—for one year. I warned, to everyone who would listen, "The nation's survival is at stake"—and I meant this in the most literal sense.

To many politicians based in Washington I seemed to be shouting into a vacuum. Helpful Republicans constantly advised me that I was too "strident," too "shrill," and I was incessantly instructed to "tone down my rhetoric." But I was not dispensing "rhetoric," and I did not modulate my voice. I knew something these advisers did not know: that my chosen "constituency" was hearing me. I knew it from the hundreds and hundreds of times that perfect strangers grabbed me, almost possessively, in airports and on street corners to thank me emotionally and to say, "Keep on fighting." My "constituency" across the nation was responding, and I knew that the day would come when Congress itself would become aware of it. That day came. Mail to Capitol Hill began to reflect my message. And when Congress returned home during the 1975 spring recess, those gentlemen discovered that "constituency" waiting for them. Many of them returned to Washington, abruptly inspired to clamp down on deficit spending. An Illinois lawmaker, a liberal Democrat, told the press, "Many of us discovered that there are an awful lot of people back home supporting Bill Simon." In fact, "an awful lot of people" were supporting the commonsense perception, lacking, above all, in Washington, that continued deficit spending would destroy the country.

It was gratifying that I had succeeded in some measure in taking my case to the people and that President Ford was able to rely on an aroused public to veto forty-five spending bills, sustaining thirty-eight of them. This was, I should add, President Ford's most significant political achievement, although it is rarely described as such. He is usually praised for unifying America after Watergate and for his own decency and earnest character, and he certainly merits those tributes. But in my view, his most important contribution to the well-being of the nation lies in that barrage of vetoes, bravely executed in the face of immense hostility. Even so, the budget deficit soared to $66 billion, the highest in peacetime history.

I have related these minutiae of my personal quarrels within the Republican hierarchy because they illustrate a tragic aspect of the country's political existence: that even within that party committed to fiscal responsibility, there is no unified or coherent support for political figures who seek to fight a principled battle. For what it is worth, I must grudgingly concede that although the liberals who fought my position were desperately mistaken—a nation simply cannot "spend itself rich," as one of my predecessors in office once put it—they, at least, believed they were fighting for a principle. Generally liberals were firmly convinced that the choice the nation faced was between inflation and jobs; they made what they conceived to be the humanitarian choice and could not grasp that inflation itself was destroying jobs. I could respect a man who fought me on the grounds of moral principle. I could not respect those in my own party who fought me and betrayed their own alleged principles and the voters as well just to placate the liberal opposition.

But having said this much, I hasten to add that I scarcely enjoyed the liberal assault on me. My public position as the administration's most vocal fighter against inflation converted me instantly into a liberal symbol of wickedness. It was hardly pleasant to be insulted as the enemy of "the poor" when I was actually fighting to keep the entire economy from crashing—a development which would scarcely have assisted "the poor"—but there was nothing I could do to penetrate that wall of economic ignorance which surrounds so much of the liberal world like a moat. I got a certain impersonal perspective on my own situation one day when F. A. Hayek, after winning the Nobel Prize for Economics, was interviewed on television and vainly sought to explain to a panel of journalists that deficit spending and inflation were the cause of unemployment. That calm and patient old man explained it clearly several times. He was listened to courteously but with total incomprehension. In my own case, however, I was neither a sage nor a Nobel laureate. I was a Republican official and a symbol of "Wall Street," and the response to me was not courteous. I gritted my teeth and took the attacks. I had no alternative.

I was not alone in the awareness of my dilemma. Many

informed men outside government were disturbed by the attacks on me. In late 1976, just before I left office, Tom Clausen, President of the Bank of America, was being considered by President Carter for the job of Secretary of the Treasury. Clausen told me he had withdrawn his name. "I know myself," he told me. "I would take the same positions that you have taken. But I couldn't take the personal abuse that was heaped on you for four years." I took that abuse not because I was a Fearless Fosdick but because I was so much more frightened by deficit spending and its power to devastate an economy and a society. By sheer force of repetition, I helped force those issues on the political agenda, where they have remained.

That, in brief, completes my explanation of the *visible* dimensions of the national economic crisis and of the role I played in combating it.

And now I come to the *invisible* dimensions of that crisis—the philosophical or ideological dimension. I said earlier that one of the most horrifying discoveries I made as I studied the various symptoms and trends in our economy was the presence of a dynamic pattern, similar to that which dominates the life of the United Kingdom. As I said earlier, "It embodied the insensate promise to the electorate of an eternal something for nothing. And since that is impossible, since wealth must be produced and cannot be conjured up out of thin air, the promise took the only practical form it could take: the pillaging of the productive for the sake of the nonproductive, both in the present and in the form of a mortgage on the future."

The trends I have described constitute a broad socialist political-economic pattern, minus outright confiscation of the means of production. It is, more precisely, a set of quasi-socialist attitudes that have been integrated into the American economy, representing that quest for "a middle ground between communism and capitalism." And it is important to know the genesis of these attitudes. First emerging from the British Fabians in the 1880s, then import-ed by our own Socialist Party in the 1920s, they were popularly enshrined in the philosophy and approach of Franklin Delano Roosevelt. They constitute, to this day, the core of the liberal "ideology," which is actually committed to a steady erosion of our wealth and freedom, although its advocates are usually unaware of it.

They are unaware of it because they no longer know the relationship between wealth and freedom. Indeed, it is not too much to say that they no longer understand the concept of freedom. FDR actually redefined that concept, corrupting it so hopelessly that, save for a few philosophical diehards, succeeding generations were never again clear as to what it meant. Political freedom means only one thing: freedom *from* the state. FDR, however, invented a new kind of "freedom": a government guarantee of economic security and prosperity. He thus equated "freedom" with cash. However desirable economic security may be—and it is profoundly desirable—it is *not* the same thing as political freedom. By equating the two, FDR corrupted the philo-sophical concept of freedom. In fact, by calling cash a "freedom" in a society where the state was pledged to protect freedom, he converted "freedom" into a monetary claim on the state. By this single ideological switch, FDR caused a flat reversal of the relationship between the individ-ual and the state in America. The state ceased to be viewed as man's most dangerous enemy, to be shackled forever by constitutional chains. It was henceforth proclaimed to be the precise *opposite*; it became man's tenderhearted protector and provider. Statism and collectivism were brought into this country by the back door—and, ironically, were heralded thereafter as the saving of free enterprise.

I remember discovering the disastrous confusion in our political and economic vocabulary just a few years ago, after a press conference at which I warned a group of Washington reporters that this country was heading toward socialism, adding that I was not making a partisan statement. Some days later I read that TRB had quoted me in the *New Republic* and reported condescendingly that my statement had been met with "titters." At the time I found it incomprehensible. I did not realize then that I was looking at the results of brainwashing. But that is exactly what it was. Our political "thinkers" today are capable of staring directly at a rising tide of collectivism and statism, labeling it as its opposite and "tittering" when the trend is correctly identified because they are the end product of four decades of doublespeak. And the original authors of this doublespeak knew exactly what they were doing.

In 1968 veteran New Dealer Rexford Tugwell, an FDR brain truster, summarized, with exceptional frankness, exactly how the doublespeak was generated. He first demonstrated a perfect understanding of limited government and of the American Constitution:

> The Constitution was a negative document, meant mostly to protect citizens from their government. . . . Above all, men were to be free to do as they liked, and since the government was likely to intervene and because prosperity was to be found in the free management of their affairs, a constitution was needed to prevent such intervention. . . . The laws would maintain order but would not touch the individual who behaved reasonably.

But, said Tugwell, the American Constitution did not allow the government to enforce various "social virtues" and, above all, to provide for "the individuals' well-being"—*i.e.*, to distribute unearned wealth. And he wrote:

> To the extent that these new social virtues developed [in the New Deal], they were tortured interpretations of a document intended to prevent them. The government did accept responsibility for individuals' well-being, and it did interfere to make secure. But it really had to be admitted that it was done irregularly and according to doctrines the framers would have rejected. Organization for these purposes was very inefficient

because they were not acknowledged intentions. Much of the lagging and reluctance was owed to constantly reiterated intention that what was being done was in pursuit of the aims embodied in the Constitution of 1787, when obviously it was in contravention of them.[1]

Tugwell is saying here, in the plainest possible English, that there was only one way to force FDR's economic collectivism into our political system, and that was to violate the Constitution. And because it required a violation of the Constitution, the New Dealers found it necessary to lie about their goals and to pretend that they were conforming to the Constitution. That is the genesis of the doublespeak that still addles Americans' brains and allows them to describe a continuous invasion of individual rights and liberty as the enhancement of freedom.

It is part of the complex cultural lie in which the FDR legacy is enmeshed that only reactionary old curmudgeons denounced him for his policies. In fact, those policies were feared by the most sensitive of true liberals, who were appalled by the invasion of state power into Americans' lives. In *The Good Society*, written by Walter Lippmann between the years 1933 and 1937, he stated:

> The predominant teachings of this age are that there are no limits to man's capacity to govern others and that, therefore, no limitations ought to be imposed on government. The older faith, born of long ages of suffering under man's dominion over man, was that the exercise of unlimited power by men with limited minds and self-regarding prejudices is soon oppressive, reactionary and corrupt. The older faith taught that the very condition of progress was the limitation of power to the capacity and the virtue of rulers.
>
> For the time being, this tested wisdom is submerged under a worldwide movement which has at every vital point the support of vested interests and the afflatus of popular hopes. . . .
>
> The fact that the whole generation is acting on these hopes

does not mean that the liberal philosophy is dead, as the collectivists and authoritarians assert. On the contrary, it may be that they have taught a heresy and doomed this generation to reaction. So men may have to pass through a terrible ordeal before they find again the central truths they have forgotten.

Lippmann's words constitute a bitter reproach to the "liberals" of our era, who have doomed our nation to that "heresy." It was a betrayal of liberalism. It emerged during the contagious years of Stalin and Hitler, which launched the tide of National Socialism across the world. It was antithetical to the very essence of America's spirit and its Constitution. And by adopting that "heresy," the most magnificently free nation in the history of man and the most productive, became committed to the regressive notion that "there are no limits to man's capacity to govern others."

To understand the present economic crisis in our country, then, is not just a matter of tracking the problem down to specific "government policies," accurate as such an analysis may be. It requires that we confront the invisible philosophy of government underlying these policies. And of all the rationalizations for authoritarian rule which now surround our form of government, the most essential is this: the belief that the state, under an FDR-like leader, has both the moral obligation and the competence to "run" the economy and guarantee its citizens economic security.

In fact, no one can "run" an economic system. Simply to translate our economy into mathematical terms would, as Oscar Lange demonstrated in 1936, require billions and possibly trillions of equations. It cannot be done. But from FDR on, American Presidents have indeed "run" the economy. And since 1947 their performances have been faithfully recorded in the President's yearly Economic Report to Congress, in accordance with the Employment Act of 1946. Since that law requires that the state guarantee the American people "freedom from want," the President must rise once each year before Congress and solemnly proclaim that either

(1) he is *about* to create prosperity and security for all or (2) he has *already* created prosperity and security for all. Those are the only two allowed alternatives. And that means essentially that America's Presidents have been legally mandated to engage in intellectual fraud.

The citizen who wants to confront the history of this fraud need merely go to the library, ask for the President's yearly reports to Congress, and read them, from 1947 on. Here are just a few of the highlights.

Harry Truman at first fulfilled the requirements of the Employment Act of 1946 by maintaining a war economy under the Marshall Plan. Just as things began to sag, as the postwar markets constricted, the country went to war in Korea. That—give or take a few inflations and recessions—allowed him to fulfill the new economic goals of the nation. In his 1953 message to Congress before leaving office, Truman declared solemnly of his administration, ". . . we achieved in great measure the kind of society of which this Act is a symbol—a prosperous and growing economy of free men, with increasing opportunity for all."

Dwight Eisenhower was also a great success for a few years, and his reports to Congress made splendid reading. As 1956 opened, the general told Congress, "Full employment, rising income and a stable dollar have been cherished goals of our society. The practical attainment of these ideals in 1955 was the year's greatest economic achievement." But the postwar markets were steadily ebbing away: the government was overspending, sparking inflation, recession and unemployment. The economy lacked the wartime glory that was FDR's and Truman's. Liberals charged Eisenhower was causing the country to "stagnate."

Then John Fitzgerald Kennedy came roaring into office, vowing to "get the country moving again." As his reports to Congress indicate, JFK launched a magic formula: (1) Cut taxes, thus supplying consumers with more money to purchase goods; (2) fill the pockets of the poor by going into debt, thus stimulating the market further with borrowed money. And for good measure, JFK intervened—modestly—in an Asian war.

The magic formula began to work and apparently launched us into a new period of prosperity. It is true that inflation was increasing slowly, but that alarmed very few observers. JFK had barely begun to contribute to the heady Presidential literature required by the Employment Act of 1946 when he was assassinated.

Then Lyndon B. Johnson came on the scene. And it is here that the President's reports to Congress began to reflect the full fraudulent potential of the myth that a President can "run" the economy. Johnson expanded the limited intervention into Vietnam into a full-scale war and announced the birth of a "Great Society" by declaring a "War on Poverty." A new kind of adviser appeared in his councils: experts from the social sciences, who became known as poverty warriors. For several years, in pursuit of his two wars, LBJ's administration incurred shattering deficits, inflated money, and transferred torrential sums of nonexistent cash to the pockets of the "poor," whose numbers and needs multiplied under the attentive supervision of the new "poverty professionals." And in 1965 Johnson made a statement to Congress which he may have believed to be true, but which was appallingly false. He said, "I am pleased to report that the state of our economy is excellent."

In 1966 the inflationary pressures were rising even more ominously, and the Presidential report to Congress was even more extraordinarily false. Johnson said, "Can we keep a destructive price-wage spiral from getting under way? Can we move ahead with the Great Society programs and at the same time meet our needs for defense? My confident answers to each of these questions is YES. . . . We have learned how to achieve prosperity."

By 1967, faced with galloping inflation, Johnson still insisted that all was well. "Prosperity is everywhere evident," he told Congress. "But prosperity is never without problems, and—in 1966—some of these were serious." They were indeed. Johnson had decided to prosecute the Vietnam War without asking for additional taxes. The national deficit leaped crazily from $700 million to $25.2 billion, and rising inflation had become a fixture of the economy. A year later, in 1968, LBJ was still insisting that these were the problems of prosperity: "Our economy has never been stronger and more vigorous than during the 1960s."

And in January 1969, as he was leaving office, LBJ declared, almost incredibly:

> The nation is now in its 95th month of continuous economic advance. Both in strength and length, this prosperity is without parallel in our history. We have steered clear of the business-cycle recessions which for generations derailed us repeatedly from the path of growth and progress. . . . No longer do we view our economic life as a relentless tide of ups and downs. . . . No longer do we consider poverty and unemployment permanent landmarks on our economic scene.

This was the very climax of the fiscal irresponsibility of our Presidents and our Congress and of the intellectual fraud inherent in the myth of Presidential omniscience. Johnson's "prosperity without parallel in our history" was to a great degree a vast speculative and inflationary bubble, blown up by devalued money and by ravenous borrowing from the capital markets and fed by a war without end, from which victory had been barred.

When Richard Nixon came upon the scene, inflation was a burning issue. Readers of the President's reports to Congress will find it difficult to describe the exact policy of this particular President because he had several. Or, more precisely, he shuttled back and forth between "conservative" and "liberal" policies, echoing the fiscal responsibility of George Shultz, then blurting out, "We are all Keynesians now." He denounced the inflation that had built up under LBJ as a result of the deficit financing of the Vietnam War and the War on Poverty, which had left him with the heritage of an "uncontrollable" budget. But he himself continued to fight the Vietnam War and he introduced his own versions of the War on Poverty. Simultaneously, he sought to obey his free market economists' frantic recommendations to cut government spending, to limit money expansion, to reduce deficits. But when inflation kept rising ominously, he succumbed to interventionist advice to clamp down wage and price controls. The controls did dam up inflation temporarily—artificially—and Mr. Nixon thus reported optimistically on the year 1973 to Congress, "The dollar is strong, we have constructive economic relations throughout the world, and we have the greatest freedom of action resulting from our great capacity to produce."

This was, of course, a huge illusion. When the controls had to be lifted, the cumulative inflationary pressures of a decade burst forth once again. And in 1974 inflation exploded, plunging America into the most severe recession since the Great Depression of 1929. The gigantic bubble had burst. The magic spend-inflate-borrow formula had stopped working.

In 1975 Gerald Ford made his first statement to Congress as required by the Employment Act of 1946. And for the first time in the history of the Presidential literature composed for that act, the report represented stark, unadorned truth. Mr. Ford's first sentence was: "The economy is in a severe recession. Unemployment is too high and will rise higher." There was nothing else the man could say. The U.S. economy was finally in crisis. The illusion that a President, guided by a small number of intellectuals, could "run" our economy had exploded in our faces.

But no one in a responsible political position actually told this to the people. Instead, the information seeped out to a very limited audience. A series of curious confessions began to appear in print from the very groups of experts whose advice to our government had helped bring about the crisis. Several were of unusual interest.

In a Brookings Institution publication, Charles Schultze,

who headed the Bureau of the Budget during the LBJ administration (and is now chief economic adviser to President Carter), declared:

> In domestic as in foreign policy, the place to start is with a sober analysis of what government can and cannot do well. Ten years ago, a review of major economic and social problems would have concentrated on asking how government might best deal with them. In today's climate of public opinion, the same kind of review must begin by asking whether government is capable of dealing with them. Ten years ago, government was widely viewed as an instrument to solve problems; today, government itself is widely viewed as the problem.[2]

In an extensive interview with *The New Yorker* magazine, Schultze conceded that the old JFK-LBJ magic formula had got the country into trouble: "We know how to get to full employment. That's not the problem. We know how to do it with the old, standard, tried and true techniques: tax cuts, easy money, putting more money into certain government programs. But when we do that, we set off the inflation."[3]

In *The Public Interest* Peter H. Schuck reported on the attempt of a group of economists to use each of the eight leading econometric models to see what fiscal and monetary policies LBJ and Nixon might have used to avoid the spiraling inflationary crisis. They were unable to solve the problem or to reach agreement on any fundamental policies. Schuck quoted one of the economists as asking, "If the best of the modern-day economic policies—even with the benefit of hindsight not available at the time—couldn't produce any better results than what actually occurred, does the economist have merely a marginal usefulness to society?"[4]

The *Wall Street Journal* interviewed several dozen of the most prominent economists in the United States on the causes of the recession and on ways to prevent a recurrence. They disagreed about virtually everything save this: that there was much economists did not yet understand.[5]

The details of the economists' ignorance are of interest, but I stress here the overriding conclusion to be drawn from their statements: *The economists who had been advising our Presidents simply had not known what they were doing.* Even retroactively the economists achieved temporary unanimity on only one issue: the need for government to *stop* deficit spending and to *stop* inflating the money supply. Economist Burton Malkiel put it delicately: "Economics is a very young science. We are learning from our mistakes." Unfortunately those "mistakes" took the form of speculating with a nation's survival and restricting its liberty. That was not "youth" at work; it was the very *ancient* belief that a tiny "elite" had the right to control the means of survival of their countrymen.

Equally revealing were the avowals of many of the sociologists and poverty warriors who had guided LBJ to the now "uncontrollable" social programs. New York *Times* reporter Joseph Lelyveld wrote:

> They might be called the Class of 1968, for they are the social engineers who toiled over the blueprints of Lyndon B. Johnson's Great Society, which promised nothing less than the elimination of poverty from an affluent society. . . .
>
> In the eight years they have been away from the corridors of power, the old poverty warriors say, the country has changed, and so have they. Asked how their thinking has changed since they left, they start with the observation that it no longer makes political and economic sense, if it ever did, to talk in terms of bold programs to eliminate poverty.

Gerson Green, formerly of the Office of Economic Opportunity, summed up the attitude of many of his colleagues when he observed caustically, "The change I discern is that none of us know what to do. In those days, we thought we did. The country has taught the social engineers a lesson."[6]

Put it all together now: The Presidents, Congress itself, the economists, and the poverty warriors had not known what they were doing. So who was running the store? The answer is: nobody. Not one human being in the whole vast realm of political control over the American economy has *ever* known what he was doing. Nobody could know. This is the precise phenomenon described by F. A. Hayek in his Nobel lecture called "The Pretense of Knowledge." For forty years the American ship of state has been lunging erratically toward economic disaster, with no awareness of its direction, guided only by a "pretense of knowledge," by intellectual fraud.

This, then, is the invisible dimension of our economic crisis. In financial terms it is desperately grave, but it is the symptom of something graver by far: an unstated philosophical commitment by our governing institutions to the "heresy" of the thirties, the belief that, as Lippmann put it, "there are no limits to man's capacity to govern others." So long as we remain in the grip of that "heresy," we must continue stumbling blindly in the direction of economic catastrophe—under the guidance of politicians armed with spurious "knowledge" who are incapable of admitting their intellectual bankruptcy to the public at large.

I genuinely do not know whether we will or will not ultimately survive the desperate damage our government has done to our economy. The potential power of the economy is immense, and its regenerative power *in freedom* is incalculably great. I am prepared to say, however, that a financial collapse is not only possible but probable unless we reverse almost a half century of irrational and unrealistic policies. And I am also certain that should such a collapse occur, we will simultaneously turn to economic dictatorship. Many, perhaps most, of our citizens have been trained by now to see the state as economically omniscient and omnipotent and to blame all economic evils on "business." Should a great economic disaster come, such people will demand a takeover of the major means of production by the state. Given our immense number of legal precedents for intervention and an ideology which morally justifies it, it would not take much to accomplish such a transition. It would be legal. And just as in

Britain, it would occur simultaneously with a thunderous proclamation from the left that we were still a "free" society.

On November 28, 1976, CBS-TV aired a very unusual program. In it, my own predictions were voiced in the most precise fashion by Nobel Prize-winning economist Milton Friedman. The program was a short documentary on the United Kingdom called "Will There Always Be an England?" CBS newsman Morley Safer reported on the British slide into bankruptcy and invited Mr. Friedman to interpret its causes.

FRIEDMAN:   The British are capable of changing drastically. If the British were to alter their course, within ten years Britain could be one of the economic miracles of the West, just as Germany was after 1948.

SAFER:   If the turnaround doesn't happen, what's going to happen to Britain?

FRIEDMAN:   It's going to continue to slide toward economic and financial collapse in the sense that it will be more and more difficult for Britain to meet government expenditures without resorting to ever higher rates of inflation, without printing more money. It will be harder and harder for Britain to compete in the world at large. The standard of life of the ordinary Briton will go down.

When will this end? Nobody knows. But one of these days, that will result . . . in a drastic political change. It will, almost inevitably, I believe, lead to a complete loss of democracy and of freedom to the establishment of a collectivist totalitarian state. . . . I don't know enough about Britain to know who will be the people who will take over, whether it will be of the left, the people who have communist leanings, socialist leanings, or whether it will be some other group. But that's the only outcome that is conceivable.

SAFER:   Do you think that we can look at Britain and learn anything?

FRIEDMAN:   Oh, there's an enormous amount to learn. We're following the same path Britain is following. Fortunately, we're about twenty years behind. But we have done exactly the same thing of expanding and expanding the role of government. Today government spending at all levels, federal, state and local, in the United States takes forty percent of our income. And government controls our lives to an even greater extent. The hordes of bureaucrats are on the rise. New York City is America's Britain. And the one fundamental difference is that New York City does not have a printing press on which to turn out those green pieces of paper we call money. As a result, it has not been able to inflate as a temporary way of postponing its ultimate collapse. It's had to face up to its realities. The United States government has a printing press, and we have been inflating. . . .

I think that we have a great deal to learn. If we continue down the road that Britain has been following, we shall have much higher inflation than we have yet had, we shall see a larger and larger part of our freedom taken over by the government, our vaunted productivity will go down. . . . I hope the American people can look at Britain, can look at New York and come to their senses before it's too late.

That is what I, too, see in America's future if we do not reverse our economic policies—and if we do not reverse the underlying philosophical and political ideas that underlie these policies. Without such a clear, conscious reversal, we must continue to lurch toward economic disaster—down what Hayek has long called "The Road to Serfdom."

# V

# New York:
# Disaster in Microcosm

The key determinant of the city,'s budget is
the politics of the municipal labor unions.
Yet the public does not elect these leaders.
On the contrary, it is they, in partnership
with the political system, who do the elect-
ing. The single most crucial reason for the
death of New York is the fact that most
critical decisions about the future of the
city are made to preserve this alliance.

—JOEL HARNETT, *Chairman,*
*City Club of New York*

In 1975 New York City collapsed financially. The catastrophe was not a result of the recession. Nor was it a result of
the energy crisis. However severe the economic difficulties
of the period, no other great American city collapsed. It was

a problem unique to New York—but unique in only one sense. The philosophy that has ruled our nation for forty years had emerged in large measure from that very city which was America's intellectual headquarters, and inevitably, it was carried to its fullest expression in that city. In the collapse of New York those who chose to understand it could see a terrifying dress rehearsal of the fate that lies ahead for this country if it continues to be guided by the same philosophy of government.

The most understandable description of the more technical aspects of New York's financial trauma was provided by Martin Mayer, author of *The Bankers*. I quote it because Mayer is splendidly uninhibited by the requirements of political diplomacy that limited my own discourse throughout the New York crisis. He writes:

> On the simplest level, the story of New York's financial collapse is the tale of a Ponzi game in municipal paper—the regular and inevitably increasing issuance of notes to be paid off not by the future taxes or revenue certified to be available for that purpose, but by the sale of future notes. Like all chain-letter swindles, Ponzi games self-destruct when the seller runs out of suckers, as New York did in spring 1975.[1]

It was a tawdry way for one of the greatest cities in the world to fulfill its philosophical destiny, but it was inevitable.

As a specialist in municipal bonds I had known for years that New York was borrowing heavily to finance the promises of its politicians to the New York electorate. The New York *Times* had observed: "No one ever won any election by proposing to give the people less." In New York people won elections exclusively by using the word "more": more public services of all kinds for the working and middle classes; ever greater salaries and pensions for the hundreds of thousands who worked for the New York City government; more extensive social programs for the less fortunate. All these had been considered political absolutes, and notes and bonds were sold to finance them. By the end of 1974 the city was seeking to sell about $600 million of bonds every month to finance delivery on the campaign promises.

Until 1974 the system worked. But in that year the borrowing pace stepped up ominously. New York's need for funds suddenly seemed to be insatiable; the city went to the market for funds eighteen times in that year alone. Warning signs began to appear in the market. Suspicious buyers, signaling an awareness of risk, were demanding more return for their investments in city notes. On November 4 tax-free city notes were going at a record rate of 8.34 percent. On top of this was the fact that the bonds offered for sale the month before had not sold well; there was a large balance for which there had been no takers. Thus, on December 2, $600 million in new notes were offered for sale at a record 9.48 percent. And on December 18 the city announced plans to persuade the trustees of the municipal pension funds to use those funds to purchase $250 million in city obligations. The city's frantic search for funds in an increasingly suspicious market had reached some kind of dead end; it was now attempting to feed on the trust funds of its employees.

At about this time I heard from a distraught Mayor Abraham Beame. He told me that New York was suffering what he perceived to be a great injustice: The city was being forced to sell its notes at the highest rate in the country. He asked the U.S. Treasury to buy the notes. I told him I had no authority to do such a thing and could not recommend it. "If we did that," I said, "the taxpayers would end up financing the campaign promises of every profligate local politician in the country." It was an unsatisfactory answer for Mayor Beame. I asked the city, however, to send us the New York balance sheets immediately so we could determine what might be done to assist the city. The Treasury did not receive those records. I did not realize, then, that the last thing on earth any New York politician desired to confront was the city's bookkeeping.

Then, in February 1975, after a young lawyer representing

Bankers Trust discovered, apparently by accident, that the city did not have the tax receipts required by law to secure a $260 million note sale, both Bankers Trust and Chase Manhattan refused to go through with the underwriting. At approximately the same time New York State's Urban Development Corporation defaulted on $104.5 million worth of bond-anticipation notes. A lawsuit was started to enjoin as unconstitutional the sale of more than $500 million of ten-year bonds, for New York City was constitutionally and legally mandated to balance its budget. Fully aware that New York might not be able to honor its debts, investors were not inclined to await the outcome of the lawsuit. By the tens of thousands they simply refused to buy any more New York paper.

There were charges that this decision was made secretly by a small group of men in a smoke-filled room. It was not. It was made in the clear light of day, visible to all, by that omniscient judge: the market. On March 13 and 20 the city, through its underwriters, offered for sale $912 million of short-term notes at tax-exempt interest rates of up to 8 percent. Even for investors of relatively moderate means, this looked on the surface like a very good opportunity. For such investors the effective yield, on a tax equivalent basis, was three times greater than that available at a savings bank. Yet weeks after the offering, despite vigorous marketing, more than half the notes remained unsold.

The market had spoken. Investors had recognized that purchase of the notes would make them just another vulnerable layer in the borrowing pyramid and that they could be repaid only by the creation of still more layers of debt in the months ahead. They simply shied away, choosing instead from a variety of competing investment opportunities. Although the returns did not match what New York was offering, the risks as perceived by the market were much lower. For New York the market had closed. The Ponzi game had "self-destructed."

The shock of New York's financial collapse was

explosive—in New York, in the rest of the country, and throughout the world. How could it have happened so suddenly? everyone wondered. In fact, it had not happened suddenly. For a decade the public had been aware that New York City was spending heavily. But in the Great Society of the sixties that was not perceived as a serious threat. The illusion was that we had found the political formula for permanent wealth: promise-borrow-spend, promise-borrow-spend. Thus, the liberal economists assured us, could we eternally "stimulate" our economy. To question the efficacy of that formula was to question the very premise of the welfare state, of government intervention into the economy, and of the redistributionist philosophy that had swept the country. It was to question liberalism itself. And to question liberalism was to be a reactionary blackguard.

No one—whether the New York politicians or the unions or the most prominent bankers of New York or the New York press—has ever given a coherent explanation of why a collapse that had been building for a decade had not been anticipated. I cannot point the finger in this respect, for I hadn't expected it either. It was particularly ironic in my case, for in the late sixties and early seventies, when I worked at Salomon Brothers, I had been a member of the Technical Debt Advisory Committee set up by Abraham Beame when he was Comptroller of New York. We supplied the city market advice on its financial transactions, but at no point during any of these sessions did any one of us seriously question the underlying fiscal condition of New York. We all worked with the numbers given to us by the city itself, just as do the advisory committees to the federal government. It never occurred to us to disbelieve those figures, which always indicated that New York would be able to repay its debt.

From today's perspective this was a naive faith in the fiscal stability and honesty of governments. But before New York collapsed, that faith did exist. No one questioned the assumptions that the city's budget would be balanced, that city officials could and would raise taxes, if needed, to honor debts, and that the city's government was fundamentally sound. I shared these assumptions, and so did all the "hardheaded" bankers of New York.

Our trust rested on a powerful historical base. With few exceptions, it had always been safe to make loans to every city and state in the country. Borrowers had first claim on all revenues, and governments were pledged to raise taxes, if need be, to meet such obligations. Even the most sophisticated financiers and the Treasury Department itself were totally unprepared for a violation of this understanding. It took months before the incredible truth was finally unearthed: that the basic legal and ethical pact between the city and its debtors had been breached. In the world of the new politicis, which constantly promised the electorate something for nothing, the moral self-regulation on which we historically relied had totally deteriorated, and we had not known it.

That is why New York's financial collapse came so "suddenly." What was "sudden" was the traumatic discovery by the financial community that it was being rooked in a Ponzi game.

There was only one response from New York's officials when they lost their "credibility," as the quaint expression goes. Faced with the closing of the market, they howled with self-pity and demanded federal aid in the form of a Treasury guarantee of their loans. I had already explained that we did not possess that authority; indeed, I could not support the idea even if we did. I made these essential points: If the federal government were to step in to guarantee New York City's bonds, we would be asking other taxpayers across the land to subsidize New York's deficit spending, and the government would inevitably be forced to supply similar protection to other cities. That, I said, would result in the erosion of one of the most crucial disciplines on local spending by generating expectations of federal money in every city in the country. It would seriously accelerate inflationary trends. It would make a mockery of the principles of federalism on which the nation was founded. And, I concluded, if the federal government did assist New York City, it could be only under the most stringent of conditions. At a Senate hearing on October 1, Senator John Tower of Texas and I had the following exchange:

> SENATOR TOWER. Of course, heavy pressure is being brought to bear on the Congress to establish legislatively some form of federal assistance for New York City, and it may very well come to pass. I haven't been convinced that we should do it myself, but my primary concern is the impact of New York's plight on the rest of the country, and I think we have to view it in the national context.
>
> SECRETARY SIMON. I agree with that.
>
> SENATOR TOWER. If we so view it, and if we initiate some sort of assistance through legislative means, in your view what would be proper form for such assistance to take? . . .
>
> SECRETARY SIMON. Mr. Tower, if the Congress in its wisdom determines that the federal financial assistance is essential in this effort, I would urge . . . a narrow and restrictive program that would be administered by the Secretary of the Treasury.
>
> I would further urge that any program prohibit assistance until the Secretary is satisfied beyond every reasonable doubt that the recipient is inexorably on the road to fiscal integrity, and I would finally urge again, as Senator Proxmire has, that the financial terms of assistance be made so punitive, the overall experience be made so painful, that no city, no political subdivision would ever be tempted to go down the same road.[2]

To my astonishment, my full line of reasoning was almost totally ignored by the press. It zeroed in to the last sentence to my answer to Senator Tower—indeed, to just two words in that sentence: "punitive" and "painful." The New York *Post* rolled off the presses with the screaming headline SIMON ON U.S. AID: MAKE CITY SUFFER. And across the country similar headlines appeared; one in Atlanta read SIMON THROWS N.Y. TO THE WOLVES.

It was obvious that these interpreters of my position did

not understand the difference between a vindictive spirit and the importance of discouraging other city governments from following in New York's footsteps. Others in the administration received similar media treatment. Their complex explanations of the danger of a federal bailout for the bondholders of New York City were evaded, and all were portrayed in the press as sadists. An article in *New York* magazine labeled Arthur Burns, chairman of the Federal Reserve Board, "New York's Lord High Executioner" and posed the question "Will he kill New York for its own good?" *Newsweek* described White House economic counselor William Seidman as exulting in New York's collapse. And when President Ford attacked the "disease" of runaway spending and criticized New York City for "asking the rest of the country to guarantee its bills," his position was summed up by the New York *Daily News* with the headline FORD TO CITY: DROP DEAD.

What the "defenders" of New York found most difficult to endure was the fact that the American public was responding to the principles enunciated by the administration, not to their demands. Mail to Congress strongly opposed a federal bailout. California Senator Alan Cranston reported that his letters ran 95 percent against a bailout. And a Charleston, South Carolina, newspaper poll produced 7604 votes to 263 against Mayor Beame and Company. *Newsweek*, reporting on this popular reaction, interpreted it as an expression of popular antipathy toward New York but conceded that Ford had touched "a real and rising concern about profligacy in government at every level."

Inevitably, as fiscal conservatives clashed with the liberal demands for federal funds, the country became ideologically polarized. Writers of various persuasions clashed in the press. These positions, which endured through the entire New York crisis and endure to this day, are readily illustrated by a few quotations.

Conservative William F. Buckley agreed with my analysis of the problems entailed in a federal guarantee of New

York's debt. He said that he found in my total position "a quality of intelligent sobriety which is increasingly rare in the passionate rhetoric of the day."[3] I deeply appreciated his statement.

The neoconservative view—*i.e.*, the view of liberals with economic common sense—was expressed by William Broyles in the *Texas Monthly*. He eloquently defended New York as "our national center of excellence" but declared that for the nation "the moral imperative was clear and inescapable": New York should not be allowed to get away with its prodigality. He went on:

> And God knows, New York was prodigal. The balance sheet fairly groans with the weight of fiscal sins too numerous to detail: ambitious social programs where economy and efficiency were unknown; outrageous contracts with public employees and a gargantuan public payroll; welfare recipients in the Waldorf; irresponsible record-keeping that disguised the city's financial problems; a less than hospitable attitude toward the apartments and businesses which made up the bulk of the city's tax rolls. These atrocities have for decades attested to New York's commendable desire to please and its reprehensible unwillingness to consider the consequences.[4]

Finally, there was the outraged viewpoint of the liberal and leftist world—a viewpoint that could not bear to admit that the city's government had committed misdeeds and argued that New York was suffering not for its sins but for its compassion to the wretched of the earth. Irving Howe, editor of the socialist magazine *Dissent*, expressed this perspective forcefully on the op-ed page of the New York *Times*:

> Our true sin, in the eyes of Philistine skinflints and neoconservative ideologues, has been the decency—if not sufficient, still impressive—with which New York has treated its poor. . . . The assault on the city is an assault on maintaining, let alone extending, the welfare state. The assault on the welfare state is an assault on the poor, the deprived, the blacks, the Puerto Ricans.[5]

That, roughly, was the ideological lineup. It had formed almost instantly the moment the news flashed through the country that New York had collapsed financially. Indeed, it had formed long before anyone had the full facts.

What were the facts? Where had New York's money gone?

The Treasury Department made an extensive analysis of New York's spending pattern based on a comparison between New York and other major American cities in 1973. The study showed that New York had gone out of fiscal control in a significant way that was not to be found in any other city. Here is what we discovered.

New York was spending in excess of three times more per capita than any city with a population of more than 1 million. When the base was broadened to include smaller cities, only Boston and Baltimore were remotely comparable, and even when compared to these cities, New York's expenses were 50 percent higher.

This was not the worst of it. New York's growth in spending over a ten-year period far outpaced that of other urban centers. From 1963 through 1973 per capita municipal expenses of other large U.S. cities increased, on the average, 2.2 times. During the same period New York's expenses increased about 3.5 times—a 50 percent greater rate.

Was New York particularly hard hit by the recession or the so-called urban crisis? No, not by comparison to other cities. But what we found was a complete lack of balance—rapidly increasing expenditures that far outstripped the growth in revenues. New York's expenditures were increasing at a rate of 15 percent a year, while its revenues were growing at only 8 percent a year. This was a formula for financial disaster.

But clearly the most significant factor in New York's financial collapse was the cost of maintaining its municipal work force. The Census Bureau shows that New York employed some 49 employees per 1000 residents. The payrolls of virtually all other major cities ranged from 30 to 32 employees per 1000 inhabitants. More striking yet were the salaries paid to New York public employees, which were among the highest in the country and far outstripped comparable salaries in the private sector. A few illustrations tell the tale.

—A subway changemaker, who was not required to change anything higher than a $10 bill, earned $212 per week. A teller in a commercial bank earned $150 per week.

—A city porter earned $203. In private industry an X-ray technician earned $187.

—City bus drivers often worked eight-hour days but were paid for fourteen. Split-shift scheduling was rare; thus, some drivers were paid for an afternoon snooze between the rush-hour periods, and they were paid at overtime rates.

—Teachers in the secondary school system earned up to $23,750, considerably more than counterparts in the private schools, and their workload had declined. Fifteen years before, a secondary school teacher had a schedule of thirty forty-five-minute periods per week and was responsible for other work. In 1975 the teacher had a schedule of twenty-five periods per week and could be asked to do nothing else.

If public salaries were absurd, the pensions of the city's workers were appalling. Between 1960 and 1970 fifty-four pension bills had been passed in New York. In 1961 the city paid $260.8 million to provide its employees with retirement and Social Security benefits. By 1972 that sum had jumped 175 percent, to $753.9 million, the growth in city employment accounting for only 30 percent of the increase. And by 1975 the city budget for retirement benefits had grown to $1.3 billion. Calculations showed that by 1985 pensions would cost New York City $3 billion a year.

These dollar totals do not tell the full story, for there are other hidden costs that accompany these extraordinary pension payments. For example, police and transit workers can retire after twenty years at half their final pay. Thus, trained men in their late thirties and early forties are able to quit and take other jobs while they collect city pensions. The leakage of trained personnel is a hidden cost to the city. In 1970, after receiving an enormous pension increase, thousands of subway and bus workers retired to take private jobs. Within one year the Transit Authority lost 70 percent of its car-maintenance supervisors, and those who remained did their work at overtime rates.

In 1976 my staff at Treasury analyzed New York's municipal wages, primarily on the basis of the work of Mayor Beame's hand-picked temporary commission on city finances chaired by one of the mayor's oldest political allies, Justice Owen McGivern. The McGivern Commission staff, headed by Ray Horton, a scrupulously honest young Columbia professor, conducted an in-depth study of labor costs in New York City. It analyzed not only the hard dollar items, like salaries and pension contributions, but also the noncash fringe benefits that contributed to the city's collapse.

What did these include? Days off for giving blood, extra-long lunch hours, guaranteed "rest" periods, uniquely generous vacations and sick leave privileges, to mention just a few. According to the mayor's own commission, these "perks," when added to other benefits, cost the city's taxpayers 68 cents over and above every dollar in wages and salaries.

This can best be evaluated by matching it with the comparable figures for both government and private industry. Such fringes for federal employees add up to 35 cents per dollar. On average, private employers and other state and local governments pay in the range of 30 to 33 cents. In other words, New York's politicians had given the municipal unions a fringe benefit package twice as expensive as the average elsewhere.

Technically speaking, this factor alone could be construed as the straw that broke the camel's back. In 1976 wages accounted for about $4.2 billion in the city budget. When that figure is increased by 68 percent, total labor costs rise above $7 billion. If, on the other hand, fringe benefits in New York were at the 35 percent federal level, total costs would have been some $1.5 billion less—the difference between a billion-dollar deficit and a half-billion-dollar surplus.

How did the unions run off with the New York budget? Essentially, the story is this. The city's unions were given the right to bargain collectively in the 1950s during the administration of Mayor Robert Wagner, but by law they were forbidden to strike. The law was unenforceable, and the unions soon discovered they had the power, by striking, to cripple the city. On entering office in 1966, Mayor John Lindsay was confronted with a strike by transit workers that brought public transportation to a virtual standstill for twelve days. Lindsay, who had presidential aspirations, was polishing up his liberal credentials, and since nothing is more liberal than "solidarity" with the "proletariat," he capitulated to the transit union. All the other city unions demanded equivalent treatment. And from then on increasingly irresponsible settlements were extracted from the city. By the time Lindsay left office in 1974 the unions had walked off with most of the city's budget. Throughout the most bitter period of the political battle over New York's fiscal crisis, Lindsay was out of the country acting in a movie. I thought at the time that he was wise to stay away. He had done more than any other human being to cripple the city's economy.

Under these circumstances, it is actually bizarre that the liberal position on the New York crisis rests on the charge that New York has gone broke because of its *welfare* burden—or, as Irving Howe put it, because of its "decency" to the "poor."

The real irony in these contentions—apart from the fact that they are not true—is that they represent a characteristic form of liberal racism. From the New York *Times* to Walter Mondale, from the New York *Post* to John Lindsay, the assumption underlying the rhetoric is always the same: Blacks and Puerto Ricans congregate in New York to go on welfare. This perpetual clamor about the "white man's burden" reflects the cruelest of liberal delusions. Members of racial and ethnic minorities come to New York to work, not to go on welfare. The typical member of a minority group in New York is working at a productive job—and paying exorbitant taxes. Moreover, median minority family income in New York is substantially above the national average. The New York welfare burden is not larger proportionately than that of other cities despite the entrenched myth to the contrary. According to the National Center for Social Statistics for 1975, 10.9 percent of New York's population received aid to families with dependent children. But this was less than the 12.6 percent in Newark, 13.9 percent in Philadelphia, 14 percent in Washington, D.C., 14.5 percent in Baltimore, and 15.8 percent in St. Louis. New York's welfare burden was great, but it was not that city's unique cross. Nine other major cities were subsidizing higher percentages of their population.

The only significant item in New York's social welfare budget which does not exist in other cities is a free municipal hospital system—built in addition to a private hospital system. The municipal hospitals carry a serious excess load of unutilized buildings and beds. A two-year study of New York's Health and Hospitals Corporation found that those nineteen hospitals have far more staff and fewer patients than the private hospitals. In fact, in September 1975 one-fourth of the city's hospital beds were vacant. New York City spends $151 per capita on health and hospitals, while most cities spend $50 or less. This is not evidence of an unusual welfare burden. It is evidence of gross mismanagement of city funds and of New York's capacity to *invent* burdens to justify the creation of government jobs for its middle classes.

And that, ultimately, is New York's unpleasant little secret. New York's subsidies to the middle classes have been overwhelmingly greater than its subsidies to the poor. Writing in *Commentary* in May 1976, James Ring Adams noted that the city's official explanation for its fiscal embarrassment "was not only misleading, it is almost the exact opposite of the truth." He continued: "The most important source of its problem . . . is *not* the city's generosity to the poor and downtrodden, but its attempt to subsidize large portions of the middle class, including its own employees."

Adams pointed out that most of the city's tax revenues go to employees' salaries, pensions, and fringe benefits—all directed to the middle class. Worse yet, the middle class absorbs a significant percentage of the funds allegedly allotted to the poor. Adams reported, for example, that day-care programs, financed by Medicaid benefits, were serving a large number of middle-class families. According to a mayoral task force report, more than one-third of the children attending day-care centers were found to be ineligible. Similarly, a recent study by Dr. Trude Lash found that some 100,000 middle-class children were receiving welfare. And ultimately, much of the budgets for New York's welfare projects end up in the pockets of their administrators, who are members of the middle class.

To assist the middle class further, New York had a city university system run at an annual cost of more than $500 million. That system was larger than forty-three of America's state universities. It offered a tuition-free education, while almost all state universities charged admission. In 1970 the city university system was found to duplicate and compete with programs offered by twenty-two other colleges in New York. Despite open enrollment policies, the free city university system was essentially a gift to the children of the middle class.

Finally, to round up the list of major gifts to New York's middle class, there was the Mitchell-Lama housing program, an undisguised middle-income handout in which each apartment was subsidized to the amount of $150 a month. By 1976, 90 of the city's 130 Mitchell-Lama projects were in arrears on their mortgage payments, which have been paid by the city budget at $45 million a year. Adams pointed out in *Commentary* that free university tuition and Mitchell-Lama housing projects alone added up to the equivalent of the payments given to families with dependent children.

The liberal cry that New York is being drained by its "decency" to the "poor" is not just a misstatement; it is virtually a psychotic—and, I submit, a racist—delusion. It is blatantly obvious that the subsidy to New York's middle class—above all, the salaries, pensions, and fringe benefits paid to the government workers—is responsible for New York's fiscal collapse. The officials of New York's budget commission concluded in 1975 that a pay freeze for all city employees could save between $400 and $600 million of Beame's $641.5 million budget gap. If New York's public employees had not been remunerated in so lavish a fashion, had they been paid by the standard of other big cities, the city would not have been in debt at all. Instead, the city would have had a *surplus* of between $500 million and $1 billion.

It has been argued by some that those extravagant wages and pensions were justified because the cost of living in New York was 16 percent higher than that in the rest of the country. That sounds convincing, but it could scarcely convince the Treasury Department, which had access to nationwide figures. New York's cost of living was indeed higher—*on an average*—but it was lower than that in a number of other large cities. It was not the cost of living that had caused these high wages. It was playing politics with the labor vote—at the expense of other citizens whose wages and pension systems in the private market did not remotely compare with those of the government employees they were being forced to subsidize.

And it is when one confronts those unsung victims that the last piece of the New York mystery falls into place. Not only had New York been subsidizing a significant portion of its middle class, but the victims—the *unsubsidized* portion of the population—had begun to disappear. Quite simply, those who were being forced to pay these extortionate subsidies to their fellow citizens were running away.

For more than a decade New York City has been slowly losing its productive backbone. Industry and skilled workers, hit by New York's excessive tax rate, have been leaking out of the city at a rapid rate. The leakage started in the early fifties, when manufacturers began to relocate to cities where the economic burdens were lower. Parts of the garment industry, large bakeries, and food processors and breweries left the city, and by 1969 they had taken about 140,000 jobs with them. The flight accelerated at a frightening pace. More than the same number of jobs vanished in the next five years. And between December 1974 and December 1975 alone, according to the Bureau of Labor Statistics, 143,000 jobs disappeared. A cautious estimate suggests that between 1970 and 1977 some 400,000 jobs vanished.

A writer in *New York* magazine, surveying this exodus on March 15, 1976, wrote:

> A "city" of businesses and taxpayers as large as San Francisco has packed its bags and left New York. . . . Both the Governor and the Mayor now realize that our economy is hemorrhaging, but they do not yet seem ready to acknowledge that the [planned] tax hikes are making matters very much worse. The most recent $600 million hike in state taxes and virtually all city tax boosts since the fiscal crisis fall exclusively on business.

And *that* is why New York City collapsed financially. If one analyzes New York's fiscal crisis in terms of its real, not its mythic, elements, one sees plainly that nothing has destroyed New York's finances but the liberal political formula. Using the "poor" as a compulsive pretext, New York politicians have formed a working coalition with a portion of the middle class to run the city for their mutual benefit at the expense of the rest of the productive population. And inevitably that productive population has slowly withdrawn, gradually destroying the city's economic base. Liberal politics, endlessly glorifying its own "humanism," has, in fact, been annihilating the very conditions for human survival.

At the height of the New York crisis some liberals—very

few—did begin to get a glimpse of the role of liberal ideology in the devastation of New York. It suddenly hit political analyst Ken Auletta, writing in *New York* on October 27, 1975, that a decade earlier William F. Buckley, Jr., had seen clearly what no liberal then could see:

> On October 7, 1965, Buckley, then a candidate for mayor, warned, "New York City is in dire financial condition, as a result of mismanagement, extravagance and political cowardice. . . . New York City must discontinue its present borrowing policies and learn to live within its income before it goes bankrupt." Judging by the reaction, one would have thought Buckley had proposed to drop the atom bomb on Israel.
>
> It took a decade for Buckley to appear "responsible." He was bucking the '60s, the Age of Good Intentions, when candidates solemnly promised to outspend their rivals. New ideas. New programs. That's what we wanted.
>
> An unwitting spokesman for the age was Mayor Robert F. Wagner who, in his last budget message in 1965, declared: "I do not propose to permit our fiscal problems to set the limits of our commitments to meet the essential needs of the people of the city."
>
> Consistent with that curious fiscal philosophy, New York City persisted in an ambitious—and compassionate—effort to care for those less fortunate by taxing those who could afford it. . . . *We have conducted a noble experiment in local socialism and income redistribution, one clear result of which has been to redistribute much of our tax base and many jobs out of the city.* [Italics mine.]

Another analyst with insight into the liberal genesis of the disaster was Theodore White. Writing in the same publication on November 10, 1975, he said:

> New York City has now reached the point where it is entirely incapable of self-government. . . .
>
> There are over a million people on welfare in this city. Our 260,000 city employees have wives, or husbands, and children. Most of them vote—and they are all united in one great purpose: "More." No one can be elected in this city who

promises "Less." So all our politicians for 20 years have promised more—more police, more schools, more playgrounds, more guidance counselors, bigger pensions, more hospital beds, more admissions to our university system. *Together the welfare population and the city employees dominate our electoral politics. As in a giant soviet, they elect their bosses and paymaster.* . . . In New York good will has not only run its course, but sped beyond all legal or social speed limits. [Italics mine.]

Both these analysts, however, were still trapped in that perspective which sees "good intentions" and "goodwill" as the genesis of New York's bankrupt "socialist experiment" and "giant soviet." But goodwill does *not* account for this pattern of destruction or for so vast a loss of contact with economic reality. Writing in the *Wall Street Journal* on December 10, 1975, Irving Kristol, a brilliant refugee from the left, presented a devastating analysis of the actual motives that underlie the liberal ideology. I cite him at length because nothing could be more imperative than to lay bare the altruist rationalizations which, alone, endow liberals with their moral influence, both in New York as in the nation:

One might call this ideology the politics of compassion, or the politics of philanthropy, or the politics of conscience, or perhaps simply the politics of social democracy. We really do not have a good and acceptable brand name for it. But we do have a clear enough conception of it. Indeed, its basic premise has been brilliantly articulated by a distinguished Harvard philosopher, John Rawls, in his book *A Theory of Justice.* . . .

This premise asserts that economic inequalities and all social policies are justifiable only to the degree that they benefit the poor and help them become more equal to everyone else. Upper-middle-class New Yorkers enthusiastically endorsed this principle long before Rawls articulated it for them. And the actual workings of this egalitarian principle, in the case of New York City, constitute a fascinating intellectual and social experiment.

The results of the experiment are conclusive, I should say: the principle is a prescription for disaster. . . . All that the

Rawls principle of "fairness" means, in effect, is that we will concentrate on apparent short-term benefits for the poor—a view which in any case commends itself to liberal-minded people and politicians who want not only to *do* good but to *feel* good and *look* good while doing good. The upshot is a species of infantile liberalism, seeking immediate gratification, spiritually and politically, while laying the groundwork for permanent frustration. . . .

[I]t is obvious to everyone who looks objectively at New York's plight that what the city's poor need, far above all else, is jobs, jobs and more jobs. . . . It follows that the overriding purpose of social policy in New York should be job retention and job creation. Unfortunately, achieving this purpose means, in the shorter term, offering encouragement to the non-poor—i.e., to businessmen and business firms. Such a policy is utterly repugnant to those who have an inflamed sense of political compassion. It may end up doing good for the poor, but it does no good whatsoever to affluent men and women who need to *feel* good while they are *seen* to be doing good for the poor. Such people cannot postpone their moral gratifications, and this moral delinquency—created by a kind of elephantiasis of the moral sentiment itself—is what makes New York's state of mind so self-destructive.

Instead of emphasizing job creation, New York's liberal elite has encouraged job destruction in the name of social reform. . . .

The failure of New York's political ideology is apparent enough to most ordinary New Yorkers, who always were somewhat skeptical of it. But the political and cultural elites in New York have made a huge investment in that ideology and are struggling desperately against the prospect of a massive write-off. They cannot believe they did harm when their consciences—magnified and rebroadcast to them by their media—assured them they were doing good. Unless and until this state of mind is itself reformed, the city will move inexorably toward that destiny which it seems to have chosen for itself: to be a moral theater for the affluent, an urban reservation for the poor. And all this in the name of equality.

In these few paragraphs Mr. Kristol strikes right at the root of New York's financial crisis. He clarifies the vested interest of so many liberals in refusing to understand what has really happened. Such understanding would, in fact, result in a wholesale adoption of "conservative" attitudes and would amount to committing ideological suicide. It is clear that most liberals would rather blind themselves eternally to the facts and let the city crash about their feet than experience such an indignity.

Intellectual evasion to protect what Kristol calls an "elephantiasis of the moral sentiment" suffices, of course, for people who merely talk and write about politics. But the evasion takes a very different form in practical politicians, who must prepare budgets and comply with constitutional and legal mandates requiring that those budgets be balanced. How did the liberal politicians resolve the conflict between their moral self-image and reality? The answer is unfortunate: They cheated. Ideological dishonesty led, inexorably, to fiscal dishonesty.

As Secretary of the Treasury I described this cheating briefly and in the most moderate language possible. I said, "In recent years, New York has faced the marketplace's demands for restraint, responsibility, and realism with spending, promises, and *gimmickry*. Capital borrowing for current expenditures, *artificially high revenue estimates to 'balance' budgets and support even more borrowing*, and, above all, an inability to say no where more spending is concerned make New York unique among our major cities." The italicized phrases were my sole references to the dishonesty of New York's accounting practices.

Others who were not serving as the financial spokesman for the administration allowed themselves more explicit language. Again, in *New York* magazine on June 2, 1975, Chris Welles described the two principal manifestations of the city's dishonesty:

> Accounting trickery evolved into a refined art at City Hall. The techniques were abstruse and varied. But basically, most involved time warps—specifically, pretending that expenses the city was incurring now actually wouldn't be incurred until

later and that revenues the city expected to receive later had
already been received. Outgo, in short, was pushed forward in
time, while income was pulled back. . . . Like other accounting gimmicks, this, of course, produced no new actual cash for
the city, only the appearance of same. . . . Over the years, the
period and extent of anticipation had grown, and the city had
mortgaged itself further and further into the future. The city
had also been selling notes in anticipation of income it knew
might never arrive at all.

By October 27, 1975, Ken Auletta, in the same publication,
had tracked down the major fiscal manipulations on the state
as well as local level, going back to the late fifties and early
sixties—covering the regimes of Governor Nelson Rockefeller, as well as those of Mayors Robert Wagner and John
Lindsay and Comptroller and Mayor Abraham Beame. What
all these fiscal manipulations had in common, essentially,
were ways of circumventing constitutional and legal controls
over auditing—and ways of increasing the power of politicians to distribute largess to the city's municipal unions.
Presenting case history after case history of these fiscal
maneuvers, Auletta described "the rollovers, false revenue
estimates and plain lies that have robbed taxpayers of
literally billions through excessive borrowing to cover up
excessive fraud. . . . People have gone to jail for less."

The same week in which Auletta's accusation appeared,
New York's conservative Republican Senator James L. Buckley reached the conclusion that the Justice Department
should investigate the city's fiscal practices. Buckley's request was based on an audit of New York's books by state
Controller Arthur Levitt that, in the words of an attorney for
the New York state legislature's Select Committee on Crime,
left "little doubt that recent city borrowings have relied upon
massive fraud in the statement of accounts pledged to repay
the borrowed funds."[6]

One might suppose that the liberals, obsessed with ethics,
applauded the idea of a probe into alleged fraud. Such was
not the case. An avalanche of abuse descended on Senator

Buckley's head from New York politicians and many in the media for his "timing." Mayor Beame put it in tones of moral outrage: "It is indeed tragic that the Senator's statement comes at a time when responsible state leaders—regardless of party—are acting in concert to stave off a disastrous collapse that cannot be contained within the boundaries of New York." In other words, just as William F. Buckley, Jr., had been declared "irresponsible" in 1965 for warning New Yorkers that their city was going "bankrupt" because of "mismanagement," so a decade later Senator James L. Buckley was declared "irresponsible" when he demanded an investigation of the "mismanagement" that had indeed led to "bankruptcy."

Thus did the "state of mind that was New York"—with the exception of a few truth tellers—throw a veil of evasion around even the most blatant political corruption and seek to render serious political criticism morally taboo.

How, finally, was the problem solved? It wasn't. Or, more precisely, there was a political uproar culminating in a cosmetic "solution" as New York fought incessantly to deny, and to escape from, the consequences of this "state of mind." The technical battle over New York's financial problems had a significance for America that transcended its own particulars, so I shall sketch it out in some detail.

The battle actually started before the market closed to New York bonds and continued unabated throughout 1975 and part of 1976. It consisted of the simultaneous and warring demands of the principals in the New York drama who were seeking to influence the Congress of the United States. The principals were a diverse group: the Treasury and the Federal Reserve; New York's municipal unions, whose wages and pension funds had consumed the bulk of the budget; and the New York banks which had been financing part of the city's debt. In addition, there were the New York politicians, notably Mayor Beame and Governor Hugh Carey, who had the official responsibility for solving the problem. There was Congress, which was seeking to evaluate all the conflicting positions. And of course, there was the press, which often participated in the battle, as well as reported on it. In reality, the voices of the principals were heard simultaneously and ceaselessly. But I will present their positions here one by one for the sake of clarity, starting with my own.

As I have already said, my position as Secretary of the Treasury had been reduced by the press to the slogan "Make City Suffer." Combined with Gerald Ford's alleged message to New York—"Drop Dead"—it was construed to be a simple expression of sadism. This was particularly ironic since my remarks about "punitive" conditions of repayment were, by definition, part of a discussion of conditions under which I thought it possible to grant New York temporary financial assistance. In fact, from the very beginning of the crisis, we at Treasury had been seeking some technical and constitutional means of assisting the city.

When the market closed to New York in March 1975, we held a series of meetings with experts in municipal finance. We were trying to identify the cause of the market closure and to see if the problem could be resolved in time to permit the city to sell $550 million of notes on April 15. As I was to put it in later testimony, we were "urgently seeking ways to sell a then unsalable product."

Simultaneously we were seeking at Treasury to establish whether the federal government could be of assistance. But for this we needed facts—facts about the city's expenses and obligations, facts about its revenue sources, facts about its debt structure. It was a severe shock to all of us when we found that no such facts were then obtainable. No one in New York City could provide us with a document that set forth the income and expenses of the city, its assets and liabilities. We soon became enmeshed in the city's Byzantine accounts and realized that after years of tortuous accounting practices, no living human being actually knew the facts we were seeking.

While we were struggling to grasp New York's fiscal situation, we heard frantic charges from Mayor Beame to the effect that the dilemma was entirely due to the federal government's shortchanging of New York City on welfare payments. HEW, he said, had failed to transmit the government's share of such payments regularly and accurately. Members of my staff and that of HEW immediately checked out the HEW assistance programs item by item. We discovered that the payments had, in fact, been scheduled regularly. But in the course of the review, we discovered that indeed, as a result of errors by the state, there had been an underpayment of $90 million to the city, and that was instantly rectified. That sum did not satisfy Mayor Beame and others in New York, who were expecting hundreds of millions to materialize magically from HEW coffers. What's more, the missing $90 million scarcely accounted for New York's dilemma—New York had been borrowing about $600 million a month in the marketplace. But the liberal compulsion to tailor reality to fit its moral self-image remained absolute. New York officials, committed to the rationalization that they had been bankrupted by their "compassion," never abandoned the view that New York's welfare budget was the key to the fiscal crisis.

Unmoved by this illusion but trying to help, we at Treasury explored all the legal possibilities of offering New York direct financial assistance. It became clear that they were severely limited. There were only two sources of meaningful amounts of cash. We could have advanced the date of payment of New York's revenue-sharing allotment and given the city a premature payment of $121 million, and we could have changed the Medicaid payment methods, giving the city an advance of $75 million on expected costs. This would have resulted in a grand total of $196 million as an emergency stopgap and would have merely postponed the city's problem for one-third of a month. So we didn't do it.

We sought, instead, to ascertain whether or not some form of federal assistance could solve New York's problem. We were looking for an authentic solution—a treatment for the cause of the problem, not a mask for its symptoms. American taxpayers could not be drained to fill New York's bottomless pit, and whatever solution we devised had to be applicable to other American cities as well, which would thereafter request comparable treatment at moments of difficulty.

It was only then, in seeking to ascertain what federal assistance measures might be acceptable to all American cities universally, that we at Treasury actually discovered the extraordinary difference between New York's handling of its fiscal life and that of other cities—the differences I have already set forth in this chapter. Not only was New York spending more per capita than any other city, not only had its increase in spending outpaced that of other cities, but New York was the only major American city to pile up a huge—and permanent—short-term debt. Indeed, apart from bond-anticipation notes, which can be considered a form of construction financing, few American cities had any short-term debt. For instance, each year Chicago issued about $300 million in notes and paid them off annually when tax payments came in. Boston had $65 million in tax-anticipation notes outstanding but retired them on schedule when the 1975 taxes were paid. Only New York was rushing headlong toward bankruptcy, committing its own citizens to constantly increasing financial burdens—and was now turning to the nation's taxpayers for even more funds.

In the course of many meetings with New York officials, we presented these disturbing comparisons over and over again and demanded a commitment to the idea that New York spending had to be brought into line with revenues. We received no such commitment. New York's political leaders were wholly bent on extracting money from the nation's taxpayers and acted as if our demands were absurd. In fact, Mayor Beame and his colleagues treated us at Treasury like naïve bunnies who did not understand the political facts of New York life. According to them, you could fight crime, you could fight pollution, you could fight ignorance, but—in New York—you could not fight the powerful forces for spending that were destroying the city. We understood quite well, of course, that if these politicians actually moved to cut out the parasitical incrustations which were strangling the city, they would be at war with their own electorate. They would not and did not act to solve the problem. And so long as they kept demanding emergency stopgaps from the federal government while postponing responsible fiscal reform, I could not and would not recommend assistance.

The truth was that there was no way that rational reform could be instituted without some type of default or bankruptcy proceedings so that the unpayable debt could be extended in time. This was well understood by the top financial and legal advisers of Mayor Beame. But Beame and other New York politicians would not tolerate so public a confession of their failure. I learned early that political facesaving was more important to them than the life of the city itself. In fact, that lesson was forced upon me in a shocking fashion, as it was on Assistant Secretary of the Treasury Robert Gerard. A brilliant man and valued friend, Gerard ultimately became Treasury's specialist in New York issues, and neither of us will forget our first brush with the gigantic hypocrisy of the New York leadership. On October 18, 1975, one day after New York had almost defaulted, we met in my office with Ira Millstein of Weil, Gotshal and Manges, the counsel for New York City, and Kenneth Axelson, the city's deputy mayor for finance. Both men told us forcefully and clearly that they hoped New York would indeed default. Bankruptcy, they said, would clear the air and would allow an orderly resolution of the city's finances.

This clashed sharply with the statements being made publicly by Mayor Beame, who at the time was asking the New York teachers' union to prop the city up with funds. Millstein and Axelson said they were privately hoping that the teachers' union would refuse to help. I was heartened by their realism, but both Gerard and I wondered when that realism would be made public. Some ten days later, when Millstein testified before the Proxmire committee, we got our answer. He presented a lengthy memo to the committee forecasting a series of horrors if bankruptcy occurred and elaborated on them dramatically in oral testimony. It was probably Millstein's testimony that turned the Proxmire committee against bankruptcy as a tolerable approach to the city's problems. But Millstein, in fact, did not believe a word he was saying. That same nightmarish hypocrisy character-ized almost every aspect of the New York crisis. From beginning to end—or at least to my withdrawal from the scene—it never ceased.

Whether the New York politicians would tolerate it or not, however, I had to examine the likelihood of a default of New York and to estimate its impact on the financial institutions of the country. An analysis was made by economists at both the Treasury and the Federal Reserve Board, who indicated that the impact of such a default might be psychologically explosive but that financially it would be highly contained and short-lived. Our analysts uniformly believed that there was enough underlying value in New York City to assure that all bond- and noteholders could eventually be paid 100 cents on the dollar. The municipal market had already experienced a major default by New York State's Urban Development Corporation and had weathered it well. Fur-thermore, the city's problems had been public knowledge for months, and the market had already reflected the risk by discounting the prices of New York's weaker issues. In one sense the market had grown stronger because of this situa-tion; the value of reliable municipal notes and bonds—such as those of Minneapolis, a well-run city—had risen. Inves-tors had grown more discriminating.

As for the banking system, it was even better able to stand the temporary shock. The New York City holdings of the major New York banks, while large in absolute terms, were *less than 1 percent* of the total assets of those institutions. Sophisticated investors—the largest depositors—were well aware of this fact and were also aware that upon a default, that portion of the banks' holdings would hardly become worthless. There was no realistic basis for fearing large withdrawals or a run on the banks. Furthermore, the Federal Reserve System was designed to handle temporary imbalances in liquidity in our banking structure. Finally, we concluded that the knowledge of New York's own responsibility for any default was so widespread throughout the country—a conclusion incessantly supported by public opinion polls—that there was little risk that it would be misinterpreted as an indication of national collapse.

Given this conviction that the economic impact of a default by New York would be brief and contained—and given the record, across the nation, of other cities whose leaders were meeting fiscal problems head-on and courageously—we reached the conclusion I have already described: that the Treasury should offer no help to New York until and unless a powerful commitment was first made to adopt a responsible fiscal program.

This could scarcely be summarized as a desire to punish New York, to see it suffer or "drop dead." Nonetheless, that is how my position was presented to the public by much of the press. If I stress this, it is not merely because I was hurt by it—I was—but because it was as serious a piece of mischief-making by the press as I have yet experienced. It obliterated the fact that a serious alternative to New York's political irresponsibility existed, it created a useful "villain" on whom to blame New York's self-created disaster, and it prolonged the period of self-pitying rationalization by New York's political leaders, who were only too anxious to see a demand for fiscal responsibility equated with "inhumanity."

Every recommendation I was to make met with the same distortion, whether it was a suggestion that New York charge tuition at its city colleges; that it scrap rent control to return the dying real estate industry to life and augment the tax base; that it replace city employees in a variety of services—above all, in health and sanitation—with private contractors, who would perform the same work at the lower prices; that it briefly boost the sales tax. To all such specific recommendations to cut New York expenses and raise its income, New York politicians and members of the press responded with personal invective: I was either "inhumane" or "Simple Simon." The suggestions themselves were never considered.

It was inevitable, I suppose, that as the election period approached, leading administration officials would attempt to decamp from the battle. One morning at the eight o'clock senior staff meeting in the White House, Donald Rumsfeld informed the assembled group, "There are to be no comments by anyone on New York City, on or off the record, save for Bill Simon." After that meeting William Seidman, one of the President's economic counselors, said tersely, "Bill, they're screwing you." They were indeed. Without, I am sure, the President's knowledge, I had been made the administration's fall guy on the New York issue. If I were successful, the White House would take the credit; if I were to fail, it would not know me.


The second protagonist in the New York drama was that group which above all had devoured and was continuing to devour the bulk of the New York budget: the municipal unions. From beginning to end the unions never acknowledged their own lethal impact on the New York economy.

When informed that cuts in jobs and in pay were inevitable, the municipal unions ran amok. It is only fair to say that Mayor Beame's cuts in the summer of 1975, under the supervision of the Municipal Assistance Corporation (MAC), were deliberately inflammatory. They were calculated for the purpose of "proving" that the city needed state and federal aid. Beame dismissed nearly 5000 policemen and more than 2000 firemen (closing twenty-six firehouses) and fired nearly 3000 of the city's 10,000 sanitation workers. The unions understood that this was an act of political blackmail, but instead of exposing it as such, they exerted counter-blackmail. In June 1975 the firemen's and policemen's unions published a four-page leaflet which they distributed to tourists. Titled "Welcome to Fear City," with a lurid skeleton's head on the cover, the pamphlet advised visitors to New York to stay indoors after 6 P.M., avoid public transportation, and, "until things change, stay away from New York if you possibly can." In July the sanitation workers went on strike illegally. They threatened to turn New York into "Stink City" and shouted from picket lines, "Wait till the rats come!"

Inevitably this blackmail was successful, 44 percent of the dismissed policemen and 35 percent of the firemen were rehired, and eighteen of the closed firehouses were reopened. That merely served to confirm the city unions' belief that a display of muscle was their best response to the fiscal crisis.

By August—six months after the markets had closed to New York City—the unions were engaged in yet another round of wage negotiations as if nothing whatever had changed. City officials and members of the Municipal Assistance Corporation—set up by the state to sequester city sales and transfer taxes as a guaranteed cover for MAC's own securities—had become frightened because even MAC bonds were not selling well in the market. They resolved to seek a wage freeze. They challenged the union officials and pointed out that city employees had received a 129 percent salary increase between 1961 and 1973, compared to an 85.2 percent increase in the private sector. The unions would not tolerate a wage freeze, but they did assent to a patched-up compromise in which they simultaneously acknowledged and denied the crisis. The compromise consisted of a *deferral* of the 5 to 6 percent pay raise that had taken effect the month before—to be postponed until the end of fiscal 1978 and paid only if the city's budget was balanced and if the city's bonds were being bought by the market. According to this agreement, higher-paid workers would defer a greater percentage of their wage increases than would lower-paid workers. But in every other respect the unions insisted that the city function as if no crisis existed: Any worker who wished to retire was to be given his pension based on the increased wages, and future contracts would be negotiated *as if* the 1975 increase had taken place. In other words, the city unions insisted on perceiving New York's financial collapse as a temporary inconvenience for which they would incur no permanent loss.

Above all, New York's unions clung tenaciously to the concept that the banks were responsible for these developments that so outraged them, as if the banks had been responsible for their own devouring of the city's budget. Victor Gotbaum, head of the largest public employee union, launched a boycott by public employees of Walter Wriston's Citibank. But Gotbaum's ultimate demon was William Simon, Secretary of the Treasury, an unabashed defender of capitalism. On one occasion Gotbaum pleaded before Congress in tones reminiscent of Little Eva, "Don't put us in the hands of Simon." On another occasion, he was on TV, snarling, "You can tell Simon, 'Up yours!'" That was the Columbia University-educated labor leader's answer to the Treasury's detailed constitutional and economic analysis of New York's predicament. Such a response was, of course, inevitable. So long as the city unions refused to acknowledge their own role in the devastation of New York City, they had necessarily to invoke a devil theory. And I was the devil.

The banks were the third important principal in the New York crisis, and—with rare exceptions—their cowardice in this situation was calamitous. These gentlemen were frightened out of their wits—but only in part because they were afraid of losing money. The amount of New York paper that they held was large—about $2 billion in total. David Rockefeller's Chase Manhattan Bank was worst off, holding about $400 million in city and MAC bonds by the end of 1975, and Walter Wriston's Citibank had about $340 million worth;

others had somewhat less. But, as I said earlier, these amounts constituted less than 1 percent of the New York banks' wealth; they were not in any serious danger. Nor were the banks in the rest of the country imperiled. A Federal Reserve Board survey ascertained that of the 4700 national banks, only 6 might be jeopardized if New York defaulted. Furthermore, Arthur Burns, chairman of the Federal Reserve Board; George Mitchell, vice-chairman; James Smith, Comptroller of the Currency; and Frank Wille, chairman of the Federal Deposit Insurance Corporation, all testified before Congress that a default by New York City was controllable within the national economic system. And most of the bankers with whom I dealt privately understood this to be the case. Indeed, in November 1975, Walter Wriston, whom I had long regarded not only as a superb banker but, also more important, as a financial statesman, defied the politicians and unions by publicly describing the administration's position as "highly responsible," declaring that "the effects of default are containable" and would have "minimal" impact on major New York banks.

The banks were not really afraid of going broke. As much as anything, the bankers' fear was *moral.* As is so often the case in our society, when the liberals orchestrate a nation-wide uproar over good versus evil, all those defined as evil suffer an acute loss of nerve. Businessmen and bankers, who seem to value respectability more than their lives, are incapable of tolerating this moral abuse. Invariably they collapse psychologically. And whatever they may think and say in private, in public they either go mute or stumble frantically over their own feet as they rush to join the moral bandwagon.

That is exactly what many bankers did during the New York crisis. They were objectively the *victims* of New York's curious bookkeeping, they had been lied to and deceived by the politicians, and they had been left holding a ton of paper which the city knew it could not honor. But instead of standing up publicly to the politicians and de-manding that New York set its house in order, they thought it safer, from a public relations standpoint, to echo the liberal line.

Even lifelong friends of mine capitulated in this fashion. The policy committees of two major Wall Street firms—men I had known for many years—refused to permit Robert Swinarton, vice-chairman of Dean Witter, and William Grant, president of Smith Barney, to support me publicly, although both did privately.

Thus, I found myself confronting a great many gutless financiers who assured me in private how deeply they appreciated my one-man battle. I can still hear their words of encouragement, the words never heard by the public: "God damn it, Bill, you're on the right track. . . . Hang in there. Don't give them a thing. . . . Make sure they do what has to be done, or the city will go right down the drain." But when I approached these gentlemen to go to Washington and testify in support of my position, they'd invariably answer, "Well . . . let me call you back." They would hold nervous meetings with their executive committees and conclude that it was wiser to "keep a low profile." It was one of the saddest days of my life when financial giants like Pat Patterson of Morgan Guaranty and Walter Wriston, who had been steadfast for so long, caved in and finally joined the others in asking Washington for federal aid.

In the entire United States very few men from the financial community were willing to support their private convictions with public Congressional testimony. I will always appreciate the courage of those who did come to Washington to testify in my behalf: Frank Spinner, senior vice-president of the First National Bank in St. Louis; Robert Abboud, chairman of the First National Bank of Chicago; William Solari, vice-president of Donaldson, Lufkin & Jenrette in New York; and Francis Schanck, senior partner of Bacon Whipple, past president of the Investment Bankers Association of America, and first chairman of the governing council of the Securities Industry Association.

There was yet a third group—those financiers who were not even aware of courage as an issue and whose fiscal understanding stretched to the ends of their noses. I was stunned when as Secretary of the Treasury I attended a dinner of the Securities Industry Association in Washington, D.C., and heard Richard Adams, vice-president of Chemical Bank, say, "Things would be all right in New York if you at Treasury would stop being so cavalier." Here were allegedly solid financiers so swept up by the propagandists that they had become hostile to those who demanded a real solution. Another instance of this sheer fiscal illiteracy was reported to me by Under Secretary of the Treasury Edwin Yeo. He went out of town to address a Securities Industry affair, and there was Brenton Harries, president of Standard and Poors, who shouted at him from across a crowded swimming pool, "Tell Simon to go back to New Jersey and run for governor! He'll do less damage there." These were people who literally didn't understand the New York fiscal catastrophe well enough to be hypocrites.

If most of the financial world did not publicly support me, what then did the banks hold as a public position? Some offered a more stylized equivalent of the unions' threats. They didn't threaten to create a "Stink City" and warn of the coming of millions of rats; instead, they raised the specter of a nationwide financial collapse. Felix Rohatyn, general partner of Lazard Freres, chairman of MAC, and unofficial spokesman for New York's financial community, testified to the Senate: "I have given it as my professional judgment that the impact of a city default would inevitably lead to a default of major state agencies and a possible default of New York State itself. I believe that the impact of such a series of defaults is not containable without major cost to the economy and to our international position. . . . A default of mammoth proportions involving city and state . . . would be an inexcusable tragedy." In effect, Felix Rohatyn—who long ago earned the nickname Felix-the-Fixer—was threatening us not with "Stink City" but with "Stink Country." The psychology was identical.

It was obvious to many members of Congress that this was

blackmail. During the hearings in October 1975 of the Senate Banking Committee, Massachusetts Senator Edward Brooke asked me, "Do you think we are being subjected to a sort of scare tactic, that the country is being alarmed, that if New York City goes into default, other cities are going to follow suit?" I answered the substance of the question, explaining in great detail why no domino effect was likely, and Utah Senator Jake Garn interjected the answer to Brooke's question about motives: "I do think we are seeing a propaganda battle that overstates the effect on the rest of this nation. Madison Avenue, or whoever is doing it, is doing a fantastic job of convincing the whole country that we are going to go down the river if New York defaults on its bonds. I think it is being greatly overplayed to put pressure on the Congress to come up with some kind of bailout program."

If the threat of a national collapse was not sufficiently frightening, many of the same people spawned an even more horrifying domino theory. If New York defaulted, they said, all financial systems in the entire world would collapse! Rohatyn announced somberly that a New York default would be perceived internationally as evidence of "the failure of capitalism." George Ball topped him by insisting that a New York default would constitute "a victory for world communism." And David Rockefeller, whose bank held the most New York paper, rushed about frantically warning financial leaders all over the world that the entire international financial system would disintegrate if New York defaulted. This was not just blackmail; it was a bizarre kind of word game. If by "default" we mean an inability to pay debts and a postponement of payments—and that *is* what a default means, even if it is called by the gentler word "moratorium"—New York was already preparing to default. Indeed, Rohatyn himself was calling for the stretching out of debt payments at the very time that the scream was going out threatening an international financial collapse if that were to occur! The horrifying scenario of international financial collapse did not materialize, of course. The world market was aware that New York could not pay its debts, and it did not fall to pieces. But facts were as irrelevant to the hysterical financial community as they were to the municipal unions.

Even some foreign leaders were roped in by the hysteria. Helmut Schmidt, the brilliant and able Chancellor of West Germany, stepped off a plane in New York one day and repeated the hideous prediction of international financial collapse at a televised press conference. I saw him on TV and said, "My God, David Rockefeller's gotten to him." But Schmidt was not completely deluded. He came to Washington to attend a White House luncheon and at one point leaned over and asked me in a low voice, "What do you think of David Rockefeller?" I told him exactly what I thought about David Rockefeller: that he had a compulsion to predict international collapse, that he had also done so at the time of the OPEC embargo, and that I thought him misguided. Schmidt listened attentively, went home, and conferred with his own financial people. One month later Hans Apel, Finance Minister of West Germany, apologized to me. He said, "Bill, we were horrified that the Chancellor could have made such a statement. We're terribly sorry." And subsequently, at the Puerto Rican economic summit, Schmidt himself apologized directly to President Ford.

France proved resistant to the propaganda. On one trip to Paris, I was met by Finance Minister Jean-Pierre Fourcade, who said to me with a twinkle in his eye, "What's this I hear about all of us collapsing if New York defaults? I wish you would explain it to me." I replied, "I wish someone would explain it to *me.*" At which point we both burst into laughter. It may not seem like a subject for laughter to a layman, but to Finance Ministers who had long known that New York could not pay its debts and that this bankrupt city had not particularly affected world markets, it was a kind of financial black humor. I hasten to add that no Finance Minister chuckles over the financial collapse of Great Britain, nor do any chuckle over the self-destructive economic policies of the United States. The Western capitalist nations are, indeed, living at the foot of a financial volcano. But to those who understand its dimensions and its causes, the New York crisis was just a boulder rolling down the side of the mountain. It was the potential disaster in microcosm; it was not the disaster itself.

And so much for the Treasury, the unions, and the banks. It is only when one understands those three powerful pressure points that one can begin to talk about the political leadership of New York—city and state. And I use the word "leadership" out of habit because "leadership" was entirely missing.

Mayor Beame functioned more like a distraught ping-pong ball than a political leader, bouncing back and forth among the three groups that he was unable to reconcile. After a prologue of monotonously blaming the bankers, he settled down to a permanent whine that New York was being punished for its generosity to the "poor." As *Time* magazine put it on August 11, 1975: "In the time-honored fashion of New York politicians, [Beame] had put off dealing with the crisis in the vain hope that it would somehow go away. At first he tried to blame the banks, as if they were to blame for incurring the city's debt. When that failed, he made a loud plea for more state and federal aid, when those governments were also hard pressed for funds." *New York* magazine, which did the most penetrating coverage of the crisis, repeatedly portrayed Beame either as a man who could not comprehend the situation or as an unreliable schemer, or as both. In August 1975 Steven Brill reported on Beame's status among "New York's businessmen, bankers, labor leaders and politicians": "All involved agree that Beame has never understood the reality of the city's problem." And Michael Kramer described Beame's pretense at budget cutting as "lies" and a "sham."

The only action that Beame took with any form of conviction was his one brand of political blackmail that I have already described: cutting and threatening to cut the most crucial necessities for survival in New York City— police, firemen, sanitation—to "prove" that fundamental reform would destroy the city. He was pushed to enact other serious cuts by MAC against immense internal resistance, railing against each cut as a personal "humiliation" and continuously devising maneuvers to make it appear that he was undertaking reforms when he was not. One aide to Beame said to the press, "Beame has spent his life finding gimmicks to get the city out of a budget crisis. He thought he could do it this time, too." To the bitter end, Beame never grasped that tricks of accounting had ceased to work, that "subjective" bookkeeping had finally collided with objective reality.

As for New York State Governor Hugh Carey, he also ping-ponged from position to position. His initial impulse, too, was to demand a federal bailout of the city and, when refused, to resort to political blackmail. When President Ford condemned the "folly" of the city's fiscal practices and declined to guarantee New York's debts, Carey charged the President with "kicking New York in the groin" and called for a mass demonstration of protest. Thousands of people responded, including the usual delegation of Hollywood movie stars who are eternally on tap for such occasions. In addition, the governor made some hefty threats of his own, declaring that riots and arson would occur if the Ford government did not bail out the city, and he cried out theatrically, "Federal funds or federal troops!" But neither the gubernatorial rabble-rousing nor the threats of violence achieved anything, so Carey settled down to devising a more sophisticated maneuver. He backed New York City with state funds until New York State itself was in fiscal danger, assuming that this would force a federal bailout. It didn't. Only then did Carey work closely with us—behind the scenes—to come up with a responsible solution.

Publicly, however, Carey had no desire to forfeit his political future as a liberal Democrat by flying in the face of

New York's liberal mythology of compassion. In October 1974, ten full months after New York's collapse, Governor Carey, while agreeing tactfully that New York's fiscal management had been inadequate, was still transmitting the ritual message that the city was dying of its welfare burden. Addressing himself to Senator Tower of Texas, he said:

> I know you well recognize that New York City got into some of its activities and actions for help to the poor, community action programs, because I was convinced by a great Texan this was a right thing to do for the cities of our country. Lyndon Johnson told us to do these things, and we did. . . .. We need a way to face some of these, as you say. We would like to see less of the money committed to welfare, which costs $1 billion of city funds for one million people in New York City. We can no longer afford that. We need time to work out from under these burdens. . . .

It never occurred to the governor to testify that if New York City threw its subsidized portion of the middle class off the gravy train, it would scarcely notice its subsidy to the poor. But that was too much to ask of a liberal governor.

There was, finally, the forum in which this drama played itself out: Congress. For the most part, Congressmen were not eager to bail out New York. The responsible men were as aware as I of the constitutional pitfalls of such a bailout, and the less responsible discovered that their constituencies would not tolerate it. They were willing, as I was, to assist New York if a mode of assistance could be discovered which would not set a destructive precedent for other cities and if New York City showed authentic signs of self-correction. Within this shared context, however, the liberal leadership—Senators Hubert Humphrey, Abraham Ribicoff, Henry Jackson, *et al.*—differentiated itself by a ritual keening over New York's crucifixion on behalf of the "poor" and by ritual denunciations of those of us in the administration who named the problem in other, more realistic terms.

Above all, the liberal Congressmen enjoyed denouncing me as "flinty," "callous," and "inhumane." The degree to which much of this was sheer rhetoric was startling even to me. The outstanding example of this playacting at moral outrage was Hubert Humphrey. Privately Hubert and I were good friends, and he knew quite well that I was no more "inhumane" than he. He got a prankish pleasure, however, out of denouncing me publicly during the New York crisis. On one occasion, when I was testifying before the Joint Economic Committee on the possible financial impact of default, Hubert put on a remarkable show. As the cameras rolled, he peered down at me grimly and ranted away about my "inhumanity"—and then, as the cameras swung away from him to capture my reaction, Hubert *winked*!

Another time, after denouncing me again in rolling rhetoric, he rose, magnificent in his wrath, and, arms waving, glasses sliding down to the tip of his nose, thundered, "Yes—and Arthur Burns will say, 'Part the waters!' and he will rescue all the Big Banks. And eight million little people will go down the drain." When the TV cameras were gone and the hearing was over, Hubert placed his arm heavily about my shoulders and said, "Bill, that came from my heart." I answered dryly, "It certainly didn't come from your head." And Hubert chuckled appreciatively. Politics required that he portray me as a monster, and he assumed that I would understand. Unfortunately I did. Hubert is a warm-hearted man who, like most liberals, is virtually illiterate in economics. He introduced me, a few months later, to a group of citizens by saying, "This is Bill Simon, Secretary of the Treasury. He has a little machine that prints money. And I am the fellow who spends it." His joke had an oversized nucleus of truth.

Nonetheless, for all the harrowing cries about my meanness, liberal Congressmen were no more willing than conservative Congressmen to put a federal guarantee behind the spending patterns of New York City which, even by the most softheaded standards, were inexcusable. But the pressure from all sides was enormous. The fear campaign and black-mail from all groups had their effect, and in a political forum, the result was inevitable: A compromise was sought. I discussed the situation at great length with President Ford, and we agreed we could not yield on principle. We could not support any federal guarantee of New York's bonds, and we could not tolerate the foisting of New York's debt on the rest of the nation. The only possible compromise we could accede to was a short-term loan, with the most stringent conditions of repayment.

Thus, in December 1975 Congress enacted and President Ford signed into law legislation authorizing me to make loans of up to $2.3 billion a year through mid-1978 to enable New York to meet its seasonal cash needs. In addition, Congress mandated a one percent override so that the Treasury would actually profit from the arrangement.

On Christmas Day, Assistant Secretary Bob Gerard, who had worked tirelessly throughout the whole New York crisis, met with me and Treasury Counsel Dick Albrecht to draw up the agreement. The loan was protected by an airtight guarantee: The revenues of New York City and New York State were earmarked first and foremost for repayment. There was not the slightest danger that the Treasury would lose one cent. In return for the loan, the city and state were required to make decisions of a type they had heretofore refused to make. In addition to committing themselves to a program of cuts with the goal of balancing the budget by 1978, they were forced to admit finally that they could not repay a substantial number of their noteholders—and to announce a three-year moratorium.

In effect, under another name New York defaulted. And needless to say, the nation did not experience fiscal panic from coast to coast, and the international financial world did not collapse.

Indeed, the market was almost the only institution that noticed that New York had defaulted. The only newspaper story I saw that revealed an understanding of what had

happened was written by Edwin L. Dale, Jr., in the New
York *Times* on December 7, 1976. Under the headline LOCAL
DEBT IN THE WAKE OF "DEFAULT," Dale wrote:

> Although the event has not received as much attention as it
> might have in the fast-moving series of developments affect-
> ing New York City, a city default of sorts had already been
> decreed by the state legislature. . . .
> The [bond]-holders were given the choice of exchanging
> their notes for ten-year bonds of the new Municipal Assis-
> tance Corporation or holding them and collecting interest, but
> not principal, for the time being. . . .
> [S]omething along these lines has been from an early stage a
> part of the New York solution envisaged by Secretary of the
> Treasury William E. Simon. . . . Mr. Simon had thought origi-
> nally of a formal bankruptcy proceeding, under a revised
> federal bankruptcy law as it applies to municipalities. For the
> note-holders, the results would be quite similar. Mr. Simon
> made clear that note-holders would not have priority over
> essential city services, including payrolls, in a bankruptcy
> proceeding . . ., but it has not been widely recognized that the
> initial "sufferers" under his solution would be banks and
> individual holders of the city debt much more than the people
> of New York. . . .
> [I]n both Congress and the Administration there has always
> been a reluctance to "bail out" the creditors of New York, as
> distinct from its citizens, and some kind of debt moratorium
> (default, if you will) was probably indispensable for any
> federal help at all.

This story is of particular interest because it was the first
time I actually saw in print the fact that my driving motive all
along had not been to serve as a PR man for the bondholders.
It was interesting in another respect as well. In it, Dale
examined the constitutional implications of this unilateral
abrogation of its contracts by a state legislature and reported
that a suit had been filed by the Flushing National Bank in
challenge of its constitutionality. This would not have happened if New York's political leaders had been willing to
declare bankruptcy openly and legally as I had recommend-

ed. They were not. So it was done hastily and in a legally questionable manner, which was later to boomerang. Even in defaulting, the city of New York had not been honest.

Most of the press, however, failed entirely to understand that New York had indeed defaulted. *Time* magazine, under the headline LAST-MINUTE BAILOUT OF A CITY ON THE BRINK, wrote:

> To wangle the loan, *which was necessary to prevent default,* city and state officials were forced to take drastic actions that went against many a past promise. For the most highly taxed city in the country, the state legislature passed a $200 million increase that includes a 25 percent raise in the city income tax. . . . *Also approved was a three-year moratorium on the redemption of $1.6 billion in city short-term debts held by individuals.* [My italics.]

In the communications world where the word so often has priority over reality, the legislature's failure to use the word "default" meant that no "default" had occurred. *Time* did not grasp that in reality a default *was* a "moratorium" on payments.

And *Time* was not alone. The short-term loan granted by the Treasury under these conditions was hailed by politicians and press as a victory for "New York" and a capitulation by the Treasury. Many in the press exulted over my alleged "cave-in." They got the notion, not from the facts but from the facesaving formulations of the New York politicians. Governor Carey pronounced the loan a "vindication of New York's cause."

It is relevant here to stop for a moment to consider the role of the press in the New York crisis. With rare exceptions— the outstanding one being *New York* magazine—the press had simply covered the crisis as though it had been a boxing match between good guys ("New York") and bad guys (Ford, Burns, and Simon). I was constantly shocked by the lack of seriousness, by the lack of concern for fact, and, where I was personally concerned, by many journalists' failure to understand that I was not simply a malignant symbol to be hissed at in ritual hate, but a representative of a serious economic and constitutional position. The press hostility took different forms, of course, ranging from a conscious intent to damage me, through a kind of conventional parroting of liberal formulas of outrage, to sheer ignorance.

The most shocking instance of conscious bias was that of Leonard Silk, a member of the editorial board of the New York *Times.* Before the opening of an NBC *Meet the Press* show on which Silk was a panelist, he said to me, "If you lay off New York, we'll lay off you." This threat was not personal. It was an expression of the same ideological malice that later showed up in Silk's "scholarly" book *The Economists,* where he subjected Milton Friedman to invective and *ad hominem* attacks. Economist Edwin G. Dolan of Dartmouth College said in a review of this book, "Silk sees capitalism as ugly and obscene."[7] In his coverage of me for the New York *Times,* Silk was simply engaged in his usual practice; he was fighting capitalism and calling it journalism.

Far less conscious, but equally virulent in effect, was the kind of "reporting" typified by New York TV reporter Gabe Pressman. On camera he lunged at me with the question "Do you mean to say you're going to let millions of innocent people go down the drain?" I'm sure he thought the question had some meaning, but it didn't. What "innocent" people? What "drain"? Would it have been morally okay to let "guilty" people "go down the drain"? And if so, who were they? I doubt that there was a clear thought in Pressman's head when he uttered this abusive statement. He was merely emitting the metaphoric noise of the liberals but imagined he was discussing economics.

As for sheer ignorance, I found it, incredibly, in the highest executive and management circles of the press, who were totally conned by the ignorance and bias of most of their own reporters' coverage. On one occasion at the height of the controversy I went to dinner at the home of Washington columnist Joseph Alsop. A number of political personalities were there, along with some members of the press, including Sydney Gruson, executive vice-president of the New York *Times.* The subject of my "callousness" to New York immediately came up, and I found myself, along with my wife, in an unpleasantly one-sided debate—about twenty-two to two. I presented the essentials of my position and the facts and reasoning which had led me to it. Then Gruson spoke up. He had scarcely concealed his scorn for me, but something was troubling him. "Why," he demanded, "haven't I seen this explanation any place?" "Because *your* reporters won't print it," I answered. "I've been explaining it for months before Congress and in speeches all over the country. If you don't know my side of the story, ask your own staff for an explanation."

It is not a coincidence that in January 1976 a damning analysis of the *Times'* frequent incomprehension and distortion of New York's financial crisis appeared in the *Columbia Journalism Review.* Nor is it a coincidence that it was written by Martin Mayer, author of *The Bankers.* Mayer himself was one of the few writers in America who understood the situation. He, too, had testified before the Senate Banking Committee, but unlike most other witnesses, he spoke in clear, unevasive English. He identified the union contracts and pensions as the critical source of New York's collapse, he analyzed the frauds and fiscal sleight-of-hand by city and state, he called for a formal declaration of bankruptcy, and although he believed that some federal aid would prove necessary, he implored Congress not to give New York assistance in any form which would allow the New York political Establishment to go on pretending that it could muddle through. His testimony had been strikingly candid:

> . . . When a man tells you he can take $1.8 billion out of debt service and he is still $1 billion short, but you should give him a guarantee, I don't see how you can listen to him.
>
> Nothing, nothing can work that pretends that a history of incompetence and fraud is really a history of social concern and bad luck, or that an insolvency problem is really a cash

flow problem. We have to face the fact—we are bust. . . .
[W]e must rewrite our contracts with those who lent us money
to reduce the interest and stretch out the amortization of our
debt . . . and we must rewrite our contracts with our workers
to eliminate the extravagances of the fringe benefits, especially the pensions. . . . Neither of these rewritings can be accomplished by the voluntary process: What we need is something
that under present law only a judge in bankruptcy can do.

And let me note that a city under Chapter IX, like a business
under Chapter XI, could gain access to the capital market. A
judge could do what MAC tried to do and couldn't, which is
establish a class of prior creditors. . . .

Nothing so simple as a Chapter IX bankruptcy can now be
attempted because the state has made itself the largest credi-
tor of the city, and the state cannot afford any stretching out of
the city's repayments. To put the matter bluntly, Governor
Carey has successfully blackmailed the federal government.
But he has paid a high price for it, calling attention to the
state's own fiscal weakness. . . .

For the city, the first question, it seems to me, must be the
fairest way to share the burden of essentially inescapable
bankruptcy. Right now we have all the disadvantages of
bankruptcy in the loss of self-government, but none of the
benefits from the scaling down of debt or the restudying of the
pension bonanza. I think the cold bath of a bankruptcy
proceeding—the sense that life is being put on a new and
rational footing—might revive the city. . . .

Either give us money or give us the functional equivalent of
a [bankruptcy proceeding], but please don't give us the sort of
federal guarantee program that would let us pretend, briefly,
that we can pay debts far beyond our means.

The clarity of Mayer's understanding was rare, and it
certainly was not shared by most of those who wrote about
New York. Indeed, the press failed in its chief function: to
serve the people as watchdogs of government. Most of the
watchdogs of New York City had never fully understood
what they were watching. They were totally bewildered by
the fraud, misappropriation of funds, deception of investors,
and ultimate bankruptcy—all "necessitated" by liberal ide-

als. They wanted to believe Governor Carey and Mayor Beame, who assured them that I had "caved in" and that New York had scored a "victory." Carey and Beame, of course, knew that it was not a "victory." Beame had been stripped of all his power. He phoned me and asked me pathetically not to bypass him in future negotiations, thus making him look like a political zero. I was sorry for him, I said I wouldn't, and I picked up the papers and continued to read about my "cave-in" and his "victory."

The most impassioned and most influential voices in the New York press, of course, were those left-liberals who were least able to confront the causes of the catastrophe. By 1976 they had retreated into incoherent rage, which, as usual, they interpreted as evidence of their moral superiority. The classic illustration of that state of mind appeared in an essay by columnist Pete Hamill in the *New York Times Book Review* of June 20, 1976. He wrote:

> It is too soon, perhaps, for a cool, rational, detached book about what has happened to New York. Those of us who choose to live here are too choked with rage. Rage at the knowledge that the South Bronx is burning to the ground, and we do not have enough firemen. Rage at the plague of crime and violence, knowing that we have too few policemen. Rage because so many of our schools and hospitals have been permanently awarded to the rats, our parks left strangled on weed and neglect, our libraries reduced to part-time outposts of civilization. Rage at the scabrous conditions of our streets, the potholes and trenches that might never again be filled, the sewers clogged with a winter's dismal refuse. Rage at the businessmen fleeing to their suburban arcadias. Rage at the loss of our local democracy. Rage at Washington. Rage at our own impotence.

Rage, rage, rage—and an almost oceanic self-pity. That was the ultimate liberal response, and it was to dominate the electoral period of 1976. During that period it was morally mandatory for all liberal Democrats running for office to portray New York as a city crucified for its compassion to the poor and to demand the federalization of welfare. The Senatorial campaign in New York City revealed the magnitude of this delusional interpretation of the New York crisis. Democrat Daniel Patrick Moynihan, who knew better, felt compelled to join the liberal chorus. He won the election. Conservative Republican Senator James Buckley, the only major politician in New York who had been immaculately honest with his constituency, was classified as "hostile to New York." He lost the election. The truth was still intolerable to the New York liberal Establishment.

On the Presidential level candidate Jimmy Carter, too, was sucked into the New York hysteria. While campaigning initially as a conservative, he had taken a hard fiscal line on New York, and he had told the New York *Times* that "it would be inappropriate to single out New York City for special favors." He had also stated his opposition to the federalization of welfare. To get the backing of New York politicians, however, he shifted and won Abe Beame's endorsement in exchange for a fuzzy promise to concern himself with New York. By the time Carter arrived at the Democratic convention, he and the Democratic Party were strongly advocating a federal takeover of welfare.

But a Democratic administration did not solve New York's problem. The election over, neither Mr. Moynihan in the Senate nor Jimmy Carter in the White House could permit themselves the act of subsidizing New York's intransigent irresponsibility. And reality kept exacting its toll of the city. Among the postelection clippings gathered from the New York *Times* while this book was being written appeared the following headlines:

NOVEMBER 20, 1976:     NEW YORK CITY DEBT MORATORI-
UM IS UPSET BY STATE'S HIGH
COURT, BUT PAYMENT NOW IS
NOT ORDERED. RULING STUNS
OFFICIALS

DECEMBER 22, 1976:     ROHATYN SAYS NEW YORK CAN'T

|  | RELY ON CREDIT MARKETS IN FULL FOR YEARS |
|---|---|
| JANUARY 6, 1977: | BEAME TO SEEK RISE IN REAL ESTATE TAX AND MORE JOB CUTS |
| JANUARY 21, 1977: | NEW YORK BANKS LINK AID TO CITY TO AN EXTENSION OF LOANS BY U.S. |
| JANUARY 24, 1977: | SENATE COMMITTEE OPPOSING EXTENSION OF NEW YORK'S LOANS |
| FEBRUARY 9, 1977: | NEW YORK IS ORDERED TO BEGIN REPAYMENT OF NOTES IN 30 DAYS |
| FEBRUARY 14, 1977: | FINANCIAL PANEL URGES A DOUBLED NYC TAX ON NONRESIDENTS |
| MARCH 1, 1977: | UNION LEADERS QUIT TALK ON FISCAL CRISIS OVER BANK'S ACTION |
| MARCH 2, 1977: | CARTER BARRING AID TO NEW YORK NOW |
| MARCH 5, 1977: | BANKS ASK NEW BOARD WITH FISCAL CONTROL, BUT BEAME REJECTS IT |

On March 9, 1977, with the pseudo "default" declared unconstitutional and with collapse a few days away, the city was faced by newly intransigent banks and a Carter Treasury which was refusing a bailout on precisely the same grounds as its predecessor. The only distinction, in fact, between the Carter and Ford administrations was that Carter kept exuding affable sounds and vague promises and reaped far kinder headlines—*i.e., New York* magazine, March 14: CARTER TO CITY: "HEAL THYSELF." Mayor Beame once again pulled a fiscal maneuver out of a hat. The city, he declared, could pay a $1 billion debt by selling Mitchell-Lama mortgages, by the city unions' agreement to forgo payment on MAC bonds they already held, and by cash from various sources. Steven R. Weisman, a New York *Times* reporter, put it accurately:

> ... So confusing and complicated was the package produced . . . that Mr. Beame and [City Comptroller Harrison J.] Goldin could not agree how to describe it.
> "Every piece of this represents a credit or a form of borrowing," Mr. Goldin said.
> "The overwhelming amount here is not from borrowing," Mr. Beame said a few minutes later.
> "Something is rotten in Denmark," said Arthur Richenthal, the lawyer who had originally gotten the State Court of Appeals to declare unconstitutional the city's moratorium on its debts.

It was the same old New York routine, but this time the bulk of the anticipated funds would come from the subsidized middle classes. New York now had no recourse except to feed systematically off its own gifts to its politically favored groups. On the basis of this alleged "solution" to the New York problem, the Carter administration approved the short-term loan to New York. It was essentially the same "solution" that had taken place under the Ford administration.

What the headlines will read when this book appears, perhaps a year from the time of writing, I cannot say. But this postelectoral crisis, two full years after New York's first financial collapse, reveals the almost incredible inability of New York's political leaders to face and solve their problems.

Some change had occurred, of course. Possibly only Mayor Beame had learned nothing. He had rushed to the Carter administration, just as he had rushed to me, demanding that the Treasury guarantee his loans. He had received soothing "hot air" from Carter, to quote Evans and Novak, but no guarantees. The banks had learned something. They were now refusing to lend money at all without hard external rule over New York politicians and criminal sanctions for disobedience—a demand that Beame, as usual, considered "humiliating."

The New York press had also learned something. It now customarily considered the "honesty" of New York's fiscal decisions. And outside the city Americans had profited by the horrifying object lesson. States across the country were scrutinizing the budget practices of their own cities. And a few liberal governors, in particular Jerry Brown of California, Michael Dukakis of Massachusetts, and Ella Grasso of Connecticut, were taking hard looks at state employment rolls and costly welfare programs. Particularly during the electoral period "fiscal responsibility" was a buzzword in all political discourse.

Yet, on the most fundamental philosophical level, little had changed. Very few liberals had yet learned that a government job was not an alternative mode of producing wealth. Liberals were still singing hosannahs to government jobs as "solutions" to unemployment and to ostentatious government programs to rescue the "poor." They still perceived business as an infinitely taxable resource. They still fundamentally believed that the real source of money was the Treasury printing press. Above all, nothing had dented the official liberal position that the whole gigantic mess in New York had been motivated by "compassion."

Before I left Washington, I had an unusual opportunity to see, in at least one case, what lay behind that position. The occasion was a meeting with Congressman Fred Richmond of Brooklyn. In public Richmond is a walking embodiment of liberal "compassion." He had been a vehement defender of New York's "right" to a federal bailout and a vehement critic of my refusal to bestow such a gift on the city. In July 1976, six months after the first short-term loan to New York had been negotiated, Richmond asked to have lunch with Arthur Burns, head of the Federal Reserve Board, and with me, to discuss New York's problems. I was somewhat reluctant to interrupt my regular weekly luncheon appointment with Burns, whom I valued as dear friend, counselor, and a man of exceptional knowledge of monetary and fiscal issues, but Richmond was insistent, so we invited him to join us. A remarkable conversation ensued.

Richmond said, "Bill, you have an opportunity to go into history as the man who saved New York City. You have to tell the city that you're cutting the loan off."

"On what grounds?" I asked. "It's a tough credit agreement, and the Treasury will be repaid."

"But that's just a short-range solution," answered Richmond. "They are not solving the long-term problem."

"That's not my mandate," I replied. "The law is very specific."

Richmond insisted, "You've *got* to cut off that loan. Tell them to sue you, but *do* it! It will force them to face their problems."

I stared at Richmond in astonishment. "Look," I said, "I know the problems—rent controls, irresponsible unions, salary agreements that are out of control. I appreciate your anxiety, but I can't do what you're proposing. I'd be setting myself up above Congress, above the law!"

"Bill, you've got to do it," Richmond insisted. "You have it in your power to save the greatest city in the United States."

"You are suggesting," I said, "that I demand now what I was demanding over a year ago: that New York set its own house in order without federal aid. But as I recall, at that time you were yelling for my head."

"I know, I know," he said, "and I realize it would happen again. Bella Abzug and people like that would be out for your skin. And so would the press. But you'd have an opportunity to be a leader, to be a statesman! Bill, you've *got* to save New York."

Arthur Burns, who had been quietly listening to all this, finally spoke. "Do you realize what you are asking Bill Simon to do?" he asked Richmond. "You are asking him to

sacrifice himself for the very people who were most antago-
nistic to him and who refused to do what he's been urging
them to do all along."

Richmond looked abashed. But he continued stubbornly.
"I realize that, but here's Bill's opportunity to lead, to go
down in history as the man who saved New York."

I looked at him with what must have been disgust. "I'll tell
you what I'll do," Richmond said quickly. "I am very close
to Mike O'Neill [editor of the New York *Daily News*]. I'll
line him up behind you. I'll round up the responsible
members of the New York Congressional delegation. I'll
make sure you have support."

I finally decided to test Congressman Richmond. "Will *you*
stand up for me?" I asked.

At this the would-be savior of New York City blanched
and recoiled. "Oh, no!" he exclaimed. "I couldn't do that
publicly. I represent a poor constituency. The best I could
manage to do would be to lay off. I couldn't *support* you."

That was the last time I ever heard from Congressman
Richmond. But it was one of my most direct encounters with
the kind of political calculation that lies beneath the mantle
of public "compassion." It is not Richmond's political hypocrisy that I stress here but, rather, his tragic political
impotence. For he, more than many others, was genuinely
terrified by the widespread political resistance to fundamental solutions and by the progressive disaster engulfing New
York. But just like his liberal colleagues, Richmond had
spent years teaching his impoverished constituency that the
source of all economic well-being was the government. They
had come to believe it profoundly. To tell them now that the
government had turned into a racket that was using the
"poor" as a cover story would destroy him politically. They
would not believe it. So Richmond did not tell his constituency what he thought. He preferred to stay in power.

This Congressman is not unique. I wish he were. The
painful truth is that he almost perfectly embodies the liberals' political dilemma. Forty years of liberal "compassion"

has created a politics of stealing from productive Peter to pay nonproductive Paul, creating a new class of Americans which lives off our taxes and pretends that its institutionalized middle-class pork barrel is all for the sake of the "poor." But no one in office today dares challenge either the formula or its rationalization, assuming he even understands it. There actually is no *political* solution in a situation where the truth has become politically lethal.

If New York were a discrete political entity, disconnected from America and committing suicide in a unique way, it would be sad but not frightening. But it is frightening, for New York is not disconnected from America. It is America's premier city and its intellectual headquarters. It is America in microcosm—America in its most culturally concentrated form. The philosophy, the illusions, the pretensions, and the rationalizations which guide New York City are those which guide the entire country. What is happening to New York, therefore, is overwhelmingly important to all Americans, and it is imperative that they understand it. If they do not repudiate the ideas that justify this system of government, if they continue to be Mau-Maued by a small political and communications elite with "moral elephantiasis," then New York's present must inevitably become America's future.

# VI

## U.S.A.: The Macrocosm

> I have no respect for the passion for equali-
> ty, which seems to me merely idealizing
> envy.
>
> —OLIVER WENDELL HOLMES, JR.

Most Americans believe that "dictatorship" means the
arrival on the political scene of a little man with a mustache,
wearing a khaki suit, shouting Marxist slogans or "Sieg Heil"
and slaughtering ethnic minorities in the name of the "proletariat" or the "race." This is extremely convenient for those
clean-shaven gentlemen in business suits who haven't the
faintest intention of slaughtering ethnic minorities and who
are seeking dictatorial powers over the American people in
the name of the "public interest." It has enabled them to lay
the groundwork for an economic dictatorship which is
expanding geometrically year after year.

The essence of dictatorship, if one understands that
concept in principle, means that the state is using its police

powers not to protect individual liberty, but to violate it. The principle is well understood by some people in some situations. For years America has resounded with the anger of those who have discovered that some of our Presidents and police institutions, such as the FBI and the CIA, have unlawfully violated the liberty of political dissenters. This indignation, while justified, is strangely selective. For while an uproar has been stirred by a few scattered incidents, there has been almost total silence about the entrenched bureaucratic dictatorship that is directly affecting millions and indirectly damaging the lives and well-being of literally everyone in the country. The direct victims are the producers of America.

In an earlier chapter I detailed the way in which arbitrary and irrational edicts by Congress and fifty-five agencies of the state had paralyzed and partially destroyed our energy industries, leading to shortages, crisis, danger to the welfare of the citizens and to the security of the nation, and ultimately yet more arbitrary and irrational state control. That was a single, elaborate case history, so to speak, of the bureaucratic dictatorship in action. But the same kind of arbitrary rule is hitting every aspect of our economy, with comparably destructive results, both in liberty and in economic well-being. The producers of America, ranging from the littlest farmer or proprietor of a mom-and-pop store to the great industrial giants, are living under an unceasing barrage of violations of their liberty, of edicts that prevent them from engaging in the simplest and most reasonable activities, of absurd, unintelligible, and self-contradictory acts of coercion. The best way to get a sense of the breadth and detail of this problem is by giving you another group of case histories, enough of them so that you cannot mistake what is happening for an occasional, even laughable aberration.

—Truckers traveling along the main cross-country interstate routes between Cleveland, Ohio, and Jacksonville,

Florida, must ride with their trailers empty even though shippers at both ends of the line are eager to give them profitable cargo. Why? Because the Interstate Commerce Commission permits the truckers to haul freight only one way. They must make the 1000-mile return trip empty.

—A bus company with an excellent safety record—Greyhound—was hauled into federal court by the Labor Department, claiming that the age qualifications for the drivers of its giant buses were discriminatory and that the company should hire people to drive no matter how old. The company was next assaulted by the Equal Employment Opportunity Commission (EEOC) on its height requirement for drivers—its safety people having set the minimum height at five feet seven inches—and along with this came a government demand that Greyhound pay about $19 million in back pay to unspecified, unknown short individuals.

—A responsible meat-packing plant—Armour—was ordered by the Federal Meat Inspection Service to create an aperture in a sausage conveyor line so that inspectors could take out samples to test. The company created the aperture. Along came another federal agency, the Occupational Safety and Health Administration (OSHA), and demanded that the aperture be closed as a safety hazard. Each federal agency threatened to shut down the plant if it did not comply instantly with its order.

—Marlin Toy Products of Horicon, Wisconsin, used to provide jobs for 85 of the town's 1400 residents. Then, in 1972, the Food and Drug Administration banned the firm's two main products, plastic rattles containing pellets, because children might swallow the pellets if the rattle cracked. The company recalled the toys and redesigned its whole product line to eliminate pellets. But the firm's name erroneously was not taken off the banned list. Although the error was called to the attention of the newly formed Consumer Product Safety Commission, the agency insisted it could not recall 250,000 lists "just to take one or two toys off." Marlin missed the Christmas season and went broke.

—The Continental Can Corporation, at a cost of $100,000 a year, safeguards its employees from noise by providing ear protectors and insisting that they be used. The OSHA acknowledges that the protectors reduce the noise level well below federal standards. Nevertheless, the OSHA demanded in 1973 that Continental Can build sound shields around thousands of machines at a cost of $33.5 million—on the ground that some workers might be too "ignorant or obstinate" to wear the ear protectors. In effect, Continental Can was ordered to create a $33.5 million insurance policy to protect a few hypothetically irresponsible workers.

—Two different federal agencies have assumed jurisdiction over the nation's toilets. First, the OSHA ruled that employers must provide special lounge facilities as part of their women's rest rooms. Then the businessmen found themselves in violation of an Equal Employment Opportunity Commission ruling that if special lounges are provided for women, they must also be provided for men.

—Construction companies working on a new dam on the Little Tennessee River were ordered to stop their work because, according to the Environmental Protection Agency, the dam would endanger the snail darter, a three-inch fish said to exist only in a seventeen-mile section of the river. The dam was 90 percent completed. Nobody had ever heard of the snail darter until 1973.

—Pharmaceutical firms are prevented from manufacturing drugs of immense value because of the FDA's extraordinary delays in approving new medicines. Although it is invaluable to epileptics, valproic acid—an anticonvulsant used in millions of doses in Europe without adverse side effects—is still not available here. Nor are more than twenty new drugs called beta blockers, which were developed in Britain more than a dozen years ago and could provide great assistance to millions of Americans suffering from heart disease.

—Manufacturers of children's sleepwear were forced by the government to process children's sleepwear with a flame-retardant chemical. When the companies shifted over to the costly new process, the FDA banned the flame-retardant chemical as a suspected carcinogen, and the manufacturers were ordered to recall their merchandise and to compensate buyers.

—All automobile manufacturers have been required by the EPA to add catalytic converters to automobiles for the purpose of controlling air pollution. After forcing this costly investment on the producer, the EPA discovered that the device itself adds to air pollution by releasing platinum and sulfuric mist into the air.

—The Labor Department took a food-service firm to federal court in New Mexico, charging that it wrongfully interpreted the overtime and coverage provisions of the Fair Labor Standards Act. The department lost this case, yet it continued to sue other companies on the same grounds, losing in seven federal district courts and two appellate courts. It costs a federal agency nothing to lose a case in court. It cost food-service companies nearly $100,000 in legal fees to "win."

—The Southern Railway Company developed a new vehicle—the Big John Car—to haul grain at rates up to one-third cheaper than conventional boxcars. The Interstate Commerce Commission banned the innovation and refused Southern permission to slash rates on the ground that it would be unfair to other railroads and to truckers. Only after spending four years and millions of dollars in legal costs was Southern finally given the go-ahead to cut costs.

—Three thousand companies have canceled pension plans for their employees after receiving the complex regulations of the Employee Retirement Income Security Act (ERISA). The requirements were so costly that the only alternative was to scrap the pension plans. Before ERISA's rulings were handed down, 5000 companies a month were requesting IRS approval of pension plans. After ERISA's edicts, the number decreased to fewer than 2000 a month.

I have compiled these case histories to give you some sense of what is happening to the productive institutions of

America. And even these examples do not really communicate what is happening because there is no way for the human mind to encompass the full reality. No one alive even knows how many federal regulations over business there are. To list all the rulings and regulations established in 1976 alone—just one year—required 57,027 pages of fine print in the *Federal Register.* As I already mentioned, ICC rulings—applicable only to the regulation of interstate transportation—number in the *trillions.* The evidence clearly indicates that the regulatory process has run amok, reaching far beyond legitimate concern over such values as health, safety, and protection of the environment. Most existing regulation is so irrational that it should be wiped out by law, along with the bureaucracies that have spawned it. This is a *disease* of government; it is not government.

The costs to American industry of this incredible torrent of governmental edicts and rulings are so immense and of so many kinds that they defy the imagination. Yet apart from the financial losses of billions of dollars, the sheer paperwork forced on these companies by Congress and the executive is draining a fortune out of the economy. According to the Commission on Federal Paperwork, government agencies print about 10 billion sheets of paper a year to be completed by U.S. businesses. Each year the government spends at least $15 billion to process paperwork.

That is scandalous enough. But the economic impact on small business is frightful. Collectively America's small businessmen are forced to spend from $15 to $20 billion simply in completing government paperwork. Businesses with fifty employees or less are required to complete seventy-five to eighty types of forms. A typical small business with a gross income of less than $30,000 is required to file fifty-three forms.

The figures become astronomical when the companies are large. General Motors must detail 22,300 employees to federal paperwork; the "affirmative action" files alone make a stack about twice as high as their New York headquarters.

The total cost of government regulation to GM was $1.3 billion in one recent year—a figure that does not include the cost of the hardware on GM products or the taxes paid by the company. The Standard Oil Company of Indiana reports that it takes 636 miles of computer tape to store data for the Federal Energy Administration alone.

When Eli Lilly & Company asked the Food and Drug Administration recently to approve a new drug for arthritis, the application ran to 120,000 pages, many in duplicate and triplicate, and two small trucks were required to transport the load to Washington. Indeed, Lilly officials are forced to spend more man-hours on federal paperwork than to research new drugs for cancer and heart disease. What's more, the $15 million that Lilly spends on government paperwork adds about 50 cents to the price of every Lilly prescription.

Clearly this is economic insanity, as well as outright victimization for its own sake. President Ford, horrified by this situation, tried to get the bureaucracy to chop the paperwork by 10 percent. I sympathized with that modest proposal and imposed it at Treasury despite the squawks of the bureaucrats, but I thought it inadequate. Sight unseen, I would cut the paperwork by 50 percent to free our productive system from this proliferating economic cancer. It is not a necessity of reasonable government; it is the expression of the petty power lust of government clerks, who are engaged in bureaucratic empire building.

Yet other severe damages to the economy of a long-range type are caused by this steady regulatory bombardment. As billions in capital and manpower are allocated to the task of obeying bureaucratic orders, there is an inevitable decline in productivity and in technological innovation. The *Wall Street Journal* in 1976 did a survey and reported on the slowdown in innovation in the chemical and drug industries caused by the serious cost increases and time delays from government regulation. The Stauffer Chemical Company said that 10 percent of its research budget is now eaten up by government regulations—compared to 3 percent in 1970. Dow

Chemical reported that before the arrival of the Environmental Protection Agency, it cost $2 million and took three years to create a new product; today, under the lash of federal "standards," it costs $10 million and takes seven years. The American Pharmaceutical Association disclosed that it now takes eight to ten years and $20 million to get a new drug cleared by the FDA and into the market. Evidence is strong that virtually all key industries—not just energy industries—are running down. The regulatory agencies are functioning as a "stop growth" force. Allegedly protectors of life, they are heralds of slow death.

In Chapter IV I noted briefly that government regulation was a major contributor to the inflationary crisis and the recession of the mid-1970s but that precise costs were impossible to calculate. All this should tell you why. Above all, what cannot be calculated are the wealth and number of jobs that would have been created had this regulatory assault not taken place and had these immense fortunes in capital been invested in production. What we know with certainty is that the regulatory process—acutely stepped up since the sixties—has had a devastating impact on investment, price stability, innovation, productivity, and economic development.

The incredible irony is that all this, allegedly executed in the interest of the consumer, has ultimately come out of the consumer's pocket. The American citizen, who is bewildered by soaring prices, the loss of pension plans, a lack of jobs, is paying for this regulatory orgy with his blood and bone. If business does not include these monstrous new expenses in its prices, it will go bankrupt. This irrational regulation, with its blind indifference to the relationship of costs and benefits, punishes everyone.

It is obvious that no such viciously arbitrary assault on the American productive system could occur were it not backed up by the police powers of the state. And in form, as well as in substance, the regulatory bureaucracy is dictatorial. Hannah Arendt, the renowned student of totalitarianism, tells us that all dictatorships use unintelligible laws as an important weapon to control the citizenry. They paralyze their victims, who are cowed by their own incomprehension, who do not know when they are innocent or guilty or when or why punishment will strike. The rulings of American regulatory agencies are largely unintelligible, and accordingly the American businessman is cowed into submission and a state of permanent fear. He has no way today of knowing what the law is or whether he is in compliance with it. Not only are many of these regulations self-contradictory and mutually contradictory, but they are also written by government lawyers in a horrendous bureaucratic jargon which increases their impenetrability. The agencies themselves cannot understand many of their own rulings.

To cite just one illustration, Chairman Robert D. Moran of the Occupational Safety and Health Review Commission, the independent agency created to hear businessmen's appeals from OSHA rulings, says that "far too many standards are, to paraphrase Winston Churchill, 'riddles wrapped in mysteries inside enigmas.' They don't give the employer even a nebulous suggestion of what he should do to protect his employees from whatever-it-is, also left unexplained, which represents a hazard to their safety and health." Offering one unintelligible standard as an illustration, Moran declared, "I submit that there isn't a person on earth who can be certain he is in full compliance with the requirements of this standard at any particular point in time."[1] Yet businessmen are persistently penalized for their failure to meet such unintelligible standards. This is the unmistakable mark of Big Brother.

And Big Brother is manifesting himself in other, cruder ways as well. For example, pending resolution of a challenge now before the courts, the OSHA can send an inspector into any American's office, plant, or factory without a search warrant. Anyone who notifies the company that the OSHA is going to make a raid, can be fined. This use of OSHA's police powers is precisely as outrageous, and for the same reasons, as any attempt by the FBI, the CIA, or the police to search people's homes or offices without warrants. It differs in only one way: Those Americans—professors, students, and journalists—who normally express vehement indignation over such violations of constitutional rights are singularly silent when the victims are businessmen.

Yet another characteristic of a dictatorial regime is that it is above the law. No checks and balances exist to limit its power. And that, too, characterizes the regulatory bureaucracies. In theory, these agencies are responsible to the executive and/or Congress and subject to review by the courts. In practice, no one has any means of supervising this monstrous collection of regulatory edicts or to check on their applications. Unless an occasional regulation arouses a public furor, as in the case of the ban on saccharin in diet drinks, Congress does not inquire into the day-by-day operations of the agencies.

Indeed, the regulatory agencies tend to operate outside the American legal system. Conventionally described as "extrajudiciary," they are outside the law in more ways than one. They actively violate every basic principle of American justice. These agencies simultaneously function as investigators, detectives, policemen, prosecutors, judges, and juries. They often apply their rulings retroactively. And it is commonplace that they hold businessmen guilty until proved innocent. In all these ways they replicate the operating principles of totalitarian "justice." Unless an American business is immensely rich and can afford to fight the long battle to take its case to a higher court, it has little or no protection from the arbitrary decisions of the regulatory bureaucracies.

Finally, I must add to all this the fact that the United States imposes a higher corporate profits tax than any other nation. Indeed, corporate profits are taxed twice—a unique penalty to which no one else in America is subjected and against which I fought vainly before an indifferent Congress. Our corporate taxation policies punish the competent producer, inhibit capital formation, and restrict industrial growth. Add to this the notoriously foggy antitrust laws which are constantly used by the regulatory bureaucracy of the Justice Department not merely to safeguard competition, but to chop down the most competitively successful companies in the very name of competition! Add further the constant Congressional impulse to extend the powers of the antitrust legislation on purely frivolous grounds. For example, there was the legislation, proposed by Senators Philip Hart and Hugh Scott, which sought to extend antitrust powers to local U.S. attorneys' offices—an unprecedented and dangerous trivializing of those powers. We at Treasury strongly opposed the legislation. One day Senator Scott phoned me and pleaded with me to reverse my position on the ground that Senator Hart had cancer, and it would make a dying man happy. I told Scott that I deeply regretted Senator Hart's suffering but that I could not respond to such logic. Congress did, however, and the bill was enacted into law.

All this gives you a picture of the almost lethal pressure on our producers. They are subjected to more arbitrary regulation than any other Western country. And they are *not* in practice protected by the Constitution. They are almost entirely at the mercy of an economic police state buried in the very heart of the American government.

It is difficult to understand how so shocking and dangerous a situation can prevail without precipitating an explosion of public indignation. I am confident that the American people would demand massive reforms if they understood the situation. But the ugly drama of this destructive regulation is almost invisible to the general public. Thanks to television, the American public is exquisitely informed about the injustices that occur in maximum security prisons, about the psychic suffering of criminals, and the violations of the sensibilities of prostitutes and pornographers, but they are almost totally unaware of injustices to businessmen. The bureaucratic dictatorship and its depredations might as well be invisible. And "invisible" is precisely the word, according to Robert A. Nisbet, Albert Schweitzer Professor of Humanities at Columbia University. In an essay called "The New Despotism," published in 1975, he writes:

> What has in fact happened during the past half century is that the bulk of power in our society, as it affects our intellectual, economic, social and cultural existences, has become largely invisible. And the reason this power is so commonly invisible to the eye is that it lies concealed under the humane purposes that have brought it into existence. . . .
>
> Congresses and legislatures pass laws, executives enforce them and the courts interpret them. These . . . are the visible organs of government to this day, the objects of constant reporting in the media. And I would not question the capacity of each of them to interfere substantially with individual freedom. But of far greater importance in the realm of freedom is that invisible government created in the first instance by legislature and executive but rendered in due time largely autonomous [and] often nearly impervious to the will of elected constitutional bodies. In ways too numerous even to try to list, the invisible government—composed of commissions, bureaus and regulatory agencies of every imaginable kind—enters daily into . . . the minor details of life.[2]

This "New Despotism" of the regulatory bureaucracies, says Nisbet, is actually "hidden" by the noble purposes that animate the regulators. It is widely assumed that only the loftiest idealism could motivate bureaucrats so strenuously dedicated to health, safety, and a clean planet. These purposes are ethically unchallengeable. Indeed, they are formulated in a way that casts those who challenge them as advocates of disease, danger, or filth. And since most people know these regulatory agencies only for their lofty aims, they have been able to wreak incessant havoc in the name of the social good.

More precisely, the havoc is wrought in the name of the public interest. Since the sixties the vast bulk of the regulatory legislation passed by Congress and the hundreds of thousands of elaborations in the forms of regulatory rulings have been largely initiated by a powerful new political lobby that goes by the name of the Public Interest movement. This movement represents neither of the conventional economic divisions of the past—*i.e.*, business or labor. It claims, instead, to speak only for the People and concentrates on the well-being of "consumers," "environment," and "minorities." These terms, too, are chosen so that one cannot with any comfort challenge them. No one, after all, wishes to be perceived as hostile to such worthy entities. But the terms, on close examination, are meaningless: *Every* group in America, including business and labor, is the People; *everyone*, including the biggest producers, is a "consumer"; *everything* that exists, including factories, is the "environment"; and in America's pluralistic society *everyone* is a member of one or another "minority." What, then, are the real purposes of the various public interest groups? One discovers them readily enough if one identifies, not the fictitious entities for which they pretend to speak, but the actual groups which are their targets and which they seek to control through the power of the state. In practice, the target of the "consumer" movement is *business*, the target of the "environmentalists" is *business*, and the target of the "minorities," at least where employment is concerned, is *business*. In sum, the Public Interest movement is a lobby, not for the People, but for expanding police powers of the state over American producers. There have been few more consistently and vehemently anticapitalist groups in the history of America.

What is even more significant about the Public Interest movement, however, is the fact that it is, above all, the political voice of the contemporary urban elite. In a now-historic essay called "Business and the New Class," first published in the *Wall Street Journal* on May 19, 1975, Irving Kristol analyzed this elite for the first time. He called it the "new class":

> This "new class" is not easily defined but may be vaguely described. It consists of a goodly proportion of these college-educated people whose skills and vocations proliferate in a

"post-industrial society." . . . We are talking about scientists, teachers and educational administrators, journalists and others in the communications industries, psychologists, social workers, those lawyers and doctors who make their careers in the expanding public sector, city planners, the staffs of the larger foundations, the upper levels of the government bureaucracy, etc., etc. . . . Members of the "new class" do not "control" the media, they *are* the media—just as they *are* our educational system, our public health and welfare system and much else. . . .

What does this "new class" want, and why should it be so hostile to the business community? Well, one should understand that the members of this class are "idealistic," in the 1960s sense of that term—i.e., they are not much interested in money but are keenly interested in power. Power for what? The power to shape our civilization—a power which, in a capitalist system, is supposed to reside in the free market. This "new class" wants to see much of this power redistributed to government, where they will then have a major say in how it is exercised.

. . . One used to call this group "the intellectuals," and they are the ancestors of our own "new class," very few of whom are intellectuals but all of whom inherit the attitudes toward capitalism that have flourished among intellectuals for more than a century and a half. This attitude may accurately be called "elitist"—though people who are convinced they incarnate "the public interest," as distinct from all the private interests of a free society, are not likely to think of themselves in such a way. It is basically suspicious of, and hostile to, the market, precisely because the market is so vulgarly democratic—one dollar, one vote.

Finally, writes, Kristol, the "new class" is almost stupendously ignorant of business and economics, to the point of being detached from reality:

It is indeed amazing that, in a society in which business plays so crucial a role, so many people come to understand so little about it—and, at the same time, to know so much about it which isn't so.

We have managed to create a generation of young people

which, for all the education lavished on it, knows less about the world of work—even the world of their fathers' work—than any previous generation in American history. They fantasize easily, disregard common observation, appear to be radically deficient in that faculty we call common sense.

Nor, it must be said, are their teachers in a much better condition. The average college professor of history, sociology, literature, political science, sometimes even economics, is just as inclined to prefer fantasy over reality. On every college campus one can hear it said casually by faculty members that the drug companies are busy suppressing cures for cancer or arthritis or whatever, or that multi-national corporations "really" make or unmake American foreign policy; or that "big business" actually welcomes depression because it creates a "reserve army of the unemployed" from which it can recruit more docile workers.

In sum, says Kristol, the "new class" displays two fundamental sets of characteristics: It combines a morbid economic ignorance with a driving power lust, and it combines hostility to democracy with the illusion that it speaks for the People. He warns that if the political ambition of this class is not checked and if it does not acquire the necessary economic education, the dangerous result must be the destruction of freedom: "We shall move toward some version of state capitalism in which the citizen's individual liberty would be rendered ever more insecure." Kristol's "new class" *is* Nisbet's "New Despotism."

There are a great many reasons for the development of an economic tyranny in the United States, and historians will eventually assign the blame. But the fault, at least in part, lies with capitalists themselves. Throughout the last century the attachment of businessmen to free enterprise has weakened dramatically as they discovered they could demand—and receive—short-range advantages from the state. To a tragic degree, coercive regulation has been invited by businessmen who were unwilling to face honest competition in the free market with its great risks and penalties, as well as its rewards, and by businessmen who have run to the government in search of regulatory favors, protective tariffs, and subsidies, as well as those monopolistic powers which only the state can grant. Milton Friedman has pointed out: "The major source of private monopoly has not been private collusion, it has been governmental activity. There is hardly a major monopoly in the United States that doesn't derive its power from government grants."[3] In the process of seeking such advantages—such protection from *freedom*—business itself has helped build up the very government powers which are now being used to damage and even to destroy it.

During my tenure at Treasury I watched with incredulity as businessmen ran to the government in every crisis, whining for handouts or protection from the very competition that has made this system so productive. I saw Texas ranchers, hit by drought, demanding government-guaranteed loans; giant milk cooperatives lobbying for higher price supports; major airlines fighting' deregulation to preserve their monopoly status; giant companies like Lockheed seeking federal assistance to rescue them from sheer inefficiency; bankers, like David Rockefeller, demanding government bailouts to protect them from their ill-conceived investments; network executives, like William Paley of CBS, fighting to preserve regulatory restrictions and to block the emergence of competitive cable and pay TV. And always, such gentlemen proclaimed their devotion to free enterprise and their opposition to the arbitrary intervention into our economic life by the state. Except, of course, for their own case, which was always unique and which was justified by their immense concern for the public interest.

My own response to such businessmen was harsh, and I warned those with whom I discussed these practices that they were indeed, as Lenin had predicted, braiding the rope that would be used to hang them. FDR used to laugh scornfully at the businessmen who came creeping to him, hat in hand, to obtain government favors while they preached about the sanctity of free enterprise. But I am not amused by businessmen of this type. They have supplied powerful ammunition to those who are anxious to demonstrate that the free market and freedom itself are intrinsically flawed.

Businessmen, too, have intensified the despotic regulatory trends by their secretive attempts to fight them—not by means of courageous open battle, but by the pathetically short-range and cowardly attempts to bribe those with political power over their destinies. As economist Murray Weidenbaum has pointed out, much, if not all, of the corruption of the business ethic that has come to light, at home and abroad, is a direct "solution" to the problem of irrational government intervention. Bribes in particular are usually attempts by businessmen to appease the bureaucrats on all levels of the government, federal, state, and local, who wield an extortionist power over trade and production. And many campaign contributions and bribes to politicians are perceived by businessmen as "insurance policies" against this extortionist power. Such actions by business are not just unlawful and unethical—which is sufficient reason not to take them—but also impractical. Revelations of these bribes have reinforced antibusiness attitudes and fed the ideological portrayal of capitalism as a criminal phenomenon. I was appalled by the flood of bribery cases which emerged while I was in office and spoke out strongly against such businessmen. I was not only angered by the lack of ethics, but also horrified by the certainty that such conduct would inevitably bring more punitive and destructive regulation upon our productive system. And it did.

Having said all this, however, I still believe it is obvious that business, seen as a whole, is more sinned against than sinning. This view clashes, of course, with the conventional liberal wisdom that business is "really" controlling the regulatory agencies. It is easy enough to arrive at an objective assessment of where the power "really" lies. Just ask yourself if the dictatorial and destructive situation I have described in the regulatory agencies could possibly exist if business "really" controlled these agencies. Would men who "controlled" them inflict 57,027 pages of new regulations on themselves in one year? Would they inflict costs mounting to the billions on themselves? Would they incessantly ban their own products? Would they drag out for years crucial decisions on which their financial lives depend? Would they devour their investment capital, destroy their own productivity, restrict their innovative capacity? Would they drive themselves into bankruptcy? Obviously not. The balance of power—and the balance of terror—lie on the side of the regulators. *Some* businessmen do indeed extract advantage from the situation, but the victimization of *all* businessmen in America is incessant. And the one crime of businessmen as a group, to which few call attention but which I condemn profoundly, is that business, on the whole, has been gripped by cowardly silence in the face of this consistent violation of its liberty and interests. It is its final, and possibly its worst, betrayal of the free enterprise system.

By far the greatest responsibility, however, lies with the reigning anti-free enterprise philosophy itself, which is now the dominant economic philosophy of our age. Starting in the last century and acquiring its modern style with the New Deal, it has rapidly engulfed a substantial portion of our educated classes. As both Nisbet's "New Despotism" and Kristol's "new class" brilliantly show, egalitarianism is the ruling value system of our urban "elite." And it is no coincidence that egalitarianism and despotism are linked. Historically, they always have been. Hitler and Stalin and Mao all offered their people an egalitarian society, disclosing only when it was too late that some would always be "more equal than others." That remarkable nineteenth-century French observer of American mores Alexis de Tocqueville wrote in *Democracy in America*:

> The foremost, or indeed the sole, condition required in order to succeed in centralizing the supreme power in a democratic community is to love equality or to get men to believe you love it. Thus, the science of despotism, which was once so complex, has been simplified and reduced, as it were, to a single principle.

And that "single principle"—equality—is precisely what the "New Despotism" in America rests on today. But because equality is also a revered concept in the American tradition of liberty, an immense confusion surrounds the issue. It merits a brief discussion.

The equality peddled by egalitarianism is *not* the equality referred to in the American Constitution, although history is being rapidly rewritten to suggest that it is. Our Founding Fathers and the liberal—*i.e.*, procapitalist—philosophers of that era were in full rebellion against an almost-unbroken human history of the divine right of kings and of legal and social tyranny rooted in hereditary privilege. When they declared that "all men are created equal," they meant something profoundly revolutionary at that time; they meant that men were equal before the law, that no legal chains forged by ancestry or caste should bind any individual to a permanent underclass. They meant that men should share an equal opportunity to face the challenges of life, each free to achieve what he could and rise to the level he could by his own wit, effort, and merit. That is the quintessentially American philosophy, the essence of the social revolution the United States brought to the world. Slavery and institutionalized racism clearly violate this principle, but in no sense do they render it less glorious.

The revolutionary effect of such a concept of legal equality created a nation with unprecedented social mobility, as men escaped by millions from the feudal prison of a hereditary class system. And as they escaped, as individuals of different kinds followed their own paths, what emerged was immense diversity and, inevitably, different levels of achievement. Since men are not interchangeable units, since they vary greatly in intelligence, discipline, effort, character, ambition, and ability, these differences in achievement are inevitable, as are the differences in the rewards and penalties they reap in life. It is America's traditional legal equality which allowed men in great number, for the first time in history, to move from "rags to riches." Our Constitution annihilated hereditary aristocracy—and replaced it with a competitive *meritocracy.*

The egalitarians' equality is of a profoundly different kind. It is one that perceives men, ideally, as interchangeable units and seeks to deny the individual differences among them— above all, the crucial differences in character, effort, and ability. The egalitarian seeks a collective equality, not of opportunity, but of *results.* He wishes to wrest the rewards away from those who have earned them and give them to those who have not. The system he seeks to create is the precise opposite of a meritocracy. The more one achieves, the more one is punished; the less one achieves, the more one is rewarded. Egalitarianism is a morbid assault on both ability and justice. Its goal is not to enhance individual achievement; it is to *level* all men.

There is, of course, only one way to level men. One levels them *downward*; mediocrity does not stretch. Since men of achievement will not—and should not—freely consent to being hacked down, in order not to tower above those less able, they must be forced to do so. Accordingly, egalitarians seek to use the police powers of the state to accomplish their goals.

In sum, the equality of the Constitution rests on *liberty*; the equality of egalitarianism rests on *coercion.* That is the fundamental source of the "New Despotism."

Needless to say, this is not the way egalitarians explain themselves to their fellow citizens. If they stated their means and ends frankly, they would be repudiated with disgust. They camouflage those means and ends under the moral concept of "social" justice—justice alone being unsatisfactory for their purposes—and claim a monopoly on "compassion." And to "compassion" virtually all Americans are responsive. It is obvious that not all men prosper in this life, and men who share the Judeo-Christian ethic are always concerned to assist those who experience calamity or disability and are unable, through no fault of their own, to support themselves. Consequently, private and state charitable institutions have always existed in America, and should exist. But charity, a desire to help the helpless and to assist those at a moment of acute need, is *not* egalitarianism. It does not imply or require the coercive leveling of men. One of the most tragic developments in America today is that millions and millions of generous, liberty-loving people are honestly mistaking the coercive leveling of egalitarianism for compassion.

What we are seeing in America today is government dedicated to both halves of the egalitarian leveling process: the chopping down of those who produce wealth and the transfer of that wealth from those who have earned it to those who have not. I have already briefly described the regulatory agencies' assault on the producers. I will now describe the transfer process. It is, of course, our welfare system.

There are a great many things to be said about our welfare system, and a thousand different books are saying them. I wish, here, to make one principal point: that its primary purpose today is a concern *not* to assist the helpless, but to redistribute the wealth. I am not speculating about people's motives here; I am talking about what is actually happening to the taxes that the government takes from the productive citizens of this land.

To see the pattern clearly, one must stand back and look at the welfare system in the full context of government spending. The context, to remind you, is this—and I use 1976 figures:

—The Gross National Product, meaning the wealth created by our productive citizenry: $1,609.5 billion.
—The federal budget, equivalent to 22.8 percent of the GNP: $366.5 billion.
—The national debt (not including the off budget items), to be paid by future taxes on the earnings of the productive: $631.9 billion.

What part of this disastrous explosion of expenditure and debt is actually going to the authentically helpless among us? The group we hear the most about are families with dependent children. It has certainly generated the most protests. In his *The Growth of American Government: A Morphology of the Welfare State*, Roger Freeman describes aid to families with dependent children (AFDC) as "a nightmare and a plague on the body politic." Since 1952, he reports, the number of AFDC recipients has increased more than five times—from 2 million to 11 million—as AFDC has become "a major nutrient in the breeding grounds of . . . social ills."[4] There is reason to agree with Mr. Freeman's assessment. We know that AFDC has been a federal invitation to fathers to abandon their families, in reality or in appearance; the system is clearly corrupt. Yet when one looks at the actual sum of money being given to this group of people, one can scarcely conclude that AFDC is breaking the back of the U.S. budget. The sum it received in 1976—calculated both in cash and in-kind services—was *$8.3 billion.*

The second group that can be legitimately viewed as meriting assistance is the disabled—the blind, crippled, and handicapped of all ages, including veterans who cannot sustain their own lives or do so with extreme difficulty. The sum—in cash and in-kind benefits—paid to this group is significantly higher than that paid to AFDC. In 1976 it was *$25 billion.*

If one takes both the dependent children and the disabled together—the two genuinely helpless groups in the nation—the budget for their support totaled $33 billion. The sum is enormous, but it constitutes less than 10 percent of the national budget. Despite the fraud and the unhealthy dynamics which inflate such programs, it has *not* been the payments to the helpless and disabled that have generated our incredible budget.

Is that calamitous budget due perhaps to defense expenditures? That, of course, is what liberals have been screaming in unison for years. As usual, what liberals scream in unison is not so. The 1976 defense budget was $101 billion, 24 percent of the budget—*down* from 46.9 percent in 1963.

Clearly, it is not the defense budget, with its declining share of the national taxes, that is hurling this nation into bankruptcy.

For what, then, is the remainder of the budget earmarked? A large chunk—$37 billion in 1976—goes for interest on the national debt. But most federal dollars go for "social programs" of one kind or another. And for whom are these programs intended? A very substantial percentage of them—certainly more than half—are benefiting the *middle class.*

This is so shockingly different from what is commonly supposed to be the case that it requires demonstration. It is easy enough to do. All that is needed is a brief inspection of the two relevant categories of federal budgeting: the official welfare programs in the national budget and the off budget items to be guaranteed or financed in the future.

First, the national budget. Sixty percent of the budget is explicitly earmarked for social welfare. In 1976 these expenditures totaled $198.3 billion (with the states and local governments spending another $133 billion). Where did the federal dollars go?

One chunk—$31.2 billion—went to pensions with built-in cost-of-living escalation for federal Civil Service employees, veterans, and retired railroad workers. This sum was only slightly less than the total sum allotted to both AFDC and the disabled. Clearly, this sum was *not* primarily of benefit to the hard-core poor. Specifically, retired railroad workers received benefits worth $3.6 billion; veterans were provided $8.7 billion; and retired federal Civil Service employees of all levels walked off with the largest amount in this category, $18.9 billion. Virtually all this is describable as middle- and even upper-class welfare.

Another chunk of the federal welfare budget went to unemployment compensation—$15.4 billion. This payment is allotted to the able-bodied who are temporarily out of work and is intended to sustain them while they actively seek new jobs. The total was unusually large because of the recession, but that by no means accounted for all of it. Like all gigantic outlays of federal funds, this one has become a magnet to free riders. A study made during the worst part of the recession in 1975 indicated that about half the people who had lost jobs were not looking for work at all but were living on unemployment compensation. In 1976 CBS-TV produced a shocking documentary demonstrating that Florida was full of cheerful middle-class people taking pleasant semitropical vacations on their unemployment checks. Indeed, for years, collecting unemployment has become a way of life for a significant number of people who hold a job just long enough to qualify for payments—collect for the full period—get another job and hold it long enough to qualify—collect, etc., etc. Today whole categories of middle-class citizens— writers, actors, musicians, and students who are "needy" by choice—sustain themselves off and on for years with unemployment payments.[5] Some significant percentage of this federal job insurance policy is now functioning as a permanent subsidy for those who prefer not to work steadily, many of them clearly describable as middle class.

The largest outlay in the "welfare" budget went to Social Security—$81.3 billion in 1976. Originally conceived as a modest assistance plan to supplement individual savings, an earned right, it is now conceived as a state-financed lifelong pension starting at age sixty-five. This program is not, of course, targeted for need. The payments go to all who have contributed to Social Security taxes during their working lives. *Most* of the money, consequently, goes to the middle class, which often has other pension systems as well, and to richer people, who do not need it. The result is that our Social Security system is breaking down under the strain. It is widely believed that our government pays Social Security out of trust funds which are kept intact and collect interest for precisely that purpose. The public has been deluded. In 1970 the trust funds were down to fifteen months' worth of benefits. By spring 1977 there were only eight months of benefits left. At this rate of depletion the trust funds would be exhausted by early 1980. The unfunded liabilities of Social Security add up to more than $4 trillion.

Social Security for the future rests exclusively on the assumed willingness of each generation of workers to provide lifelong pensions of increasing magnitude to the preceding generation. The burden will grow even heavier as the rate of population growth slows and the elderly become a larger and larger proportion of the population. It is already obvious that the present Social Security tax cannot finance lifelong pensions for the entire working population. Today one-half the nation's wage earners are already paying more in Social Security levies than they are in income taxes. Experts like Martin Feldstein of Harvard and R. David Ransom of the University of Chicago warn that the Social Security tax will have to be increased by 50 to 100 percent if those born during the "baby boom" are to receive payments from those born during the "baby slump." It is just a matter of time— according to Ransom, twenty-five to thirty-five years— before the tax burden becomes so onerous that the entire Social Security system collapses.

Social Security is often described as the keystone of our welfare system. It is actually a commitment in perpetuity to assist predominantly middle-class citizens, most of whom could very well assist themselves if taxes and inflation were not destroying their capacity to reap the rewards of savings at commercial interest rates.

And even the immense sums I have already listed do not account for the full $198 billion federal welfare budget. A substantial percentage of it is still unaccounted for— disbursed in hundreds of other health, education, and welfare programs. What are they? Most people have no idea. Just as the regulations that govern business attain a high degree of invisibility because of their number, so do these social programs. Only specialists in the welfare field claim to know what they are and what they do, and even these people disagree; the perceptions vary strikingly from expert to expert. I did not understand these disparities until I obtained my first glance at the organizational charts of the great welfare bureaucracies. To look at them is to know why certainty is impossible. A chart listing federal educational programs is literally indecipherable. Lines—broken and unbroken—of various hues link up little boxes representing various programs. A magnifying glass is necessary to sort out the programs, subprograms, and subsubprograms, which include:

Information Clearing Houses
Guaranteed Student Loan Program
Special Programs for the Disadvantaged
Ethnic Heritage Studies
Cooperative Education
State Student Incentive Grants
Fulbright Hays Fellowships
Language and Area Training
Supplemental Opportunity Grants
College Work Study
Basic Opportunity Grants
Higher Education Facilities Loan Insurance Fund
Mining Fellowships
Ellender Fellowships
Veterans Cost of Instruction
Legal Fellowships
State Post-Secondary Commissions
University Community Services
Aid to Land Grant Colleges
College Teacher Fellowships
Public Service Fellowships

Direct Loans Capital Distribution
Direct Loans to Institutions
Direct Loans: Teacher Cancellations
Deaf Blind Centers
Gifted and Talented
State Grants
Packaging and Field Testing
Dissemination
Planning and Evaluation
Developing Institutions: Basic Program
Developing Institutions: Advanced Programs
Consumer and Homemaking
Curriculum Development
Work Study
Education Professions Development: Elementary and Secondary
Other Education Professions Development
Community Schools
Consumer Education
Metric Education
Adult Education
Grants for the Disadvantaged (Title I—ESEA)

Support and Innovation
Educational Broadcast Facilities
Emergency School Aid: State Apportionment
Emergency School Aid: Civil Rights Advisory
Emergency School Aid: Evaluation
Drug Abuse
Follow Through
Libraries: Consolidation
Environmental Education
Schools in Federally Affected Areas: Maintenance and Operation
Schools in Federally Affected Areas: Construction
Library Training and Demonstration
College Libraries
Media Centers
Recruitment and Information
Regiònal and Adult
Regional Resource Centers
Specific Learning Disabilities Research
Early Childhood Education
Special Education Manpower
Severely Handicapped
Basic State Program
Special Needs
Cooperative Education
Vocational Innovation
State Advisory Councils
Public Libraries
Educational TV Programming
Emergency School Aid: National Priority Projects
Undergraduate Instructional Equipment
Indian Education
Arts in Education
Women's Equity
Career Education
Right to Read National Reading Improvement
Teacher Corps
Bilingual Education

These educational projects, which are proliferating more rapidly than any other category of welfare, exist *in addition* to a nationwide network of government-subsidized public education, public libraries, state universities and community colleges, and an extensive scholarship system. In no sense can these extra programs be construed as essential to the survival of the authentically helpless in our midst. Nor, to judge by the scandalously declining literacy rates and national test scores, are they contributing to a rise in the quality of education.

Numerous other social programs also subsidize the middle class. Health, Education, and Welfare Secretary Caspar W. Weinberger discovered that nearly *half* the families receiving benefits from the food stamp program had incomes "well above the poverty level." A substantial number were college students, who by no stretch of the imagination can be classed as America's neediest. Similarly, many milk and nutrition programs are not targeted to the needy; the beneficiaries are mainly middle-class children. Day-care programs, too, are being widely used across the nation by middle-class, as well as welfare, mothers. Economist Alan Reynolds sums it up: "Even if the requirements were as loose as requiring that half the money go to poor people, it is doubtful that many HEW programs . . . would qualify."[6]

Some of the benefits to the middle classes are indirect. The administrators of the welfare programs themselves siphon off some 10 to 25 percent of the budgets of these programs in salaries and expenses; they are paid, like all Civil Service employees, at levels higher than those in the marketplace and ultimately receive costly federal pensions for their pains. On top of this, these programs have become important vested interests for business, labor, and professional groups. Weinberger observed that when President Ford sought to cut down the middle-class riders on the food stamp program, these vested interests reared up to protect their economic fiefdoms:

> One of the first attacks on the President's proposals came not from many of the so-called poverty groups but from the head of the Amalgamated Meat Cutters Union. This indeed is typical of the support and sponsorship for many of these in-kind programs. For example, the principal supporters of the school milk program, not surprisingly, turns out to be the Associated Milk Producers Inc.; and it turned out that among those who were prominently supporting the ill-advised proposals for health insurance for the unemployed under which the government would pay the premiums of only those unemployed who had been working for employers who had health insurance plans were the American Medical Association, the American Hospital Association and the unions whose welfare funds would have been depleted had they been called upon to pay the health insurance premiums of union members who were unemployed.

In fact, in-kind programs, rather than programs which simply give poor people cash to spend as *they* decide, are nearly always sponsored by special groups who benefit either from the increased sale of the particular product or from having payment of their bills guaranteed by government programs.[7]

So much for the federal welfare budget. There are other programs, but this largely suffices to make my point: Welfare is *not* keyed to the acutely needy among us. To a very serious degree it is subsidizing the "nonneedy," and it should be cut to the bone, along with the bureaucracies that are placing millions of middle-class citizens on the dole.

In a 1976 lecture at Hillsdale College, M. Stanton Evans made a disturbing calculation. He observed that there were by official definition 25 million poor people in the United States. And he also noted that between 1965 and 1975 the total expenditure on social welfare programs increased some $209 billion to a staggering total of $286.5 billion. He said:

> If we take those 25 million poor people and divide them into the $209 billion increase—*not* the whole thing, just the increase—we discover that if we had simply taken that money and given it to the poor people, we could have given each and every one of them a stipend of some $8000 a year, which means an income for a family of four of approximately $32,000. That is, we could have made every poor person in America a relatively rich person. But we didn't. Those poor people are still out there.
>
> What happened to the money? The answer is that some of it did get into hands of the people who are supposed to get it. But a lot of it didn't. I would say the majority of it went to people who are counseling the poor people, working on their problems, examining the difficulties of the inner city, trying to rescue poor families and devise strategies for getting them out of their doldrums. It went to social workers and counsellors and planners and social engineers and urban renewal experts and the assistant administrators to the administrative assistants who work for the federal government.

While it is not exclusively the bureaucrats who are devouring the bulk of the money, Evans is right when he says that it is not the poor. He is also right when he says that, given the enormous expenditures on welfare, the poor by now could theoretically have become relatively rich. But of course, they haven't. They haven't because in a nation politically dominated by egalitarian thought, *leveling*—not liberating the wretched from misery—is the true goal. To a sickening degree, in fact, the "poor"—who are invoked to justify almost all contemporary political actions—are merely a means to an end. Lawrence Chickering, Jr., executive director of the Institute for Contemporary Studies, once put it ironically: "If there were no poor, the liberals would have to invent them."

And they do invent them. They keep the official number of poverty-level citizens artificially high by reporting only on cash income, leaving out such subsidies as medical care, food stamps, and housing. And every year the welfare bureaucrats redefine "poverty" so that it encompasses a yet greater number of people, all of whom are instantly proclaimed to be in a dire state of helplessness and in great need of new and costly "programs." A growing population of dependents—a growing corruption of the population—is now a vested interest of the egalitarian world. The destiny of the "new class" can be realized only by dictating to greater and greater numbers of "helpless" people how they shall live.

America is not a welfare state even in the old New Deal sense of the term. This country today is purely and simply a redistributionist state, endlessly shaking down Peter to pay Paul. Not orphaned Paul, not crippled Paul, not aged Paul, not black Paul, just *Paul*.

We can now stand back and look at the overall pattern built into our government. Here is what we see: (1) We see the arbitrary assaults on business and the slow destruction of our productive system, which is the source of all wealth. (2) We see the redistribution of increasing amounts of wealth to a combined clientele of the acutely needy and a growing portion of the middle class. (3) We see the tax burden growing steadily to finance the redistribution process. (4) We see an abyss of governmental debt piled on debt, much of it hidden from the public by budgetary manipulation. (5) We see a commitment to a vast network of lifelong pensions to government employees and others in the middle-class populace. *We see something eerily similar to the fiscal pattern of New York City.*

When I said earlier that New York's present was America's future, I meant it seriously. There are differences, of course, between a city and a nation. New York cannot print and inflate money to escape, deceptively, from its debts; the federal government can. The producers and nonsubsidized citizens, whose life's blood is being drained, can flee from New York; they cannot flee from the United States. In a certain sense, New York is fortunate. It took only a comparatively few years for the Ponzi game to self-destruct— precisely because people were free to run away. But the national Ponzi game will go on much longer.

On February 5, 1976, as Secretary of the Treasury I told the Senate Committee on the Budget:

> Deficits cumulate over time. Total federal debt has increased from $329.5 billion at the end of fiscal year 1966 to an estimated $633.9 billion at the end of fiscal year 1976—a rise of 92 percent in only ten years' time. Over the past ten years, the average maturity of the debt has declined from five years and three months to two years and five months. What this means is that the U.S. Treasury must be a more frequent visitor in financial markets simply to roll over outstanding securities, let alone to raise funds for current deficits. In this fiscal year (1976) the U.S. Treasury will absorb over 70 percent of all moneys in the securities markets; government at all levels will absorb over 80 percent.

I might as well have been talking about New York City running frantically to the marketplace to borrow as its wealth ebbed away. As this incessantly compounding debt and ravenous devouring of investment capital coincides with a nonstop regulatory assault on our productive system and a nonstop redistributionist assault on our productive classes, the national Ponzi game too must ultimately self-destruct. Our government has not been *warring* on poverty; it has been *creating* poverty by attacking every value and every institution on which the generation of wealth depends. And with this, inevitably, it is corroding our liberty. Unless the lethal pattern is changed—which means, unless the philosophy that shapes this pattern is changed—this nation will be destroyed.

# VII

---

## The Road to Liberty

All that is necessary for evil to triumph is
for good men to do nothing.

—EDMUND BURKE

There is tragically little awareness in the United States
today that a guiding philosophy lies behind the destruction
we are seeing. So far that knowledge is restricted to the
relatively few citizens concerned with political and moral
theory. Indeed, it is commonly denied that "ideology" has
anything to do with American politics at all. There is,
however, a substantial awareness in our political leadership
that our fiscal and economic policies have gone awry and
that the multiple promises of cradle-to-grave security for our
citizens can no longer be responsibly expanded, if indeed
they can be fulfilled. This is true not only in America, but
also in all the Western social democratic nations that are
guided by the same egalitarian-redistributionist philosophy.

During my four years in Washington I had countless private conferences with the leaders of those nations, and I witnessed the progressive loss of confidence in their economic policies. Chiefs of state and finance ministers of America's Western allies told me with great concern that they no longer knew how to sustain the levels of economic support which their citizens had come to believe was their "right." All were counting on America to save them. But America was in the same position.

Their anxiety surfaced during the American elections of 1976. That was the time, as some will recall, when the most critical questions being discussed in the public forums of the country were: How would the Democratic candidate, Jimmy Carter, apply the old formulas of liberal economics to the problems of recession, inflation, and high unemployment? What magic combination of taxation, deficit spending, and monetary stimulation would he adopt to "solve" our problems? Should he expand the deficit by $15 billion? By $30 billion? By $70 billion? Those were the questions being asked because few knew any other kinds of questions to ask. In fact, where government is concerned, there are no others. Those are the only economic alternatives available to an interventionist state. It can confiscate; it can redistribute what it has confiscated; it can spend more than it possesses by borrowing and by printing baseless money. There is only one thing it cannot do: produce wealth. The leading politicians of Europe listened with mounting alarm to the level of America's campaign debate, and finally they spoke up.

In September British Prime Minister James Callaghan, in a speech to the Labor Party Conference, declared, "We used to think that you could just spend your way out of a recession and increase employment by cutting taxes and boosting government spending. I tell you in all candor that that option no longer exists and that insofar as it ever did exist, it only worked by injecting a bigger dose of inflation into the economy, followed by a higher level of unemployment. That is the history of the past twenty years."

And shortly thereafter West German Chancellor Helmut

Schmidt, speaking at the International Socialists Conference in Geneva, warned all the socialist and social democratic nations that they were sinking economically because they were "stimulating" their economies by printing fake money.

They were speaking not only to their own countries and to Europe, but also, I believe, to the American government. Those were accurate statements. I had been saying the same thing for years in the United States. But they were something more; they were confessions of governmental impotence. The wisest politicians and economists, in America and Europe, have learned a bitter lesson from the experimentation of the past decades. Today they know clearly what the state should *not* do. They no longer have any clear idea of what the state *should* do. Today the only ones with "certainty" are the advocates of dictatorial centralized planning.

Normally in life, if one finds oneself in a situation where *all* known courses of action are destructive, one reassesses the premises which led to that situation. The premise to be questioned here is the degree of government intervention itself—the very competence of the state to function as a significant economic ruler. But to question that premise is to hurl oneself intellectually into a free market universe. And that the social democratic leaders will not do. A few may actually understand—as did the brilliant Chancellor Erhard in postwar Germany—that the solution to shortages, recession and unemployment, and an ominous decline in technological innovation is to dispense with most intervention and regulation and allow men to produce competitively in freedom. But they know that if they proposed this, they would be destroyed by the political intellectuals of their countries.

Those intellectuals, in Europe, as in the United States, are still in the grip of Lippmann's "heresy" of the 1930s—the belief that "there are no limits to man's capacity to govern others and that therefore no limitation ought to be imposed on government." They have lost the knowledge "born of long ages of suffering under man's dominion over man . . . that the exercise of unlimited power by men with limited minds and self-regarding prejudices is soon oppressive, reactionary and corrupt." They have lost this knowledge because today—although in their collectivist "idealism" they cannot grasp this—*they* are the reactionary, corrupt oppressors.

They do understand one thing perfectly, however: that the greatest threat to their power is a free market economy which sets stringent limits on the state. A significant move to free the market would decimate the "New Despotism," and the ruling group would try to destroy any politician who proposed such a course. The powerful political intelligentsia that determines the trends in social democratic nations today is as stubborn and ruthless a ruling elite as any in history and worse than many because it is possessed of delusions of moral grandeur.

So here we are, with most of our politicians careening toward more and more central planning and our society ruled by a small band of moral and economic despots who, as Kristol says, *are* our universities and *are* our foundations and *are* our media and *are* our bureaucracies. They constitute the vocal intellectual superstructure of this country, the functioning "mind" of our society. What then can we do?

We can do a number of things, and they will perhaps be better understood if I first eliminate the things we cannot and should not do. The *last* thing to do is to fight conventionally in the political arena, on the assumption that getting Republicans or conservatives of both parties into office is a solution. I am partisan enough to wish to see members of my party hold office, but I have learned that it solves nothing fundamental. Such men are merely faced today with a tidal wave of egalitarian projects and proposals for increasingly authoritarian controls over the economy, and the best and most principled among them merely find themselves saying no. The outpouring of Ford vetoes was the most heroic aspect of his administration. But consistent negativism is not a constructive or even intelligible long-range position.

Similarly, one should not come up with programs of one's own. Not only would they turn out, in the current context, to be modified egalitarian-authoritarian programs, but also the very approach is itself a symptom of the interventionist disease. The incessant spawning and modification of laws, regulations, programs, and "national purposes" are the expressions of a state which sees its primary function as a controller of citizens. The tragic fact is that today this proliferation of programs is the only "respectable" form of political thought—the definition of "respectable" coming from the Establishment technocrats who emerge from the universities to compete for government jobs. These clever young men win the coveted power by publishing articles and books, which offer minute new wrinkles in the use of state power. Shrink it a little here, expand it a little there, the technocrat says, and the machine of state will creak a little less ominously and grow more "efficient." He aims, of course, at being hired to supervise that growing "efficiency."

This kind of exercise produces the liveliest manifestations of political thought today. Our technocrats have taught people that only learned bickering over microscopic matters constitutes "expert" or "profound" political discourse. But learned bickering over trivial aspects of a pathological situation and the struggle to make that pathology more "efficient" will not help us. That is the language of centralized planners, and we don't need more of it. And we certainly don't need a more "efficient" government in *their* sense. On the contrary, so long as our government remains in its present state, we are far better off with extreme inefficiency. Life can still be lived in the loopholes and in the crevices between the government contradictions. I fully share Herman Kahn's sardonic view that Americans are fortunate *not* to get all the government they pay for!

What we need today in America is adherence to a set of broad guiding principles, not a thousand more technocratic adjustments. And so, at the end of this book, I shall not waste my time or yours with a set of legislative proposals. Instead, I will suggest a few of the most important general principles which I would like to see placed on the public agenda. They are actually the conclusions I have reached in the course of working on this book.

—The overriding principle to be revived in American political life is that which sets individual liberty as the highest political value—that value to which all other values are subordinate and that which, at all times, is to be given the highest "priority" in policy discussions.

—By the same token, there must be a conscious philosophical prejudice against any intervention by the state into our lives, for by definition such intervention abridges liberty. Whatever form it may take, state intervention in the private and productive lives of the citizenry must be presumed to be a negative, uncreative, and dangerous act, to be adopted only when its proponents provide overwhelming and incontrovertible evidence that the benefits to society of such intervention far outweigh the costs.

—The principle of "no taxation without representation" must again become a rallying cry of Americans. Only Congress represents American voters, and the process of transferring regulatory powers—which are a hidden power to tax—to unelected, uncontrollable, and unfireable bureaucrats must stop. The American voters, who pay the bills, must be in a position to know what is being economically inflicted on them and in a position to vote men out of office who assault their interests, as *the voters* define those interests. Which means that Congress should not pass bills creating programs that it cannot effectively oversee. The drive to demand scrupulous legislative oversight of our policing agencies, such as the CIA, is valid; it should be extended to *all* agencies of the government which are also, directly or indirectly, exercising police power.

—A critical principle which must be communicated forcefully to the American public is the inexorable interdependence of economic wealth and political liberty. Our citizens must learn that what keeps them prosperous is production and technological innovation. Their wealth emerges, not from government offices or politicians' edicts, but only from that portion of the marketplace which is *free*. They must also be taught to understand the relationship among collectivism, centralized planning, and poverty so that every new generation of Americans need not naïvely receive the Marxist revelations afresh.

—Bureaucracies themselves should be assumed to be noxious, authoritarian parasites on society, with a tendency to augment their own size and power and to cultivate a parasitical clientele in all classes of society. Area after area of American life should be set free from their blind power drive. We commonly hear people call for a rollback of prices, often unaware that they are actually calling for the destruction of marginal businesses and the jobs they furnish. People must be taught to start calling for a rollback of the bureaucracy, where nothing will be lost but strangling regulation and where the gains will always take the form of liberty, productivity, and jobs.

—Productivity and the growth of productivity must be the *first* economic consideration at all times, not the last. That is the source of technological innovation, jobs, and wealth. This means that profits needed for investment must be respected as a great social blessing, not as a social evil, and that envy of the "rich" cannot be allowed to destroy a powerful economic system.

—The concept that "wealth is theft" must be repudiated. It now lurks, implicitly, in most of the political statements we hear. Wealth can indeed be stolen, but only *after* it has been produced, and the difference between stolen wealth and produced wealth is critical. If a man obtains money by fraud or by force, he is simply a criminal to be handled by the police and the courts. But if he has earned his income honorably, by the voluntary exchange of goods and services, he is not a criminal or a second-class citizen and should not be treated as such. A society taught to perceive producers as criminals will end up by destroying its productive processes.

—Conversely, the concept that the absence of money

implies some sort of virtue should be repudiated. Poverty may result from honest misfortune, but it also may result from sloth, incompetence, and dishonesty. Again, the distinction between deserving and undeserving poor is important. It is a virtue to assist those who are in acute need through no fault of their own, but it is folly to glamorize men simply because they are penniless. The crude linkage between wealth and evil, poverty and virtue is false, stupid, and of value only to demagogues, parasites, and criminals—indeed, the three groups that alone have profited from the linkage.

—Similarly, the view that government is virtuous and producers are evil is a piece of folly, and a nation which allows itself to be tacitly guided by these illusions must lose both its liberty and its wealth. Government has its proper functions, and consequently, there can be both good and bad governments. Producers as well can be honest and dishonest. Our political discourse can be rendered rational only when people are taught to make such discriminations.

—The "ethics" of egalitarianism must be repudiated. Achievers must not be penalized or parasites rewarded if we aspire to a healthy, productive, and ethical society. Able-bodied citizens must work to sustain their lives, and in a healthy economic system they should be enabled and encouraged to save for their own old age. Clearly, so long as the government's irrational fiscal policies make this impossible, present commitments to pensions and Social Security must be maintained at all cost, for the bulk of the population has no other recourse. But as soon as is politically feasible—meaning, as soon as *production* becomes the nation's highest economic value—the contributions of able-bodied citizens to their own future pensions should be invested by them in far safer commercial institutions, where the sums can earn high interest without being squandered by politicians and bureaucrats. American citizens must be taught to wrest their life savings from the politicians if they are to know the comfort of genuine security.

—The American citizen must be made aware that today a relatively small group of people is proclaiming its purposes to be the will of the People. That elitist approach to government must be repudiated. There is no such thing as the People; it is a collectivist myth. There are only individual citizens with individual wills and individual purposes. There is only one social system that reflects this sovereignty of the individual: the free-market, or capitalist, system, which means the sovereignty of the individual "vote" in the marketplace and the sovereignty of the individual vote in the political realm. That individual sovereignty is being destroyed in this country by our current political trends, and it is scarcely astonishing that individuals now feel "alienated" from their government. They are not just alienated from it; they have virtually been expelled from the governmental process, where only organized mobs prevail.

—The growing cynicism about democracy must be combated by explaining why it has become corrupted. People have been taught that if they can get together big enough gangs, they have the legal power to hijack other citizens' wealth, which means the power to hijack other people's efforts, energies, and lives. No decent society can function when men are given such power. A state does need funds, but a clear cutoff line must be established beyond which no political group or institution can confiscate a citizen's honorably earned property. The notion that one can differentiate between "property rights" and "human rights" is ignoble. One need merely see the appalling condition of "human rights" in nations where there are no "property rights" to understand why. This is just a manifestation of the socialist myth which imagines that one can keep men's minds free while enslaving their bodies.

These are some of the broad conclusions I have reached after four years in office. Essentially they are a set of guiding principles. America is foundering for the lack of principles; it is now guided by the belief that *unprincipled* action—for which the respectable name is "pragmatism"—is somehow superior. Such principles as I have listed do not represent dogma. There is, as I said, nothing arbitrary or dogmatic about the interlocking relationship between political and economic liberty. The history of every nation on earth demonstrates that relationship, and no economist known to me, including the theoreticians of interventionism and totalitarianism, denies this. If liberty is to be our highest political value, this set of broad principles follows consistently.

In fact, these are not particularly original principles. They were the fundamental precepts of American society when the nation was expanding healthily. It is evident today that our nation is being ruled by precisely the opposite principles and that our growing degeneration, both political and economic, is the result of that philosophical reversal.

The single most important thing I can conceive of in the realm of American political life is to make Americans aware that this has happened; that the fundamental guiding principles of American life have, in fact, been reversed; that we are careening with frightening speed toward collectivism and away from individual sovereignty, toward coercive centralized planning and away from free individual choices, toward a statist-dictatorial system and away from a nation in which individual liberty is sacred. It is imperative to launch a national "dialogue" on these very issues. They should be publicly discussed, publicly debated, and that debate should extend to every home. There is nothing in the nature of the American people (or of any people) which forbids this. I know of no people, including the very young, who are not interested in such broad ethical questions. The eyes of Americans glaze over when they are asked to remember who their "representatives" in government are, since clearly they feel unrepresented by them. Their eyes glaze over when asked to recall a legion of alphabetical agencies and when asked to pay reverent attention to technocratic analyses of the minutiae of economic decisions. Their eyes do *not* glaze over when broad issues of moral principle are raised. Those, in fact, are the only issues that get the electorate excited. The electorate tends to be far more abstract and philosophical than most of its contemporary leaders.

There is only one way to generate a public awareness of the issues I have listed and to launch a broad challenge of the assumptions and goals presently underlying our political life. It cannot and will not emerge naturally from the ruling intelligentsia, which has no interest in challenging its own assumptions and goals and invests vast energies in evading them or even actively denying them. What we desperately need in America today is a powerful counterintelligentsia that will issue such challenges. There are many thousands of authentic intellectuals who are not of the authoritarian breed and who do not aspire to dictate the course of the lives of their fellow citizens. There are millions of intelligent people in every profession, every trade, and every craft in the country who have come to distrust both "big government" and the ruling intelligentsia. And the overwhelming majority of Americans, 83 percent, according to a Gallup poll of May 1, 1977, are opposed to the coercive leveling of egalitarianism, at least in the realm of employment, and name "ability" as the desired standard for hiring. A powerful counterintelligentsia can be organized to challenge our ruling "new class" opinion makers—an intelligentsia dedicated consciously to the political value of individual liberty, above all, which understands its relationship to meritocracy, and which is consciously aware of the value of private property and the free market in generating innovative technology, jobs, and wealth. Such an intelligentsia exists, and an audience awaits its views.

Because the need for this is so intense and because it is a logical development in a nation historically dedicated to individual liberty, we have been seeing the birth of just such a movement in recent years. It has been spontaneously generated in three parts of our culture. The oldest, of course, is the educated pro-free enterprise conservative movement. The most brilliant and dedicated intellectuals of the right are classical liberals, adherents of limited government and a minimally regulated free market economy, and are totally aware of the unbreakable link between political and economic liberty. These people have built themselves a fortress in the heart of academe, particularly in the economics departments of the University of Chicago and UCLA. There are many hundreds of such scholars, European and American— Nobel Laureates Hayek and Friedman being the most visible in the mass media since their awards—and they are the authors of a constantly growing body of theoretical free market literature. They have kept the torch of economic liberty burning and are passing it on to younger generations.

The younger generations tend, in fact, to be more militant about the free market than their elders, a good many today being laissez-faire purists. The most publicly visible are the young libertarians. In 1975 one of their number, Robert Nozick, a philosophy professor at Harvard, won a National Book Award for an exposition of libertarian theory and a challenge to egalitarianism, which was discussed in the major opinion journals in the land. Nozick sent a ripple of laughter through the world of political theorists with his witty defense of freedom for "capitalist acts between consenting adults." One of the most remarkable documentaries I myself have seen on the problem of government violation of both our civil and economic liberties is *The Incredible Bread Machine,* a brilliant film by a libertarian, Ted Loeffler, once a Yale liberal. As Secretary of the Treasury I gladly contributed a commentary to that documentary, as did economists Milton Friedman and Walter Heller. Courtesy of Loeffler's Campus Study Institute, it has now been seen by 15 million people, and 1200 prints are circulating around the country. I wish it could be seen by the entire nation.

A tiny fragment of the American body politic, the libertarians are so well furnished with academic degrees and so intense in their dedication to freedom that their impact on the intellectual world transcends their numbers. Like all radical scholarly groups, they serve as a goad to their elders and attract the liberty-loving young. Utopian, idealistic, and immoderate—to them "extremism in the defense of liberty is no vice"—they are the connecting link between America's free enterprise past and future and refute the canard that economic liberty is a value to rich old men alone.

The second group concerned with liberty has sprung from within the very heart of the liberal world and has become known, however inaccurately, as "neo-conservative." These people are essentially anticommunist scholars of a New Deal stripe. Some are former leftists; some are affiliated with organized labor, in particular with the strongly anticommunist leadership of the AFL-CIO. All have gradually become aware that certain components of their own interventionist philosophy are destroying political liberty, academic liberty, and jobs. Shocked into an awareness of the destructive trends by the totalitarian instincts of the New Left, by HEW controls over universities, and by the conflict between many regulatory agencies and the productive process, they have begun to challenge the most irrational collectivist and egalitarian developments, and some go so far as to question centralized government controls. Among the most prominent members of this group are distinguished intellectuals like Irving Kristol, James Q. Wilson, Nathan Glazer, Daniel Bell, Michael Novak, and Sidney Hook. In May 1977 Hook, the oldest of the group and once an internationally known socialist, explained his political evolution to a libertarian publication, *Reason*. I quote part of that revealing interview here because it illuminates the background of this entire segment of American political opinion, which rarely surfaces in the mass media:

> REASON: A lot of people on the left or new left maintain that Sidney Hook, who used to be a great leader in the left in the United States, has become a conservative, and you maintain that it's quite the opposite—they have changed their position.
>
> HOOK: Well, I would not put it like that. I would hate to admit to having lived 74 years in this world without having

learned something new and abandoned inadequate ideas. I must confess that in the '30s there were two things that played a decisive role in my thinking. First was the fear of Fascism. I saw Nazism developing when I lived in Germany in 1928 and 1929. . . . [Secondly, we] had the Great Depression in this country. . . . [T]o most of us, 1929 seemed to be the heyday of free enterprise, and the crash seemed to be the death knell of capitalism.

With respect to Fascism, we assumed that the Soviet Union would fight Hitler. We also assumed that the Soviet Union would move toward a more humane society. Instead, our dream turned into a nightmare. As soon as Hitler came to power in 1933, . . . I realized that Stalin's theory of social Fascism had been instrumental in Hitler's success. I turned very strongly against the Communist Party and all its works. . . . What Solzhenitsyn discovered in the '50s we already knew in the '30s, but we did not have the eloquence to persuade the world.

The welfare state, anticipated by neither Adam Smith nor Karl Marx, emerged. I began to see that there were ways of achieving what I regarded as the good society that made the democratic process itself central. Since then I have regarded myself primarily as a democrat, and I support only socialist measures that I believe will strengthen the democratic way of life.

REASON:  Isn't there a problem there, in that socialist measures, because they depend upon control of people's lives, pose a direct threat to democracy?

HOOK:  I must admit that I have become increasingly skeptical of centralized government control. Perhaps the greatest challenge to my socialism has come from the observation of what bureaucrats can do with respect to university life with guidelines that distort the original principle of affirmative action. Initially this outlawed all discrimination on grounds of race, religion, sex or national origin. When I saw how the bureaucrats, aided by academic timidity, transformed it into a mandate for reverse discrimination and a quota system, and when I realized that these rulings were not derived from laws passed by the Congress but were decrees interpreted and enforced by bureaucrats, it gave me an intellectual and emotional shock from which I have not completely recovered. Now I look very hard at government programs in order to see if they are properly authorized and controlled by legislative authority.

The liberals and laborites in this "neo-conservative" group are still interventionists to a degree that I myself do not endorse, but they have grasped the importance of capitalism, are battling some of the despotic aspects of egalitarianism, and can be counted as allies on certain crucial fronts of the struggle for individual liberty.

And the third broad movement in opposition to prevailing trends is to be found in the world of business itself, where the most intelligent and courageous leaders have faced the fact that they must fight for free enterprise before it is too late. The action taken by such men and companies usually consists of public education projects in free market economics and high-powered advertising campaigns in the mass media, where they present the ideas and arguments on behalf of the free market that are conventionally ignored or suppressed by those media.

These three groups are not large, speaking numerically, and their views are by no means uniform. But they have widening spheres of influence in our society, at least in that portion of it which is concerned with ideas. And ideas are weapons—indeed, the only weapons with which other ideas can be fought. All attempts to combat by purely political means the hostile collectivism unleashed in the sixties have failed ignominiously. In fact, such attempts have precipitated the very scandals—*e.g.*, Watergate—which today are *causes célèbres* of the left, for if one does not combat ideas with ideas, one is reduced to combating them with force. And that is both a confession of intellectual failure and a violation of the constitutional rights of the opposition. If we are to fight the "New Despotism" effectively and respect the very individual liberty for which we are fighting, we can only do it by building up the influence of the counterintelligentsia, whose views, if known, would command a respectful hearing in the marketplace of ideas.

The problem is that the existing counterintelligentsia has comparatively little access to that broad market of ideas. The reason for that is shocking: There are few voluntary institutions in America today that are organized to finance intellectuals who fight for economic, as well as political, liberty. Most private funds—inevitably from business itself—flow ceaselessly to the very institutions which are philosophically committed to the destruction of capitalism. The great corporations of America sustain the major universities, with no regard for the content of their teachings. They sustain the major foundations which nurture the most destructive egalitarian trends. And with their advertising, they sustain the mass media, which today inevitably serve as a national megaphone for every egalitarian crusade. In the last analysis, American business is financing the destruction of both free enterprise and political freedom.

Why this is so will doubtless preoccupy scholars of future generations. From my own experience, as reported in this book, I conclude that most businessmen today, at least until very recently, have been more concerned with short-range respectability than with long-range survival. Most appear to be mortally afraid of antagonizing the egalitarian gurus of our society. They do indeed seek to protect their enterprises, but with little understanding of the philosophy that justifies their actions. Consequently, they do so secretively, and often guiltily, in the form of lobbying, financing politicians, and, not infrequently, bribing them. Even more disturbing, they also seek to protect their enterprises by endorsing the very values of their worst enemies and financing their causes. If American business consciously wished to devise a formula for self-destruction, it could not do better than this. This is appeasement on a breathtaking scale. The only saving element, in fact, lies in that growing nucleus in the business world which has come to understand the devastating futility of this kind of appeasement.

And that, essentially, is where to begin in organizing a powerful countermovement—with that courageous group of businessmen who have decided to fight openly for the free-enterprise system. But there is one condition that must be met: These businessmen must not just preach free enterprise; they must practice it. They cannot be hypocritical leeches on the state, who mouth platitudes about the free enterprise system, then come hat in hand to Washington. This practice totally destroys their credibility as spokesmen for a principled cause. No citizen has any reason to believe a businessman's charge that the state is violating both liberty and productive efficacy when that businessman himself continually asks for state protection and state favors. A group of genuinely principled businessmen must be organized who will refrain from asking for one cent of the taxpayers' money, who will honorably accept the risks and penalties of freedom along with its great rewards. Only such a group can earn the respect of the American people and begin to exert a moral influence. Only such a group can start the arduous process of giving the business world itself some backbone and a clear vision of how to protect its—and our—freedom. Once organized, such a group can start the needed crusade to divert the immense corporate funds presently earmarked for education, "public relations," and "institutional advertising" into the organizations needed to sustain and expand the counterintelligentsia.

What this means is nothing less than a massive and unprecedented mobilization of the moral, intellectual and financial resources which reside in those who still have faith in the human individual, who believe in his right to maximum responsible liberty and who are concerned that our traditional free enterprise system, which offers the greatest scope for the exercise of our freedom, is in dire and perhaps ultimate peril. I mean nothing less than a mobilization of those who see a successful United States as the real "last best hope of mankind" and who are not afraid to be counted among those who do. What, then, will this crusade or this mobilization involve?

1. Funds generated by business (by which I mean profits, funds in business foundations and contributions from individual businessmen) must rush by multimillions to the aid of liberty, in the many places where it is beleaguered.

Foundations imbued with the philosophy of freedom (rather than encharged with experimental dabbling in socialist utopian ideas or the funding of outright revolution) must take pains to funnel desperately needed funds to scholars, social scientists, writers and journalists who understand the relationship between political and economic liberty and whose work will supplement and inspire and enhance the understanding and the work of others still to come. This philanthropy must not capitulate to soft-minded pleas for the support of "dissent." Indeed, it is the economics and the philosophy of capitalism which represent "dissent"—dissent from a dominant socialist-statist-collectivist orthodoxy which prevails in much of the media, in most of our large universities, among many of our politicians and, tragically, among not a few of our top business executives.

Those capitalists who, in the interests of "fairness," have financed the intellectual opposition have seen their foundations literally taken over. The textbook case of such infiltration was dramatized recently when Henry Ford III resigned from the Ford Foundation. I called Mr. Ford on reading of this in the newspapers and asked him to explain how this had happened. He answered: "I tried for 30 years to change it from within but couldn't." Of course he couldn't, not after he had allowed the Ford Foundation to become a veritable fortress of the philosophical opposition. One does not work from "within" the egalitarian world to change it; one can only work from without—and this absurd financing of one's philosophical enemies must not be tolerated in the new foundations. On the contrary, they must serve explicitly as intellectual refuges for the non-egalitarian scholars and writers in our society who today work largely alone in the face of overwhelming indifference or hostility. They must be given grants, grants and more grants in exchange for books, books and more books. This philosophical restriction placed on the beneficiaries of the new foundations will not result in a uniformity of intellectual product. There is an enormous diversity of viewpoints within the center-to-right intellectual world which endorses capitalism. The point is simply to make sure that the thinkers on that broad band of the American spectrum are given the means to compete in the free market of ideas. Today they constitute an impoverished underground.

2.   Business must cease the mindless subsidizing of colleges and universities whose departments of economics, government, politics and history are hostile to capitalism and whose faculties will not hire scholars whose views are otherwise.

Again, the essence of this is a recognition of the fact that in the universities of which I speak, capitalism is no longer the dominant orthodoxy. That has important implications. There was a time, 40 or 50 years ago, when capitalism *was* the dominant orthodoxy, not just in government and in the marketplace but in our universities as well. At that time, it was urged that it was for the good of the society as a whole that the dissonant voice be heard on those campuses—that the critic of capitalism, the dissenter from its philosophy, its economics, its mores be given a hearing—and, characteristically, capitalism responded by doing precisely that. Indeed, it is through the very generosity and tolerance of capitalism that the enemies of capitalism have come to dominate our campuses today. However, now that they have achieved dominance, there is no longer any reason for capitalism to support them, and it is ridiculous for them to claim (as they loudly do) some sort of "entitlement" to support from a system which they openly despise and lose no opportunity to disparage.

This has nothing to do with trying to govern what any individual professor teaches, nor is it an attempt to "buy" docile professors who will teach what businessmen tell them to. That notion is as ridiculous as the idea that anti-capitalist professors are entitled to support by capitalism. No non-professional has any right to attempt to dictate what and how a teacher teaches. He can, however (and, I argue, he must), decide whether or not that teacher—either by virtue of his competence or lack of it, or the nature of the doctrine he espouses—is entitled to his support. There is a world of difference between attempting to govern what is taught and simply refusing to support those whose teachings are inimical to one's own philosophy.

In sum, America's major universities are today churning out young collectivists by legions, and it is irrational for businessmen to support them. Conversely, business money must flow generously to those colleges and universities which do offer their students an opportunity to become well educated not only in collectivist theory but in conservative and Libertarian principles as well.

This is no interference with the First Amendment rights of the intellectuals presently working in our universities. They remain free as the wind to express the views they choose. It merely ensures that the citadels of anti-capitalist thought will be deprived of the funds generated by a system *they* consider to be corrupt and unjust.

3. Finally, business money must flow away from the media which serve as megaphones for anticapitalist opinion and to media which are either pro-freedom or, if not necessarily "pro-business," at least professionally capable of a fair and accurate treatment of procapitalist ideas, values and arguments. The judgment of this fairness is to be made by businessmen alone—it is their money that they are investing. Again, I stress, this is no violation of anyone's First Amend-

ment rights. If a newspaper or magazine or broadcasting station wishes to serve as a voluntary public relations agency for those who assault the capitalist system, it should be entirely free to do so. Without capitalist money. The First Amendment guarantees freedom of speech and of the press from governmental intervention. It does not require that any citizen finance those that seek to destroy him.

These are the three fronts on which to act aggressively if we are to create a sophisticated counter-force to the rising despotism. One of my own first actions on leaving the post of Secretary of the Treasury was to accept the job of president of the John N. Olin Foundation, whose purpose is to support those individuals and institutions who are working to strengthen the free enterprise system. I do this in the fervent hope that my children will have the same freedom, the same opportunities to succeed or fail that I did.[1]

I know of nothing more crucial than to come to the aid of the intellectuals and writers who are fighting on my side. And I strongly recommend that any businessman with the slightest impulse for survival go and do likewise. The alliance between the theorists and men of action in the capitalist world is long overdue in America. It must become a veritable crusade if we are to survive in freedom.

Only when this complex process has begun will we see in America the most important aspect of a cultural regeneration—an authentic public dialogue on the problems of our era. This may seem an odd statement to those who are aware of the incessant "controversies" that have roared about our heads, particularly during the past two decades. These controversies, however, have been sterile clashes of opinion in which the issues have never been joined. At the best, exchanges have been like hostile ships passing in the night, firing shots across each other's bows. Never have the basic premises of these controversies been opened up for public inspection. Invariably the anticapitalist groups, the collectivists, and the advocates of centralized planning have set the terms of the debate and determined the issues to be placed on the public agenda. The function of a counterintelligentsia is, above all, to challenge that ideological monopoly: to raise the unnamed issues, to ask the unasked questions, to present the missing contexts, and to place a set of very different values and goals on the public agenda. Only then will American citizens be offered a choice—not between more or less of the same destructive trends, but between alternative solutions to problems, between a social system increasingly based on force or one increasingly based on liberty.

It is often said by people who receive warnings about declining freedom in America that such a charge is preposterous, that there is no freer society on earth. That is true in one sense, but it is immensely deceptive. There has never been such freedom before in America to speak freely, indeed, to wag one's tongue in the hearing of an entire nation; to publish anything and everything, including the most scurrilous gossip; to take drugs and to prate to children about their alleged pleasures; to propagandize for bizarre sexual practices; to watch bloody and obscene entertainment. Conversely, compulsion rules the world of work. There has never been so little freedom before in America to plan, to save, to invest, to build, to produce, to invent, to hire, to fire, to resist coercive unionization, to exchange goods and services, to risk, to profit, to grow.

The strange fact is that Americans are constitutionally free today to do almost everything that our cultural tradition has previously held to be immoral and obscene, while the police powers of the state are being invoked against almost every aspect of the productive process. Even more precisely, Americans today are left free by the state to engage in activities that could, for the most part, be carried on just as readily in prisons, insane asylums, and zoos. They are not left free by the state to pursue those activities which will give them *independence.*

That is not a coincidence. It is characteristic, in fact, of the contemporary collectivist, in both America and Europe, to clamor that freedom pertains exclusively to the verbal and emotive realms. It allows the egalitarian socialist the illusion that he is not trying to weave a noose for the throats of free men, and it renders him all the more dangerous to the credulous. It is difficult, indeed, to identify as a potential tyrant someone who is raising a righteous uproar over your right to fornicate in the streets. But in this as well, our contemporary "liberators" are not original. I transmit to you a warning by Professor Nisbet, professor of humanities at Columbia University, included in his essay "The New Despotism." He says something that I consider vital for the contemporary citizen to know because it is the final reason for the invisibility surrounding the destruction of some of our most crucial liberties:

> [M]ore often than not in history, license has been the prelude to exercises of extreme political coercion, which shortly reach all areas of a culture. . . . [V]ery commonly in ages when civil rights of one kind are in evidence—those pertaining to freedom of speech and thought in, say, theater, press and forum, with obscenity and libel laws correspondingly loosened—very real constrictions of individual liberty take place in other, more vital areas: political organization, voluntary association, property and the right to hold jobs, for example. . . .
>
> There are, after all, certain freedoms that are like circuses. Their very existence, so long as they are individual and enjoyed chiefly individually as by spectators, diverts men's minds from the loss of other, more fundamental social and economic and political rights.
>
> A century ago, the liberties that now exist routinely on stage and screen, on printed page and canvas would have been unthinkable in America—and elsewhere in the West, for that matter, save in the most clandestine and limited of settings. But so would the limitations upon economic, professional, education and local liberties, to which we have by now become accustomed, have seemed equally unthinkable a half century ago. We enjoy the feeling of great freedom, of

protection of our civil liberties, when we attend the theater, watch television, buy paperbacks. But all the while, we find ourselves living in circumstances of a spread of military, police and bureaucratic power that cannot help but have, that manifestly does have, profoundly erosive effect upon those economic, local and associative liberties that are by far the most vital to any free society.

From the point of view of any contemporary strategist or tactician of political power, indulgence in the one kind of liberties must seem a very requisite to diminution of the other kind. We know it seemed that way to the Caesars and Napoleons of history. Such indulgence is but one more way of softening the impact of political power and of creating the illusion of individual freedom in a society grown steadily more centralized, collectivized and destructive of the diversity of allegiance, the autonomy of enterprise in all spheres and the spirit of spontaneous association that any genuinely free civilization requires.

I cite this for another reason. Like others whom I have quoted at length at several points in this book, Mr. Nisbet stands as a living illustration of what I mean by a counterintellectual. It is only the scholar with a profound understanding of the nature of liberty and the institutions on which it rests who can stand ultimate guard over American cultural life. It is only he who can offer the American citizen the authentic and profound choices that our political system and our press no longer offer him.

I do not mean to imply here that it is only on a lofty, scholarly level that the fight can be conducted, although it unquestionably must begin at that level. At any time and on any social level the individual can and should take action. I have done so in my realm, and you, too, can work for your liberty, immediately and with impact.

Parents must take an active role in the education of their children. Join parent-teacher associations; examine the courses and material that your children are receiving. Do not hesitate to protest strenuously. Run for local school boards, if necessary, to make sure that the leaders of tomorrow are not being indoctrinated in the philosophy of statism.

Get involved in politics—in campaigns from the town council to the White House. Support only those candidates who will not waver on the issue of liberty. For too long we have willingly accepted the "lesser of two evils." Run yourself. Government is far too important to be left to the professional politicians, the wet-finger-in-the-wind types whose purposes are uncontaminated by principles. But the most urgent counsel I can give you is this:

*Stop asking the government for "free" goods and services, however desirable and necessary they may seem to be. They are not free. They are simply extracted from the hide of your neighbors—and can be extracted only by force. If you would not confront your neighbor and demand his money at the point of a gun to solve every new problem that may appear in your life, you should not allow the government to do it for you. Be prepared to identify any politician who simultaneously demands your "sacrifices" and offers you "free services" for exactly what he is: an egalitarian demagogue. This one insight understood, this one discipline acted upon and taught by millions of Americans to others could do more to further freedom in American life than any other.*

There is, of course, a minimum of government intervention needed to protect a society, particularly from all forms of physical aggression and from economic fraud and, more generally, to protect the citizen's liberty and constitutional rights. What that precise minimum is in terms of a percentage of the GNP I am not prepared to say, but I do know this: that a clear cutoff line, beyond which the government may not confiscate our property, must be sought and established if the government is not to invade every nook and cranny of our lives and if we are to be free and productive. It is with *our* money that the state destroys our freedom. It is not too soon to start the process of tightening the leash on the state on the individual level, above all, by refusing to be a parasite.

In the lowest-income groups in our nation there are men and women too proud, too independent to accept welfare, even though it is higher than the wages they can earn. Surely such pride can be stimulated on the more affluent levels of our society.

Ultimately, of course, it is in the political arena that we must definitely solve these problems. The difficulties will be great because Congress today, much of the judiciary, and for the moment the executive are dominated by a coercive, redistributionist, and collectivist philosophy. The Democratic Party is the primary vehicle of economic authoritarianism, and President Jimmy Carter has already demonstrated—through his energy proposals—strong authoritarian impulses. The only party with a philosophical heritage which might permit it to be the Liberty Party in the United States is the Republican Party. But the Republican Party today is inert—reduced to spineless inconsistency by a half century of compromises on principle. The immense irony is that by compromising on the principle of free enterprise, the Republicans have simply ended up being the party of "business" in the sense of a specific pressure group, and that is a profoundly different thing; it is the difference between idealism and cash. Until the Republicans become a party of principle, aware that a fundamental assault on our freedom is transforming the country, and until its politicians are willing to stand up and fight for that freedom with moral conviction and passion, it has no future. Americans do not need a dime-store version of the "New Despotism" in the Republican Party when in the Democratic Party they've got the real thing.

The only thing that can save the Republican Party, in fact, is a counterintelligentsia. Without such a reservoir of antiauthoritarian scholarship on which to draw, it is destined to remain the Stupid Party and to die. It may even deserve to die. A political party which declares itself philosophically committed to freedom but allows an economic dictatorship to emerge in the United States without stirring up the fiercest political donnybrook in American history has asked for the oblivion to which it is presently being consigned.

It is with a certain weariness that I anticipate the charge that I am one of those "unrealistic" conservatives who wishes to "turn back the clock." There is a good deal less to this criticism than meets the eye. History is not a determinist carpet rolling inexorably in the direction of collectivism, although an extraordinary number of people believe this to be the case. The truth is that it has unrolled gloriously in the opposite direction many times. Above all, the United States was born. There is nothing "historically inevitable" about the situation we are in. There is also nothing "realistic" in counseling people to adjust to that situation. That is equivalent to counseling them to adjust to financial collapse and the loss of freedom. Realism, in fact, requires the capacity to see beyond the tip of one's nose, to face intolerably unpleasant problems, and to take the necessary steps to dominate future trends, not to be crushed passively beneath them.

The time plainly has come to act. And I would advise the socially nervous that if our contemporary "New Despots" prefer to conceive of themselves as "progressive" and denounce those of us who would fight for liberty as "reactionary," let them. Words do not determine reality. Indeed, if language and history are to be taken seriously, coercion is clearly reactionary, and liberty clearly progressive. In a world where 80 percent of all human beings still live under harrowing tyranny, a tyranny always rationalized in terms of the alleged benefits to a collectivist construct called the People, the American who chooses to fight for the sanctity of the individual has nothing for which to apologize.

One of the clearest measures of the disastrous change that has taken place in this country is the fact that today one must intellectually justify a passion for individual liberty and for limited government, as though it were some bizarre new idea. Yet angry as I get when I reflect on this, I know there is a reason for it. Seen in the full context of human history, individual liberty *is* a bizarre new idea. And an even more bizarre new idea is the free market—the discovery that allowing millions upon millions of individuals to pursue their material interests as they choose, with a minimum of interference by the state, will unleash an incredible and orderly outpouring of inventiveness and wealth. These twin ideas appeared, like a dizzying flare of light in the long night of tyranny that has been the history of the human race. That light has begun to fade because the short span of 200 years has not been long enough for most of our citizens to understand the extraordinary nature of freedom. I say this with genuine humility. I came to understand this late in life myself, inspired by a very special perspective: I was flying high over the land of one of the bloodiest tyrannies on earth. But having understood it, I cannot let that light die out without a battle. It is my profound hope that this book will inspire the same determination in others.

# NOTES

## Chapter II

1. Okun, Arthur. *Equality and Efficiency: The Big Tradeoff*, The Brookings Institution, 1965, p. 38.
2. For detailed information on the industrialization of the USSR by western capitalists, and on the failures of centralized planning, see: Keller, Werner. *East Minus West = Zero—Russia's Debt to the Western World 1862–1962*, G. P. Putnam's Sons, New York, 1962; Nutter, G. Warren. *Central Economic Planning: The Visible Hand*, American Enterprise Institute, 1976; Sutton, Antony. *Western Technology and Soviet Economic Development 1945 to 1965*, Hoover Institution Press, Stanford University, Stanford, California, 1973.
3. Harris, Ralph. *Great Britain: The Lessons of Socialist Planning*, published in *The Politics of Planning*, Institute for Contemporary Studies, San Francisco, California, 1965, pp. 41–59.
4. *The Hudson Letter*, published by Hudson Research Europe, Ltd., 12 Whitehall, London, S.W.1. May 17, 1976.
5. Krock, Arthur. *Memoirs*, Funk and Wagnalls, New York, 1968, p. 406.

## Chapter III

1. *Small Business and the Energy Shortage*, Vol. I, Hearings of the Subcommittee on Special Small Business Problems of the Permanent Select Committee on Small Business, House of Representatives, Washington, D.C., May 22, June 6, 21, 22, July 10, 1973.
2. News from Senator Edward W. Brooke, Massachusetts; "Brooke Urges Deregulation of 'New' Natural Gas", June 14, 1975.
3. Nobel Prize winners in physics and chemistry: Eugene Wigner, Hans Bethe, Willard F. Libby, James Rainwater, Felix Block—as well as James Van Allen, discoverer of the "Van Allen radiation belt"; Edward Teller, head of the Lawrence Radiation Laboratories; Norman Rasmussen, Professor of Nuclear Physics at the Massachusetts Institute of Technology, and Ernest C. Pollard, a leading authority on the effects of radiation on living cells.

## Chapter IV

1. Tugwell, Rexford G. "Rewriting the Constitution", *The Center Magazine*, publication of the Center for the Study of Democratic Institutions, Vol. 1, No. 3, March 1968.
2. Owen, Henry and Charles Schultze, *Setting National Priorities: The Next Ten Years*, The Brookings Institution, September 1976.
3. Interview with Charles Schultze, *The New Yorker*, September 13, 1976.
4. Schuck, Peter H., "National Economic Planning: A Slogan Without Substance", The Public Interest, No. 45, Fall, 1976.
5. The *Wall Street Journal*, August 18, 1976.
6. The New York *Times*, November 27, 1976.

## Chapter V

1. Mayer, Martin. "Default at The New York *Times*", *Columbia Journalism Review*, January/February 1976.
2. *New York City Financial Crisis*, Hearings before the Committee on Banking, Housing and Urban Affairs, United States Senate, October 1, 1975.

3. Buckley, William. "Underestimating Simon", New York *Post*, October 23, 1975.
4. Broyles, William. "An Aye from Texas Is Upon Us", *Texas Monthly*, reprinted in *New York Magazine*, January 12, 1976, pp. 9–11.
5. Howe, Irving. "Balanchine and Larchmont", The New York *Times*, November 27, 1976.
6. "Buckley Asks Ford to Order an Inquiry into the City's Borrowing Practices", The New York *Times*, October 24, 1975.
7. Dolan, Edwin G. Review of *The Economist* by Leonard Silk, *The Alternative*, Vol. 10, No. 6, March 1977.

## Chapter VI

1. Quoted by Murray L. Weidenbaum, *Government-Mandated Price Increases*, American Enterprise Institute, February, 1975.
2. Nisbet, Robert A. "The New Despotism", *Commentary*, June 1975.
3. Friedman, Milton, interviewed by World Research INK, Vol. 3, 1976.
4. Freeman, Roger. *The Growth of American Government: A Morphology of the Welfare State*, Hoover Institution Press, 1976.
5. For a detailed report on this phenomenon, see Marx, Lenny, "Confessions of An Unemployment Cheat", *The Washington Monthly*, May 1977. Mr. Marx writes: "For me, and people like me, unemployment insurance had become that long-cherished liberal dream: government funding of the arts. . . . For others with no artistic bent, the unemployment program is allowing them to live out the fantasies of their undergraduate days. . . . 'Work for six months and go on unemployment' is their new motto, and it's working out just fine, thank you. Unemployment offices are beginning to resemble youth hostels with nomadic college grads checking in for their weekly out-of-state employment reports. . . . Meanwhile, to cover the costs of the program, their employers are paying taxes into state and federal treasuries, and throwing up their hands in despair at the rapid turnover of workers. . . . [T]hey are penalized with higher taxes up to a state maximum if there is a big worker turnover."
6. Reynolds, Alan. "Competition in Welfare", *National Review*, December 10, 1976.

7. Weinberger, W. Caspar. *The Reform of Welfare: A National Necessity* (original draft).

## Chapter VII

1. I agreed to head the John N. Olin Foundation because I learned in conversations with Mr. Olin that he and his associates shared utterly my own views regarding the virtues of the free enterprise system and the traditional American values of individual political freedom and the responsibility which it represents. They also shared my concern over the grave threat which has increasingly been posed to those institutions.

For my part, I endorsed these objectives of the Foundation, which were to contribute to the battle of ideas—to the ongoing war between the free society and those who would make it less free or destroy it altogether—by seeking and supporting scholars and programs which would competently and persuasively expound those ideas. In short, without any sacrifice of integrity or quality, the Foundation would seek scholars whose orientation was *toward* freedom, rather than against it (as is the case with the army of scholars who urge ever-increasing regulation and ever-encroaching government upon us as the only solution to all of the ills which ever-increasing regulation and ever-encroaching government have already visited upon us!).

No scholar supported by the Olin Foundation is or ever will be instructed as to what he shall teach or what research he shall pursue or what conclusions he shall reach or what papers he shall write. Our standards seek only to assure that a given scholar either has excellence or the potential for excellence and that he is not in principle *against* what the founder of our Foundation and its Board of Trustees, including myself, are for. Let him satisfy those standards, and the chips may fall where they will. Scholarly competence and scholarly integrity are paramount. Beyond that, our Foundation seeks only to add to that body of scholarship which exposits the operation of markets and the behavior of free men under free conditions, and it is left to the student or the reader to determine whether freedom is better than its absence.

# INDEX